Ethics from Experience

The Jones and Bartlett Series in Philosophy

Robert Ginsberg, General Editor

Ayer, A. J., *Metaphysics and Common Sense*, 1994 reissue with corrections and new introduction by Thomas Magnell, Drew University

Beckwith, Francis J., University of Nevada, Las Vegas, Editor, *Do the Right Thing: A Philosophical Dialogue on the Moral and Social Issues of Our Time*

Bishop, Anne H. and John R. Scudder, Jr., Lynchburg College, *Nursing Ethics: Therapeutic Caring Presence*

Caws, Peter, The George Washington University, *Ethics from Experience*

DeMarco, Joseph P., Cleveland State University, *Moral Theory: A Contemporary Overview*

Gert, Bernard et al., Dartmouth College, *Morality and the New Genetics*

Gorr, Michael, Illinois State University, and Sterling Harwood, San Jose State University, Editors, *Crime and Punishment: Philosophic Explorations*

Haber, Joram Graf, Bergen Community College, Interviewer, *Ethics in the '90s*, a 26-part Video Series

Harwood, Sterling, San Jose State University, Editor, *Business as Ethical and Business as Usual: Text, Readings, and Cases*

Heil, John, Davidson College, *First-Order Logic: A Concise Introduction*

Jason, Gary, San Diego State University, *Introduction to Logic*

Minogue, Brendan, Youngstown State University, *Bioethics: A Committee Approach*

Moriarty, Marilyn, Hollins College, *Writing Science Through Critical Thinking*

Pauling, Linus, and Daisaku, Ikeda, *A Lifelong Quest for Peace, A Dialogue*, Translator and Editor, Richard L. Gage

Pojman, Louis P., The University of Mississippi, and Francis Beckwith, University of Nevada Las Vegas, Editors, *The Abortion Controversy: A Reader*

Pojman, Louis P., The University of Mississippi, Editor, *Environmental Ethics: Readings in Theory and Application*

Pojman, Louis P., The University of Mississippi, *Life and Death: Grappling with the Moral Dilemmas of Our Time*

Pojman, Louis P., The University of Mississippi, Editor, *Life and Death: A Reader in Moral Problems*

Rolston III, Holmes, Colorado State University, Editor, *Biology, Ethics, and the Origins of Life*

Townsend, Dabney, The University of Texas at Arlington, Editor, *Aesthetics: Classic Readings from the Western Tradition*

Veatch, Robert M., The Kennedy Institute of Ethics, Georgetown University, Editor, *Cross-Cultural Perspectives in Medical Ethics: Readings*

Veatch, Robert M., The Kennedy Institute of Ethics, Georgetown University, Editor, *Medical Ethics, Second Edition*

Verene, D. P., Emory University, Editor, *Sexual Love and Western Morality: A Philosophical Anthology, Second Edition*

Williams, Clifford, Trinity University, Illinois, Editor, *On Love and Friendship: Philosophical Readings*

Ethics from Experience

Peter Caws
The George Washington University
Washington, D.C.

Jones and Bartlett Publishers
Sudbury, Massachusetts

Boston   London   Singapore

Editorial, Sales, and Customer Service Offices
Jones and Bartlett Publishers
One Exeter Plaza
Boston, MA 02116
1-800-832-0034
617-859-3900

Jones and Bartlett Publishers International
7 Melrose Terrace
London W6 7RL
England

Library of Congress Cataloging-in-Publication Data
Caws, Peter.
    Ethics from experience / Peter Caws.
       p. cm. -- (Jones and Bartlett series in philosophy)
    Includes bibliographical references and index.
    ISBN 0-86720-970-4
    1. Ethics.   2. Applied ethics -- Case studies.   3. Experience.
I. Title.   II. Series.
BJ1031.C38   1996
171--dc20   95-32866
                                            CIP

Acquisitions Editors: Arthur C. Bartlett and Nancy E. Bartlett
Production Administrator: Anne S. Noonan
Manufacturing Buyer: Dana L. Cerrito
Editorial Production Service: Seahorse Prepress/Book 1
Typesetting: Seahorse Prepress/Book 1
Printing and Binding: Edwards Brothers
Cover Printing: New England Book Components, Inc.
Cover Designer: Joyce Weston

Cover Photograph by Nancy Breslin, M.D.

Printed in the United States of America
99 98 97 96 95   10 9 8 7 6 5 4 3 2 1

For Elisabeth and her generation

Contents

Preface

Reading in Context

The intended audience for the arguments that follow is both general and professional, but like most academics I hope that my work will be useful to undergraduates—as many of them as possible. An ethics course based on this book will not be a standard introduction to the subject, either historical or systematic or topical. It will be something more interesting: the working through of a robust and livable moral position, testable against individual experiences and intuitions and suited to an age of science, technology, and communication. I offer the result not merely as a theoretical point of view but as a practical stance that, if generally adopted, would make the world a better place.

In the course of this working through the reader will encounter most of the major problems and many of the major figures in the history of ethics, so that the use of the book as a framework for something like the standard course can be justified if that is what the curriculum requires.

One conclusion of my argument is that a fully moral life cannot be lived in ignorance. The Socratic claim that no one could know the better and do the worse is challenged by the evidence that apparently educated human beings are still capable of terrible evil, though we may well ask in such cases just what their education has brought them to *know*. But at least this much might be said: that no one is likely to do the better, except by accident, without knowing what it is. Some great minds (Jesus, Jefferson, Kant, Tolstoy) have suggested hopefully that knowing the good is fairly straight-forward. But even with a simple view of the good, knowing the better may still require hard thinking and hard evidence. It cannot be known independently of the factual context surrounding whatever is to be done, for better or worse.

Socrates, 469–399 B.C.E., Greek philosopher and teacher of Plato. For Socrates, wisdom lay in knowing one's own ignorance, and in knowing when *not* to act. The source of evil in the world was,

> he thought, a general lack of knowledge, especially self-knowledge.

This suggests that there should be a lively connection between ethics courses on the one hand and courses in the natural and social sciences on the other. For unless we know something of the properties of things in the world, the likely reactions of other people, and above all our own capacities and dispositions, we will not be free agents, much less moral ones.

So moral philosophy should be a challenge to knowledge and self-knowledge as well as to behavior. This applies to teachers as well as students. We all live in a social context and are affected by the moral beliefs and habits of others. In the special context of the ethics course, the relevant other for the students is their professor of moral philosophy. Students can be expected and should be encouraged to test the professor's behavior, as it affects them, against the principles they are working out. It is not a moral imperative that this behavior be up to the test; as I shall argue, the validity of moral arguments is independent of the example of those who make them. But it is a pedagogical recommendation.

In the social world of students there are, predominantly, other students, but there are also administrators, politicians and other public figures—and parents. One of the great functions of college teaching is to influence the previous generation, and students should similarly be encouraged to raise questions about the moral beliefs and behavior of their elders. I remember a student from a prosperous family in New York who wrote a paper about the morality of crime; the criminal, she said, was just like any other citizen trying to make a living, and should not be discriminated against. I hope that the conversations we had about the paper helped her to think again about how her relatives supported themselves.

That was an extreme case, but the point holds generally: the nearest examples of ethical problems do not happen in lifeboats or wars, nuclear or otherwise, important as those are. They happen in connection with paying taxes and rearing children, with living in neighborhoods and driving automobiles, with smoking and drinking and taking drugs, with buying and selling and advertising, with working and voting and entertaining, with taking exams and writing term papers, and with the constellation of activities springing from the agent's physical needs and desires, especially his or her sexuality and habits of gratification. What happens if I hold up my own behavior in these areas to moral scrutiny? What happens if I do the same to the behavior of my friends and colleagues, my parents and professors?

How such questions are raised is itself a moral issue: inquiry has consequences. Social arrangements involving high moral claims—religious movements like Puritanism, political regimes like Communism—become oppressive, degenerating into witch-hunts or public self-criticism. Nobody wants students to become intolerant hardliners, full of righteousness and denunciations. At the other end of the scale, a merely tolerant curiosity may lend itself to rationalization and complacency in the face of behavior that is harmful or destructive.

The first aim of practical moral inquiry is understanding, not judgment. But the process does not stop there. To understand all is to forgive all, says an old French saying (*tout comprendre c'est tout pardonner*), but that does not mean we have to put up with all; understanding is the first step toward change. Denouncing morally objectionable behavior is not of much help, but analyzing it may be. Just to have it pointed out to me that something I am doing hurts someone else in ways I was not aware of may give me pause, for a moment at least, and that may provide the opportunity for someone else to suggest an alternate behavior.

Equally powerful, or even more so, may be the realization that my immoral behavior hurts *me*. Socrates used to say that it was better to suffer evil than to commit it, because the former only harms my body but the latter corrupts my soul. We might interpret "corrupting the soul" as making me a lesser person than I might be or than I would wish myself to be. This may seem a stern doctrine but it can be conveyed convincingly to students. How to change, though? Moral philosophy requires examples of good lives as well as criticisms of bad ones. The biographies of the great are not of much help here. Creative or even saintly lives are not necessarily good in the straightforward moral sense; too many people may have suffered to make them possible. But the modest lives of truly good people are not likely to be written down.

Here I have found that students themselves are among the best sources of material. Nearly all of them know or have known some person they consider good. Soliciting stories about such people and inquiring what about the person's life or behavior warrants the attribution of goodness can open up discussion of moral issues in a productive way. Similarly, although I offer some cases of moral dilemmas in vignettes at the end of the book, personal and topical issues make a better basis for lively exchanges of ideas, and tests of theoretical positions, than invented examples, however ingenious.

The position worked out in this book is practical and robust enough to be tried out on every day's headlines, whether on the front page or in some other section, business or medicine, world or local news. Moral issues are played out in the real world. That is where moral argument belongs also.

Acknowledgments

This book was mostly written during a sabbatical year at the University of Kent at Canterbury. Roderick French and Stephen Joel Trachtenberg of the George Washington University made the sabbatical possible, and Darwin College and the Philosophy Board of Studies at the University of Kent provided conditions and colleagues friendly to ideas. I am indebted to them all. A special word of thanks goes to Richard Norman and Sean Sayers.

The idea of turning an old work into a new one was prompted by an inquiry from Robert Ginsberg; he also proved a demanding but stimulating editor. I am grateful to him and to Arthur Bartlett for their friendly encouragement. Arthur Bartlett prodded me into the uncharacteristic decision to have illustrations in the book; this proved challenging and led to some reflections on popular morality that have found their way into an appendix.

To readers who have read all or part of the manuscript at various stages—Nancy Breslin, Vere Chappell, Virginia Held, Charles Karelis, Jeffrey Reiman, Jeannie Ridings, David Rothenberg, Michael Slote, and Henry West—go my thanks for provocative and reassuring criticisms and comments. I acknowledge also stimulating discussions over the years with Andrew Altman, Hilary and Jonathan Caws-Elwitt, and David DeGrazia, which have helped shape my views even if some of those views remain at odds with theirs.

I thank Karen Greisman for her secretarial help.

To Nancy Breslin, my wife, I owe more than I can say.

Peter Caws
Washington, D.C.

Introduction

The aim of this book is to present a moral theory based on the experiences of individuals. Individuals can share their experiences, so each moral agent does not have to build his or her own outlook from scratch. But in the end the individual has to validate the theory in terms of personal experience. I use "theory" and "outlook" interchangeably here because their root meanings are the same: a theory is a way of looking at things.

> *Experience:* Latin *experior* is "to try, test, prove" (as in "proving ground" rather than in the commonly understood sense of mathematical proof). One of its root forms is *periculum,* "a trial or test," which survives in contracted form in the English word "peril." So experience is not just anything that happens but something one undergoes or is put through, sometimes even at risk. Experience does not form a useful basis for anything if it is not appropriated and reflected upon with some seriousness.

There is an obvious parallel between moral theory and scientific theory. For centuries science rested on authority, and for many people morality is still a matter of authority, sometimes religious, sometimes social. But in the last few hundred years it has become possible for ordinary individuals, suitably instructed, to see how science is validated on the basis of their own experience. The same development is possible in the case of morality.

> *Theory:* The *theoros* in Athens was an official observer, who accompanied people when they competed in the games or consulted the oracle so as to ensure that things were done fairly

and in proper order. *Theazein* meant to be a spectator; "theater" comes from the same root. Some philologists have suggested that *theoros* may be from *theos*, "god," and *ora*, "care," the one who had the word of the god in his care—"his" because *theoros* is a masculine noun.

The present book borrows its theme and some of its material from an earlier one, published in 1967 under the title *Science and the Theory of Value*. For me, this represented a departure from work in the domain of the natural sciences and their philosophical critique. University duties meant I had to teach ethics, and I came to two disturbing conclusions about it. First, moral theorists seemed not to have learned much about the nature of theory, as clarified in connection with the sciences. Second, ordinary people did not seem to have access to the kind of robust conclusion in moral matters that they had come to count on in scientific ones. In the preface to that work I said:

> This book has been written in the conviction that a great deal of what has been learned since the scientific revolution of the sixteenth and seventeenth centuries is regularly left out of account in dealing with problems of value. I have in mind less the facts discovered by science (important as they are) than the principles of empirical knowledge which the discovery of those facts has brought to light. The significant thing about science is that it is knowledge attained, organized, and established in a certain way. It has seemed worth while to inquire whether knowledge about value might not be attained, organized, and established in an analogous way and to ask further, if so, what such knowledge might consist of.
>
> The answer to these questions, as it emerges in what follows, is that the structure of scientific knowledge can, *mutatis mutandis* [with suitable modifications], be transferred to our knowledge of values, although the necessary changes lead to a crucial difference between the two kinds of knowledge. Value can be furnished with an empirical warrant while still retaining its distinctive character as value. The theory of value does not become a science, but it appropriates some of the methods of science and no longer needs to depend on theological or political or romantic presuppositions. And in this way it achieves a basis for universality and a practical relevance which are urgently needed.[1]

These remarks are still on target a quarter of a century later. I am now, however, less inclined to invoke the reputation of science in my title. The claim that science is the best available example of how to get knowledge out of experience used to be generally accepted. The claim is still valid, but this is no longer so obvious, because since the 1960s science has come under attack from at least two quarters, one popular, the other philosophical. In both cases the critics have misunderstood what science is and does, but its reputation has suffered nonetheless.

On the popular side was a great disillusionment on the part of many members of the 1960s generation, who mistrusted science because they thought it was responsible for the Bomb, for technology out of control, for their parents' lack of feeling. A good example of this argument was found in Theodore Roszak's *Where the Wasteland Ends.*[2] Roszak's "wasteland" followed T. S. Eliot, who—in his turn following late medieval romances— had written a famous poem called "The Waste Land" in the twenties. *Where the Wasteland Ends* dealt eloquently—but, I think, mistakenly—with the alienation from science and technology that so many people felt at the time. Its theme was the corruption of nature by technology, the undermining of religion by science, the overwhelming of feeling by knowledge. It argued for a revival of religious awareness, going back to roots older than the already Westernizing doctrines of Judaism and Christianity, and offered a scathing critique of contemporary institutions and attitudes unfriendly to this.

On the philosophical side was a powerful attack, from several directions, on science as objective knowledge. Science was said to be historically and culturally relative, just one discursive practice among others at this point in human development. Its basis in fact was challenged on the ground that facts do not exist. Its convergence toward consensus was called into question.

What the popular argument against science most often amounted to was a complaint that knowledge and reason were not experience and feeling. Reason was represented as cold and abstract, feeling as warm and human. No doubt many people, in the pursuit of rational explanations, have neglected to cultivate intuitive sensibilities. That is their loss. Also, the dominant educational values of our time have stressed knowledge and slighted feeling. The balance is beginning to shift a little. More and more, instruction is accompanied by sensitization, which is all to the good, although we have a long way to go. But attempts on the part of well-meaning reformers to develop feeling *at the expense of* knowledge have usually made things worse.

Relativism: the view that what is true or good in one context or epoch may not be so in another, that no judgment can be final or absolute. You may be tempted to conclude that, in this general form, relativism is absolutely true! Even if true, however, relativ-

> ism does *not* mean that there can be no way of adjudicating between conclusions reached in different contexts or epochs. There may be a more inclusive context or epoch from whose point of view conflicting conclusions can be compared.

It can only obscure the real issue to attribute to the development of science as objective knowledge—knowledge of whatever can be known, including human behavior—the overcrowded and impersonal circumstances of life in our times. Scientific knowledge has helped technological development, some elements of which in thoughtless or greedy or power-hungry hands have posed dangers to the environment or to civil order. But we would again be wrong to charge these misfortunes to science as such, when the real problem is its misuse by shortsighted and unscrupulous people. What human beings have done, human beings can undo, but only if they are guided by appropriate values and have at their disposal reliable knowledge of the sort that science can provide.

What of the attack on the very idea of objective knowledge?[3] Much of it has rested on a misperception: the assumption that science thinks of itself as absolutely objective, that it makes sweeping claims about the certainty and completeness and cosmic scope of its findings. If some scientists have made such claims, that is not (as in the case of the technologists) to be held against the discipline, but against the pretensions of those who overestimate it (and themselves). Scientific knowledge can never be fully objective, in the sense of being wholly independent of human interests. But as knowledge grows more inclusive, as it becomes available across a wider spectrum of cultures, as it survives more tests of its reliability and predictive power, we can say—conditionally but with some confidence—that it acquires objectivity. This means chiefly that knowledge developed in this way resists demands from *particular* religious, ideological, political, or economic interests. It cannot be overturned or discredited by anyone's whims, whether private or institutional.

As to the charge of cultural relativism, people from every cultural background have been persuaded by and have contributed to this trend away from the local and sporadic to the general and systematic, so that *those who have become proficient in it* no longer regard science as particularly "Western," even though its historical roots happen to lie mainly within what is called Western culture.

Are there matters of fact on which science can rest? Again, we need not claim that any factual account of the world is final; a radical skepticism is always possible. For example, we know that perceptions change according to conditions: colors look different under different lights, everything looks different when we are tired or intoxicated, we do not recognize things or people in unfamiliar settings or perspectives, and so on. We can easily imagine extreme cases in which we would be unsure about everything: dreaming without hope of waking, drugged beyond recovery, or caught forever in a great computer game, in "virtual reality" with no access to the familiar world.

Such scenarios deserve to be taken seriously, but they can safely be put aside for two reasons: first, if one of them were the case, we could not know this from within; second, we would have a use even then for the distinction between the factual and the nonfactual. The word "fact" came into being to serve a genuine use. In contrast to "fantasy," "conjecture," "assumption," and other terms that indicate unreality or uncertainty, it stands for things done or achieved, settled states of affairs about which, practically speaking, we no longer have any doubt. Some things and states do meet this description; there is no reason to deny them the status of fact, and it is on them that the edifice of science rests. Some facts are contrived, made to happen in the laboratory, and the same fact may correspond to more than one description, depending on the theoretical stance of the observer, but these qualifications do not jeopardize their factual status. Observers can agree about experimental facts as well as about natural ones, and descriptions may be shown to be equivalent. The science that is based on these facts will always be provisional, but that is an accepted feature of human knowledge.

Fact: Latin *factum* was the past participle of *facio*, "to do or make," hence a deed or exploit, something accomplished. A "fact" need not be definitive or unchangeable; that concept is captured by the related word "perfect," describing something *thoroughly* or *completely* done.

The question of the convergence of scientific theories—a suitable answer to which might deflect charges of historical and cultural relativism—is a more difficult one. The thesis of convergence holds that we are getting closer to a true account of the world, but relativism replies that we cannot know this, because we are always trapped in the language and prejudices of our own history and culture. Science is admittedly very recent and has examined only a small corner of the universe; in spite of its remarkable progress, convergence at the level of the most abstract theorizing remains to be consolidated. History may yet take a divergent turn, and we should be careful not to be presumptuous, or to dismiss alternative accounts out of hand.

In spite of these reservations, a central body of confirmed and teachable scientific knowledge, at the level of the modeling of everyday phenomena for explanatory and predictive purposes, is available to anyone. It is agreed upon by everyone suitably instructed, and helps us to make our way reliably about in our world. If we could learn from it, the way in which this body of knowledge has developed on an empirical basis might provide a model for the grounding of our moral knowledge.

To avoid misunderstanding, let us dwell on this point for a moment. Science is exciting and controversial at its frontiers. That these frontiers are marked by uncertainty and rapid change may persuade excitable people that the whole enterprise is shifting and unstable, and hence a poor example for moral theory. I have sometimes found useful a contrast between the distant frontiers and what I call the "flat region," the middle ground we all inhabit from day to day, where space is Euclidean, time Newtonian, events local, and things macroscopic.

Objects in the flat region are available for inspection; they can be seen and touched. Nothing is microscopically small or cosmically large or relativistically fast. Even scientists live for practical purposes in the flat region; the results of their researches into the distances or the depths have to be brought back there, in forms that can be seen or handled by ordinary human eyes and hands. Reports about quarks or DNA or the Big Bang or the K-T extinction event—the recently confirmed meteoric impact that signed the death warrant of the dinosaurs 65 million years ago—show up uniformly on $8\frac{1}{2}$ by 11 inch paper.

Euclidean space, Newtonian time: The Greek mathematician Euclid (fl. 300 B.C.E.) envisaged a three-dimensional space, with what we would now call rectangular coordinates, that would extend to infinity without gaps or curvature. The English physicist Sir Isaac Newton (see p. 69) thought of this space and everything in it as subsisting through a time that "flows equably." In the nineteenth century it was realized that other consistent spaces were possible (being curved, having more than three dimensions, etc.); in the twentieth it became clear that far away from the flat region actual physical space is non-Euclidean, and time may behave in a nonlinear fashion.

In the flat region Archimedes' principle still holds, and so do Newton's laws. Knowing these and a host of similar principles enables people to weigh, measure, calculate, build, and operate. The accumulation of human experience over centuries has brought the world under effective control *in the flat region*, although forces of nature—hurricanes, fires, epidemics—still remind us of our finitude. This robust knowledge with its practical applications, rather than the exotic and technical knowledge of science at the frontiers, provides the model for what moral knowledge based on experience might hope to become. In moral life we find analogies for events far from the flat region, events so marked by horror or terror that moral agency is overwhelmed and paralyzed and moral theories are inadequate. But such events, and the moral perplexities they provoke, do not invalidate the enterprise of trying to get the central theory right. That is the task of the pages that follow.

Archimedes' principle, Newton's laws: Archimedes (287–212 B.C.E.) discovered that when solids displace fluids their weight is decreased by the weight of the displaced fluid. Sir Isaac Newton (see p. 69) formulated laws of motion for bodies with mass: they keep going uniformly unless acted on by external forces, in which case they accelerate or decelerate in the direction of the external force. When bodies are extremely tiny or when they move incredibly fast, these and similar generalizations no longer apply, but these limits are reached only in a minute fraction of the cases with which human beings have to deal. Most of us never come anywhere near them.

Notes

1. Peter Caws, *Science and the Theory of Value* (New York: Random House, 1967), pp. 5–6.
2. Theodore Roszak, *Where the Wasteland Ends: Politics and Transcendence in Postindustrial Society* (New York: Doubleday, 1972).
3. I have dealt with this problem at length in *Yorick's World: Science and the Knowing Subject* (Berkeley and Los Angeles: University of California Press, 1993), especially Chapter 18.

I

The Apparatus of Moral Argument

1. The Content of Moral Philosophy

This chapter will introduce some of the technical language of moral philosophy. These terms and concepts have been devised by philosophers over the years in the attempt to clarify urgent issues that have affected the lives of human beings since culture began.

> *Argument:* An "argument," in logic, is a series of propositions that lead by the application of rules from something given (the "premises") to something acquired (the "conclusion"). If the argument is valid and if the premises are true, then the conclusion is true also. But the activity of argument need not conform to this technical description. The term derives from Latin *arguo*, "to throw light upon," and refers back to the mythological Argus, who was employed by Zeus to guard his lover Io, whom he had disguised as a young cow. Zeus's wife, Hera, killed Argus and chased Io away, which suggests that seeing things clearly is not always advantageous or safe. Argument is best thought of as a process of clarification or even of enlightenment.

What is the good life, and how can we attain it? How should we act, and how can we judge the actions of others? Different cultures, and different individuals and groups within the same culture, have widely divergent views about the scope and foundation of moral judgment. What some consider matters of taste or individual preference, such as diet, dress, or sexual orientation, are of high moral concern to others. At the same time the grounds for this concern often seem arbitrary and capricious, or to consist of little more than inherited prejudice. So at first glance the scope of morality is vaguely defined, while its foundations are at best uncertain.

All these issues involve the values that people hold. The concept of value is crucial, so we should be clear about its meaning from the start. The main root meanings of the term are "strength" and "worth." The things that are worth most to us are those that are strong: tools that last, friendships that endure through adversity, principles that can be depended on. They are things that evoke strong feelings. No wonder value and morality are tightly interconnected, and no wonder these topics generate such controversy.

Value: Valeo in Latin meant "to be strong," and this sense survives in our "valor." It is not an active component of the word in current English usage; the transition to "value" comes through a secondary meaning of *valeo*: "to be strong (enough) for some purpose," hence "to be worth."

Is it possible to devise a moral theory that will command general agreement, even when values are diverse? It will have to be minimal rather than comprehensive: to catch what is common to divergent human attitudes, not to try to cover all their vagaries. And it will have to appeal to principles accessible to all, not to local beliefs that exclude the rest of the world. One aim of this book is to develop such a theory, one that will be of modest scope but rest on firm foundations, that will make morality simpler but stronger. Its method borrows what it can from science, so one of its incidental purposes will be to determine what the limits of such borrowing are and to distinguish between the proper objects of scientific theory and those of theories of value, moral or otherwise. But it begins on the ground of traditional moral philosophy.

Ethics, morals: "Morals" derives from *mores*, how things are done in a given group or society or culture; compare "ethics," from *ethos*, tribal or group behavior. *Mores* and *ethos* are the Latin and Greek versions of the same idea. That anyone *ought* to conform to the *mores* or the *ethos* is not part of the original meaning; presumably people just did. One way in which "ought" may arise from "is," the normative from the descriptive, is suggested by current English usage. When the descriptive "That's not the

> way we do it here" is said to a newcomer in a group, it means the
> normative "Don't do it that way!" (See section 3.)

In standard usage the distinction between "ethics" and "morals" is not clear. In the following examples the two terms are often used interchangeably:

- "Ethical" and "moral," describing good persons or right conduct
- "Ethics" and "morals," designating principles held by good persons, or standards of right conduct
- "Ethics" and "moral philosophy," designating critical and theoretical reflection on the nature, meaning, and validity of goodness and rightness

I find it helpful to think of moral philosophy as the more reflective part of ethics. Ethics has come to include a great deal of practical reflection that is more technical or legal than philosophical—for example, on the appropriate codification of standards of right conduct for particular professions. This is why I take it to be more inclusive than moral philosophy. Most of the argument of this book will belong to moral philosophy proper; experience may be relevant to ethics in some nonphilosophical ways, but the present project is to consider its strictly philosophical relevance.

What people call morality has to do with the way they behave, how they describe and conceptualize their behavior, and the feelings they have about that behavior, including the justifications and excuses that may be offered for it. Moral philosophy sometimes looks at the behavior itself, but it concentrates more on the descriptions and conceptualizations, the feelings, the justifications, the excuses. Philosophy itself can be characterized as the persistent and reiterated posing of a set of questions about meaning, mattering, truth, and consequences.

Not all behavior is morally relevant. We can tell whether an aspect of behavior should fall under moral scrutiny by considering how it affects others. Morality, as I shall claim later on, is *essentially* a social matter; if something I do has *no* effect, even indirectly, on any other person (or any other being with moral standing—possible candidates are animals, or God), then it does not fall under the scope of morality. Anything I do that *does* have such an effect is potentially a matter for moral judgment.

These bald statements will need qualification when put to the test of philosophical scrutiny, and not all moral philosophers would agree with them. It may be better to postpone making such claims for the moment and to turn to a brief consideration of some of the elements of moral philosophy as it has been practiced in recent times. In this book I shall argue for a particular ethical position, which I will eventually call *minimal consequentialism,* but it is only fair to you to point out that many alternative views have been advanced.

Also, for constructing and adjudicating philosophical arguments between alternatives, a repertoire of definitions and distinctions has been developed over the years in the search for clarity. You should be aware of these and make use of them. In the remainder of this chapter I set out, in a series of brief statements, some of the issues that have dominated argument in moral philosophy in the past century or so. This is not a systematic presentation, or a historical one; nor is it the last word (even in this book) on the topics covered. Its purpose is to introduce some basic terms and concepts.

2. Ethics and Meta-ethics

The Greek preposition *meta,* which means "through" or "alongside" or "beyond," shows up in various philosophical contexts. The longest established is metaphysics; indeed for a long time it stood alone. Metapolitics emerged briefly in the nineteenth century, as a name for the political philosophy of Kant and Rousseau, but it did not catch on. In this century "metalanguage" has appeared on the scene, meaning the use of a language to refer to something linguistic, rather than to something in the world. "The cat is on the mat" is an expression in the English language and refers to a cat; "'cat' has three letters" is a metalinguistic expression and refers to a word, an element of language. The common feature in all these cases—metaphysics, metapolitics, metalanguage—is that attention moves up one level in a hierarchy of abstraction or "aboutness." Physics deals with truths about the world, metaphysics with truths about truth; politics deals with the exercise of power, metapolitics with theories about that exercise; language is about things, metalanguage about language. The term "metaphilosophy" has been introduced to describe philosophizing about philosophy.

> *Metaphysics:* Metaphysics deals with necessary truths, as contrasted with the contingent truths of the physical world and thus seeming to transcend them. But the name "metaphysics" comes from a quite contingent episode in the editing of Aristotle's works by Andronicus of Rhodes. Andronicus chose to put next to the book *Physics* an as yet untitled book that dealt with "first principles." The title he supplied for editorial purposes was purely descriptive: "the book next after the Physics," *ta meta ta phusika.* Whether he intended to exploit the ambiguity of *meta* is

not clear; he may not have had it consciously in mind in placing that particular book where he did. In any case, "metaphysics" came to be thought of as an inquiry dealing with something beyond the physical. This usage was firmly established by medieval times. However, "meta-ethics" is not usually taken to transcend the ethical in this way.

In a similar way, many writers in the last several decades have suggested that the philosopher's task in relation to ethics is not to deal directly with the moral world, with what is right or good, but to deal with the language of morals, with what people mean when they talk about the right and the good—in short, to work not at ethics but at meta-ethics. More generally, the contrast is between what J. L. Mackie has called the "content" and the "status" of ethics.[1] This is a useful distinction in thinking about the recent history of the subject (when operating, that is, at a level that is "meta-" with respect to the distinction between ethics and meta-ethics!), but its importance in ethics itself has been exaggerated.

The distinction is difficult to sustain because recommendations about moral language have an immediate impact on moral behavior. For example, if people who used to think of an activity as stealing come to see it as the reappropriation of what has been expropriated, this may free them to engage in it in spite of their former scruples. Even if there are no objective moral truths at the content level (as Mackie, I think rightly, maintains[2]), the fact that people believe in and claim to refer to such truths makes them operative at the content level in the moral world, and does not merely provide matter for second-order or meta-ethical reflection.

3. The Descriptive and the Normative

If we were inclined to think of ethics as a kind of natural history, or even ethnography, we might examine common behavior or common beliefs and simply extract from them the general principles of morality. The behavior, however, may well be inconsistent with the beliefs. From such an inquiry might emerge cultural practices and rules of thumb—the Golden Rule (see p. 30), for example, or its variants—or various views of the ultimate object of moral endeavor as a philosophical *summum bonum* (highest good): pleasure, the intellectual love of God, the greatest happiness of the greatest number of people, progress, the classless society, the performance of duty, self-realization, engagement in an authentic project, and the like. This would be to do ethics "descriptively" or "historically."

But if we think of ethics as moral teaching, a regulator of human behavior in civil society, then the inquiry will look quite different. The fact that people in various times and places have followed established patterns of conduct, or believed that such-and-such was the highest good, does not mean that their behavior or conclusions were right. Expressions like "so many million consumers (Americans, Baptists, etc.) can't be wrong" are without argumentative force. All those people *can* be wrong—most people can have been wrong about most things since the beginning of time. A few of them probably got some of it right, and we hope that as time goes on more will do so, but these things cannot be assumed; the case has to be made. Thus we will be looking not for what anybody actually did or believed, but for what everybody (or, more modestly and more to the point, what *we*) *ought* to do or believe. This is to do ethics "normatively" or "prescriptively." A prescription records ahead of time what is to happen—usually what medicine we are to take—rather than describing what did happen, after the fact.

Normative: Norma, in Latin, meant a carpenter's square. A "norm," then, is a standard, and "normative" means adhering to or recommending such a standard.

You will not be surprised to learn that in this book ethics will be looked at normatively. That people behave in certain ways is of historical or sociological interest, as is the fact that they hold certain opinions. But philosophy being the questioning activity it is, opinions become philosophically interesting only when we can also discover some of the reasons why they are held. Similarly, patterns of behavior become philosophically interesting only when we can discover some of the reasons behind them. When the opinions are moral opinions and the behavior moral behavior, then these reasons will inevitably have a normative cast. For that matter, moral opinions will themselves be normative, though this fact about them could be treated descriptively. Note that among the moral opinions will be an opinion about what is properly described as moral behavior.

4. Naturalism and Intuitionism

A related contrast appears when we ask how we know what ought to be done or believed. Does this knowledge rest on a descriptive basis or a prescriptive one? In the latter case the "ought" will be doubled: you ought to know what you ought to do. This is not very helpful to someone who doesn't know, who is wondering what to do. Intuitionism offers comfort here by saying that you do know, that to find out you have only to look within, which is exactly what the word "intuition" has come to mean. To know something intuitively is to know it directly, but not on the basis of evidence or argument: we just *see* that it must be the case. This certainly happens in logic, for example, when we see the necessity of the conclusion of a simple argument form (like *modus ponens*—see p. 73) on the basis of the premises. To be able to do something similar in moral matters would mean showing that ethical intuitions are universal and that they do not arise from unconscious acculturation.

Intuition: Tueor in Latin, past participle *tutus*, is "to look or watch"; a tutor was originally someone who looked after or watched over you. *Intueor* is "to look carefully or attentively," not necessarily to look inward; "sensory intuition" is found in English translations of Kant, for example. "Intuitionism," however, normally refers to moral (or mathematical) intuitions, not sensory ones.

If intuitionism were correct, morality would be a relatively simple matter. Equally simple is the position known as naturalism, which holds that if we only stay close enough to nature we will find that the good comes naturally. Naturalists share with intuitionists the view that we can discover something that will offer a ground for moral rightness. Naturalists think we will find it by looking outward to a description of how human beings naturally are, while intuitionists think we will find it by looking inward, to what our feelings of satisfaction or of guilt prescribe in respect of our behavior—in short, to our conscience. For ethical naturalists, goodness is a special but nevertheless observable property of things or actions. The fact that we may not recognize goodness at once is no argument against this position; picking out goodness among all the other observable properties might take training. Certainly we learn to recognize good performances or good wines in this way; the question is whether *moral* goodness is something we can learn to spot directly, without supplementary inquiry or argument.

Naturalism is continuous with some forms of descriptive ethics, since a natural basis for morality can be expected to be incorporated in social practices, especially among primitives not yet corrupted by greed or power, and to be observable there. The difficulty with both positions, naturalism and intuitionism, is what to do with conflicting evidence. There is doubt about the existence of cultural universals, let alone moral ones. What seems naturally right in one context may not seem so in another; the natural may turn out to be culturally determined. Again, if the intuitions of two individuals or cultures disagree, no intuitive ground can be appealed to that would require one party to yield to the other.

5. Deontology, Teleology, and Consequentialism

With specific cases—that is, acts performed by individual agents, on which moral judgment is to be passed—the question arises as to what about a given act carries the moral weight. Here I distinguish three main positions:

1. The *deontological,* according to which the rightness of an act lies in what kind of act it is
2. The *teleological,* according to which the rightness of an act lies in the end it is intended to achieve
3. The *consequentialist,* according to which the rightness of an act lies in its foreseeable consequences

In making these distinctions I am not following a standard usage in ethics. Many philosophers take (3) to be a special case of (2), but I find it useful to keep them separate. The concepts of consequence and end must be carefully distinguished. I may perform an act, aiming quite genuinely at a given end but in ignorance of the fact that this end could never be the consequence of that act. I am reminded of a story about the owner of a maple-sugar bush in Vermont, who was not a native of the state. His assistant, a taciturn Vermonter, watched him every year tap into a particular tree with no result. One year the owner said, "It's an odd thing, this tree never gives any sap," to which the Vermonter replied, "Twon't neither, 'tis a butternut."

Deontology: From Greek *deo,* "lack" or "bind," hence dealing with what is required, or obligation. "Deontic logic," the logic of *must* and *may,* is a branch of modal logic, the logic that deals with sentences in modes other than straight assertion—with probabilities, for example, or beliefs. "Must" and "may," and the corresponding concepts of obligation and permission, are related to one another in interesting ways. For example, "it is not the case that you must not do X" is equivalent to "you may do X," while "it is not the case that you may not do X" is equivalent to "you must do X." Whether there is any obligatory act and what acts are permissible are basic ethical questions.

Teleology: From Greek *telos,* "end," hence dealing with what is aimed at or intended. The term is most frequently encountered in discussions of purposiveness in Nature. Teleological views are contrasted to evolutionary ones; in the former, developmental changes tend toward some intelligible goal, and in the latter they are driven by random mutations under environmental pressure. This distinction has nothing directly to do with the use of the term in an ethical context.

Similarly, the fact that I was aiming at one end when some other unfortunate consequence followed does not excuse me from taking responsibility for that consequence. Even though the latter was not an end I intended, my act did bring it about. The doctrine that "ends justify means" offers an excuse in such cases, but there can be no general justification for that doctrine itself. No matter how good the intended end, each act taken as a means to it needs to be considered independently in the light of its separate consequences. This becomes obvious when the ends and means are grossly disproportionate—for example, if my laudable intention is to crack a nut, but I use for the purpose a sledgehammer that wrecks the kitchen. In this case I may well succeed in realizing my primary intention, but often enough the bad consequences follow without the achievement of the good end. An old saying has it that "the road to hell is paved with good intentions"; in other words, in the event of a final judgment, no claim that I meant well will get me off the hook if the outcome of my deeds was evil. Even if the outcome was good, however, I am accountable for each consequence separately if some of the acts that led to it had unacceptable side effects.

The term "consequentialism" incorporates the idea of a sequel, that is, what follows upon an act through the working of cause and effect. Consequentialism requires me to accept responsibility for what happens as a result of my act, even if I did it according to the most impeccable deontological principle or with the purest of teleological intentions. It does not, however, judge acts only according to their consequences, or assign responsibility only on the basis of consequences the agent actually foresees. It also judges and assigns responsibility according to what is *foreseeable.* This view of consequentialism differs in some respects from the way it is represented in the philosophical literature, especially by its critics. The argument of this book will be largely concerned with setting out and defending a consequentialist position.

6. Acts and Rules

One well-established version of consequentialism is utilitarianism, which was developed in the nineteenth century by John Stuart Mill from the ideas of Jeremy Bentham and James Mill, who were influenced by Enlightenment doctrines about the perfectibility of human happiness through rational action. The utilitarians held that those acts were best that had as consequences "the greatest happiness of the greatest number." This quantitative approach involves difficulties that make utilitarianism a poor representative of the consequentialist position. For example, two oppressors capable of great sadistic happiness would seem to outrank one victim with sensibilities dulled to pain, and the "greatest happiness" principle might be seen as legitimizing their cruelty.

John Stuart Mill (1806–1873), English philosopher, made memorable contributions to logic, political philosophy, ethics, and feminism. For Mill "the ultimate end with reference to and for the sake of which all other things are desirable . . . is an existence exempt as far as possible from pain, and as rich as possible in enjoyments, both in point of quantity and quality."[3] The idea of a *quality* of pleasure was Mill's improvement on Bentham.

However, one distinction that has been much debated in connection with utilitarianism does apply to a broader consequentialism as well: the distinction between *act utilitarianism* and *rule utilitarianism*. The "act" view holds that moral judgment must in the case of each individual act be brought to bear on the consequences, actual and foreseeable, of that specific act. The "rule" view holds that moral judgment bears instead on the rule under which the act was done, and what the consequences would be if everybody followed that rule. One difficulty with rule utilitarianism (or rule consequentialism) is that we often act without reference to any rule, either because we just don't bother to think about it or because no available rule governs the case. But rule utilitarianism shares another and more serious difficulty with the deontological and teleological positions: it allows us to disavow responsibility for bad actual consequences by arguing that we were following a good rule. The most powerful recommendation for consequentialism is precisely its refusal to let people hide behind principles and intentions. In this light rule consequentialism would be self-defeating, not a kind of consequentialism at all.

7. Contracts and the State of Nature

Some of the perplexity of moral action may be removed if its principles can be shown to follow from something obvious and agreed upon. For example, if I have promised you to do something, the question of whether or not I ought to do it does not arise: promising *means* putting myself in the position of being obliged to perform what is promised, not because promise keeping is a deontological principle but because not to accept the obligation would involve me in a contradiction. This does not mean that, in practice, I cannot break my promise, but if I do so I shall not be able to help feeling that I have failed morally, even if I am compelled by overriding circumstances. The external world is not always friendly to my desires to be moral. In an important but generally neglected class of cases, *nothing* I can do, even if I do nothing, can meet moral standards.

A promise is a form of *contract*, an agreement between two or more people governing their future behavior toward one another; some examples are the paying of debts and the provision of goods or services. Contractarian theories suggest that such agreements underlie all moral behavior. Since many acts to which moral judgment applies are not explicitly contractual, the idea of an implicit contract may be appealed to. Sometimes this is dramatized as an original contract that must have been made between our ancestors in order for any moral order to emerge in society at all. *State of nature* or *original position* theories envisage a time chronologically prior to the establishment of morality, or a situation conceptually prior to the formulation of moral rules, and outline ways in which agreement between agents might have been arrived at.

The main advocates of this view in the history of ethics are Thomas Hobbes, Jean-Jacques Rousseau, and John Rawls. In Hobbes's state of nature human beings are generally hostile to one another; in Rousseau's they are generally innocent. Rawls's original position imagines human beings behind what he calls a "veil of ignorance," where they do not know whether they are rich or poor, strong or weak, but only that they will have to live when they do know these things according to rules chosen when they did not know. In all three cases individuals under these conditions are assumed to arrive at contractual agreements with one another, the implementation of which can be seen to lead to, and account for, present arrangements. Some artificiality is always involved in theoretical approaches of this kind. The mass of human beings never were as warlike or as pure or as blind as the theories in question require. Indeed, in Rawls's case the original position is acknowledged to be purely hypothetical, a device to clarify moral reasoning.[4] But as argumentative strategies such theories can be useful and enlightening.

Thomas Hobbes (1588–1679), English philosopher. In *Leviathan* he maintained that the natural state of human kind was a "war of all against all" in which life was "mean, nasty, brutish, and short." His solution to this situation was not moral but political: only if ruled over by a power that could keep them in awe could human beings live together in peace.

Jean-Jacques Rousseau (1712–1778), Swiss philosopher, wrote *The Social Contract* and *Emile*, a novel about education according to nature. Rousseau thought that the first person to say "mine" and "thine" had introduced discord into the world. He also believed that each human being could arrive at a conception of the good for all, and that these conceptions would express a "general will" transcending particular wills.

John Rawls (1921–), American philosopher, is the author of *A Theory of Justice.* He is known for his doctrine of justice as fairness.

8. Rights and Duties

Much recent moral argument has centered on the concept of *rights,* entitlements that individuals can call on other individuals or institutions to honor. Some rights clearly rest on explicit contracts: if I pay fees or taxes, or earn a degree, or am admitted to a club, then I have rights to services or privileges that will be spelled out by the law, the guarantee, the diploma, or the charter. But some rights seem to antedate any contract. One way to ground such rights is to attribute them to a higher power; for example, the Declaration of Independence asserts as a self-evident truth the universal possession of certain inalienable rights endowed by the Creator. Another way is to discover a basis for them in the natural order.

Do human beings have natural rights? We might explain why some rights *seem* natural by arguing that they follow from an implicit contract; once the contract is in place, whatever form it might take, I have a right to expect others to honor it. Here it might be more accurate to say that the contract would secure *basic* rights rather than *natural* rights. The concept of nature itself, however, was extended by the Greeks to cover what they called "second nature," the learned rather than instinctual behavior that was characteristic of civilized life. If after some point in human social evolution *everyone* were taught some form of civilized behavior toward others, so that all understood that behaving in that way was a condition of acceptance as part of the human community, then everyone could count on everyone else to behave in that way toward them.

If such a situation ever did arise, we would no longer need to use the language of rights. I would not have to call upon anyone to do anything, because they would already be doing it naturally. A more realistic view correlates rights with duties, but natural duties are even more problematic than natural rights. The context of rights arguments has often been a situation in which group A is demanding something from group B as owed to the members of A (for example, because of a history of oppression on the part of group B's ancestors), while group B refuses to acknowledge any duty to provide what is demanded. To say that group B *ought* to acknowledge this is not helpful; my rights are empty if I cannot find someone who has *and will accept* the corresponding duty.

Duty: A derivation from the Latin verb *debeo*, "to owe" (from which we also get "debt" and "debit"). *Debeo* in turn is a contraction of *de* and *habeo*, roughly "to have from," that is, to have something of someone else's. My having a right to something means, according to the correlation of rights and duties, that someone else has it and owes it to me, that is, has a duty to render it to me.

---

9. Virtues and Reasons

A full-fledged natural right theory would claim that people have rights because that is part of their nature as human beings, independently of anyone else's having learned to honor those rights as part of second nature. This view is hard to maintain against the hostility of the rest of nature. But if we restrict attention to human nature, especially as exemplified in the relations of human beings to one another, the case might be made that *if* part of basic human nature (not second nature) is to have positive dispositions toward others, *then* a corresponding part of human nature might be something like a right to expect that others will have such dispositions toward oneself. If, for example, the nature of mothers is to protect their offspring, we might say that the young have a natural right to maternal protection or something equivalent. (This would not work in the case of negative dispositions. For example, a natural tendency toward violent behavior on the part of some would not imply a *natural* right of others to be protected from violence, even though we would certainly want to build such a right into the structure of any civilized society.)

We can invoke the concept of virtue at this point. According to classical teaching (especially Aristotle's), a virtue is an attribute the possession of which fulfills the individual's nature as a human being. Practicing virtue is what makes human lives good lives. According to this view we can say that human beings *ought* to be virtuous, and hence require that others be virtuous in their conduct toward us, to behave in such a way as to honor our rights as human beings. It will even be virtuous for us to know what those rights are and to claim them.[5]

But a virtue-based society, if fully operational, would like a duty-based society make rights redundant. In either case we could ask if people are not doing their duty, or manifesting the necessary virtues, what might persuade them to change their ways? Except in small communities of dedicated people we can count on many hardened cases—perhaps the majority—who will not naturally be dutiful or virtuous and who will be deaf to moralistic urgings to become so.

Virtue: Latin *virtus* meant "manliness" or "manly excellence," from *vir*, "man"; it came to be applied especially to bravery and to moral worth. No comparable value term seems to have been derived from *mulier* or *femina*, both meaning "woman." *Mulier* may be related to *mollis*, "soft," so it may be worth citing *mollitia*, meaning among other things "gentleness" or "tenderness." This, however, has no derivative in English except the cognate "mollify," which suggests appeasement rather than any positive value. The only candidate for a value term in English to stand against the masculine connotations of "virtue" seems to be the adjective "maternal." This tells us something significant about the development of our male-dominated culture.[6]

If we cannot appeal to duty or to virtue, we may still appeal to reason. The ethical strategy based on *good reasons* for acts assumes an underlying rationality in all normal agents, though what that rationality consists of is not always clear. Let us consider two contrasting views of reason, which I will call the "maximal" and "minimal" views.

The maximal view takes reason to be a problem-solving ability; people endowed with it can grasp the structure of problem situations and work out strategies for resolving them. Experience suggests that not too many people are habitually rational according to this definition. This is not to say that most people are constitutively *irrational*. The defect might lie in a lack of imagination or initiative, or in a lack of instruction.

The minimal view takes reason to be a solution-recognizing ability; people endowed with it can readily tell whether a presented solution will do the job, even if they cannot think of a single solution themselves. Otherwise unimaginative people turn out to be quite good at choosing the better of two solutions if more than one candidate is offered. The development of a rational ethics, if it is to be realistic, will have to adopt this second view; it must be within the reach of the majority, not just of those who happen to be specially endowed. Everything will then hinge on the provision of imaginative accounts of the moral life between which thoughtful agents will be able to choose.

10. Egoism and Universalizability

For the most part people do bring reason in this second sense to bear on aspects of their personal lives. Imaginative accounts of the good life for individuals—or what is represented as the good life (since many possible options involve bad consequences, overt or covert)—are readily available. Some people have claimed that rational self-interest, consistently followed by all, will result in a situation that will be good for everyone. In the economic theory of Adam Smith this tendency for individual actions to converge to public good is attributed to an "invisible hand," and advocates of the notion of an "efficient market" still hold that all will be well if informed individuals are left to make private decisions that consult only their own interests and preferences. The course of human history since the formulation of this principle suggests that the principle is false or that agents are generally ill-informed. Both may be the case.

Choices made according to the values held by individuals in their own self-interest are sometimes called "agent-relative." However, an egoistic standpoint is not the only possible one; I can, if I make the required effort, take into account the interests of others. It will normally be quite easy to do this for particular others, those to whom I am related by blood or gratitude or common interest, but more difficult for others generally. In most cases, I might feel inclined to say, "I do not even know what their interests are." Suppose we were to ask, "What would *just anybody* want in a given situation?" This would be to adopt an "agent-neutral" position, in which I deliberately ignore the special interests that I bring to the situation and try to see it from an unprejudiced point of view.

Adam Smith (1723–1790), Scottish economist, wrote *An Enquiry into the Nature and Causes of the Wealth of Nations,* the first great treatise on economics, and also *Theory of the Moral Sentiments.* He thought that the appearance of intelligent planning in a situation where individuals, acting freely and independently, pursued only their self-interest, arose from competition. But if each agent were also motivated by the moral sentiment of sympathy, that would presumably have something to do with the happy outcome.

This is to some degree artificial. Auguste Comte, the French creator of the original form of positivism, coined the term "altruism" as an alternative to "egoism." "Altruistic" has usually come to mean self-sacrificing: I do not merely take the interests of others into account, but I consider their welfare *more* important than my own. Even that might be managed in special cases, for the sake of a spouse or children for example, but it is certainly not required in order to be moral. What is wanted is a principle that treats everyone equally, including the agent. One such principle, which has been important in the history of ethics, is arrived at by turning the problem on its head: instead of trying to put myself in everyone else's position, I imagine what it would be like if everyone were in my position. What would happen if everybody did what I want to do? The argument implied here is called the *generalization argument.*

Auguste Comte (1798–1857), French philosopher. He held that human society develops through three stages: theological, metaphysical, and positive, the last being characterized by freedom from unwarranted assumptions about divine powers or abstract principles. *Positivism* is the view that claims to knowledge should be restricted to what can be positively shown, without recourse to theology or metaphysics.

Altruism: From Latin *alter,* "other," originally meaning one of two; *alternus,* from which we get "alternating" and "alternative," meant taking turns.

The most famous exponent of the generalization argument was Immanuel Kant, whose *categorical imperative* in its first formulation states "act only according to that maxim by which you can at the same time will that it should become a universal law."[7] An imperative is an expression of something that *must* be done, though not necessarily because a person in authority commands that it be done. Many such expressions are conditional; that is, the imperative holds only under specific conditions. For example, "if you wish to be considered for financial aid, you must submit your application by the deadline"; the condition (the application) must be fulfilled as prerequisite to the result (being considered for aid). This for Kant would be a *hypothetical imperative*. A *categorical* imperative, by contrast, would be *un*conditional.

Immanuel Kant (1724–1804), German philosopher. Kant's critical philosophy sought to show the structure and limits of reason, and how it enables us to reconcile the domains of nature and of freedom ("the starry heavens above and the moral law within"). He developed a strict deontological ethics, holding that nothing done from inclination or interest counts as good, but only the act of a good will done from a sense of duty.

Imperative: From Latin *impero*, "to impose a requirement," for example on a community, hence to give orders or command. Our word "emperor," from Latin *imperator*, has the same root.

Can we cite any rule that we just *ought* to follow, regardless of circumstances or desires? Kant's answer—or one version of it—was the formulation of the categorical imperative given above. The position I shall adopt is like it: we ought to behave in such a way that anyone similarly situated could behave in the same way and no one would be disadvantaged. In other words, we ought not to consider ourselves privileged over other people.

Categorical: From a Greek root meaning a public assertion or accusation made in the *agora*, the place of assembly, hence straightforward, without quibbles or qualifications.

Practically speaking, the generalization argument has to be qualified by common sense observations about the world and human nature. Suppose we want to go to the beach. We ask ourselves, "What would happen if everybody went to the beach?" The answer is that the beach would become impossibly crowded. So we conclude that we ought not to go to the beach. This is silly. Suppose we ask instead: What if everybody who happens to want to go to the beach today goes—do we have the right to stop any of them to make it easier for us to go? Applying the generalization argument in a modified form, we might conclude that the beach may still be pretty crowded, we had better leave early, and if we cannot find a parking space we may have to come back another day.

The main point here is that everyone is on an equal footing. We take the risk along with all the others that a good in short supply may have run out by the time we get there, but we are interchangeable with them. The situation is symmetrical; if we make it on to the beach, we have still claimed no privilege over those who came later and were turned away.

11. Casuistry and Double Effect

At the opposite end of the scale from the generalization argument is the idea that cases of the application of moral principles are unique and must be dealt with, as the expression goes, "on a case-by-case basis." The term "case" is ambiguous, in that it can mean a member of a class similar to all the others (another case of the flu, for example), but it can also mean a quite specific situation, for example a court case, such as *Brown v. Board of Education of Topeka*. The senses are linked: if *I* have the flu then what preoccupies me is *my* case. The old saying "Circumstances alter cases" suggests that general rules are liable to exceptions. This introduces a difficulty and a danger. The difficulty is to know how to decide what falls under the rule and what does not. The danger is that the decision will not be made disinterestedly.

Casuistry: The interpretation of strict rules as they apply to cases, to problem situations in daily life. The word "case" comes from Latin *cado*, "to fall," *casus*, "a fall"—what is the case being what "falls out" or "befalls," to use old-fashioned English. Casuistry has been practiced for millennia, mainly by representatives of religious bodies having claims to ethical leadership (rabbis with the Talmud, priests with Church doctrine). It acquired a bad name because the Jesuits were alleged to have used specious

> casuistic arguments to condone acts that would ordinarily have been regarded as wrong, such as gaining wealth at the expense of the poor or eliminating rivals.

A special case of an argument of this kind has been called the principle of *double effect*. This principle holds that if an act done for the purpose of achieving a worthy effect (for example, liberating a city) has at the same time other effects not quite so worthy (for example, killing many of its citizens), the unfortunate effects may be excused on the grounds of the overriding value of the intended effects. The force of the principle is not to make the world better but to salve the consciences of the agents responsible for the effects —a prime function of casuistry in its chief historical form. Casuistry is enjoying a new lease on life as a case-based method for doing ethics, but it is still subject to the old danger. I do not see how any morally sensitive person can use the principle of double effect to legitimize evil side effects. In any event, the consequentialist position to be developed in this book will rule that out.

Notes

1. J. L. Mackie, *Ethics: Inventing Right and Wrong* (Harmondsworth: Penguin Books, 1977), p. 9.
2. Ibid., p. 15.
3. John Stuart Mill, *Utilitarianism* (Indianapolis, Ind.: Bobbs-Merrill/ The Liberal Arts Press, 1957), p. 16.
4. John Rawls, *A Theory of Justice* (Cambridge: The Belknap Press of Harvard University Press, 1971), p. 12.
5. See for example Alasdair MacIntyre, *After Virtue: A Study in Moral Theory*, 2nd ed. (London: Duckworth, 1985), p. 154.
6. See Sarah Ruddick, *Maternal Thinking: Toward a Politics of Peace* (Boston: Beacon Press, 1989), for a thoughtful treatment of this issue.
7. Immanuel Kant, trans. Lewis White Beck, *Foundations of the Metaphysics of Morals* (Indianapolis, Ind.: Library of Liberal Arts, 1950), p. 105.

II

The Role of Moral Theory

12. Moralists and Moral Philosophers

The previous chapter was intended to introduce, in no special order, a series of technical terms whose understanding will provide you with a good background for following the rest of the argument. It was not meant to advocate a particular ethical position. But you will have gathered that in more than one way a preference for such a position—announced explicitly in the first section—underlay the way in which the exposition proceeded. This illustrates the difficulty of doing moral philosophy without being a moralist.

A "moralist" is someone who has a moral point of view and advocates it, criticizing (at least implicitly) the behavior of those who do not share it and often trying to persuade them to do so. The term has become pejorative because moralists typically have demanding views that are seen as interfering with other people's freedom. *Moral philosophers*, on the other hand, might be expected to preserve neutrality about the principles they are criticizing, even if they do not claim to be working at a meta-ethical level—which, as we have seen, would involve a somewhat different distinction, between language and substance rather than between commitment and detachment.

A striking fact is that the status of moral philosophers as human beings predisposes all of them to recognize roughly the same problems as moral ones, and for the most part their analyses of familiar problems of moral behavior accord with the common sense of their time. If this were not so, the philosophers would not be listened to. We may suspect, though, that the common sense often dictates the analysis and not, as might have been hoped, that the analysis independently justifies the common sense.

The argument that moral philosophers should not justify anything, but that their analyses are secondary activities—"meta" with respect to the primary business of the moral life, and with no commitment to one moral conclusion rather than another—is thus difficult to maintain. In ethics, of all the branches of philosophy, such detachment is suspect. Ethics deals with the nature and justification of moral argument. What makes an argument moral is never merely its form but always also the use to which it is put and the practical consequences of that use. Moral arguments must be of use in solving moral problems, and the decision as to what counts as a moral problem and what does not already commits the moral philosopher to some ethical position or other. Sometimes the disclaimer of any such commitment arises from a natural reluctance to assume a position of apparent moral superiority, which might involve hypocrisy if the philosopher fails to live an exemplary life.

This reluctance rests on a confusion: the commitment to an ethical position is not a moral commitment but an intellectual one, and philosophers' lives belong to a different logical category from their teachings. "Be not too hasty to trust, or to admire, the teachers of morality," says Dr. Johnson; "they discourse like angels, but they live like men."[1] A thoroughly immoral theorist might propound a correct moral theory, and it would be correct nonetheless. The theory would condemn the theorist, as it would condemn anyone else who acted similarly, but the fact that it was that person's theory would not make the condemnation any worse. The theorist's behavior might, it is true, have something to do with the attitude that other people took to the theory, but if they rejected it for the wrong reasons the responsibility would be primarily theirs. Moral philosophers should be aware of their role as exemplars, but they need not hesitate to make recommendations about and impartial assessments of the various arguments with which they deal.

Samuel Johnson (1709–1784), English writer and critic. He was known for his pithy sayings, many of which have the form of philosophical arguments in miniature.

If moral arguments are to be useful in solving moral problems, they must be intelligible to people who confront such problems. Since everybody confronts moral problems, this makes a demand on ethics more challenging than any demand made, for example, on metaphysics or logic or the philosophy of science. Doesn't everybody confront logical and scientific problems too? Yes, but the cases differ significantly. Science is a refinement of ordinary experience. The commonsense solutions that ordinary people find to the problems that arise routinely in their dealings with the physical world are not yet explicitly scientific, nor should they be held to scientific standards.

Something similar is true for logic. Everyday discourse obeys a form of logic that has become an object of inquiry for ethnomethodologists, scholars who examine the methods people use to arrive at conclusions in nontechnical settings, like juries and committees. These methods are highly functional but nonformal. Ordinary simple arguments are often quite strictly logical, and can sometimes be formalized for teaching purposes. Yet people can be illogical if they like. Nothing compels them to engage in logical reflection.

But morality is part of ordinary experience. Many of the commonplace problems of ordinary people, which arise in their dealings with others, are full-blown moral phenomena that require no refinement to become the subject of ethical discussion. We may say that people can be illogical if they like, but not that they can be immoral if they like. They *can*, being free, but the rest of us cannot safely remain indifferent to this as we usually can in the case of logic. This immediate and down-to-earth character of the moral does not mean that ethics has no room for technicalities and refinements. It does mean that these must not be allowed to obstruct the primary task of ethics, which is *the construction and criticism of arguments relevant to the concerns of everyday life and robust enough to withstand the uses to which plain people will put them.*

Nothing prevents philosophers from spending their lives in secondary activity; it can be "quite good fun for those people who like that sort of thing."[2] Too evangelical a tone is not considered good form among philosophers. But, in spite of professional qualms, there is no good reason why philosophy should not take upon itself the authority in moral matters to which religion and nationalism have proved unequal. The chaotic state of public morality suggests that it ought to do so. To meet this challenge, philosophers have to produce arguments capable of carrying everyday burdens, as well as arguments suitable to the more technical interests of professors.

13. Criteria for a Practically Useful Moral Theory

Producing such arguments, however, is not as easy as it looks. The conditions they must meet are stringent. Their premises (or initial assumptions) must be generally accessible and convincing; their terms must be unambiguous and generally intelligible; their steps must be generally plausible and easy to follow; their applicability to cases must be straightforward; and they must be analytically rigorous, that is, they must be able to stand up to critical scrutiny and to withstand counterarguments.

Some arguments that apparently satisfy these criteria have been in practical use for a long time, but their success has usually been due to an overloading of the premises with emotionally charged material, religious or patriotic, to such an extent that the argument itself becomes a mere appendage. The fear of God or the love of country, together with a set of commandments or exhortations, can have the practical effect of making conduct unproblematic, of providing a rule for every situation. Many people, for example, have claimed that everything needed for the right conduct of life is to be found in the Bible. Others have taken their codes of behavior from ideals of chivalry or of scholarly or artistic integrity or of a national way of life. Some stripped-down codes (such as the Ten Commandments) once had an emotive basis but have largely lost it. Others (such as the Golden Rule) never had such a basis. But these codes are of limited applicability. Bertrand Russell said of the Golden Rule, "Do not do unto others as you would have them do unto you—their tastes may be different."

The *Ten Commandments* can be found in the books of Exodus, 20:3–17, and Deuteronomy, 5:7–21. They are among the several hundred commandments God is said to have given to Moses on Mount Sinai for the government of the Jewish people, who were on their way from Egypt to the Promised Land.

The *Golden Rule* is traditionally formulated as "do unto others as you would have them do unto you." A negative (and perhaps more effective) version is also found: "do not do unto others as you would not have done unto you."[3]

Bertrand Arthur William Russell, third Earl Russell (1872–1970), English philosopher. He did important work in logic (with Alfred North Whitehead [see p. 155]) and the philosophy of mathematics, but became widely known for his popular writings, which were lucid and often radical. His appointment at City College in New York in 1940 was blocked on the grounds of immoral character. He was imprisoned during World War I for pacifist activities and won the Nobel Prize for Literature in 1950.

In religious or nationalistic cases, a more or less overloaded set of premises will be an integral part of the code. People may disagree about how to interpret these premises, but such disagreements will be treated as theological or political matters, rather than moral or philosophical ones. The problem of implicit premises is one of the most crucial in ethics. It undercuts the meta-ethical claim that the task of the moral philosopher would be done if the meanings of the terms used could be clarified and the rigor of moral argument guaranteed. The examination of a theory of what is good may show that accepting it involves some belief about the structure of society, perhaps, or the grounds of obligation: for example, that nothing done from inclination can be morally worthy, or that human beings and their jobs are absolutely more important than endangered species of owls or fish, rather than being factors to be weighed in a larger ecological context. Without this background belief, the meaning of the good would be quite different. If valid reasons existed to judge the belief as either groundless or compelling, the analysis would not be complete unless they were specified.

The ultimate premises of moral argument may be called *moral principles*. The implicit premises of traditional codes of ethics no longer carry much weight as moral principles. In the absence of satisfactory replacements people may come to believe either that no principles exist or that principles must be a matter of blind and arbitrary faith, which amounts to the same thing. Professional philosophers have rarely been forthright in discarding the old principles or imaginative in proposing new ones. Scholarly disengagement does not encourage this. Descriptive ethics can describe the principles that human beings have in fact adhered to at various times and in various places without passing judgment on them. The analysis of ethical language may uncover implicit presuppositions, but it can deal with their logical relations to the rest of the system independently of their truth. The solution to these difficulties does not lie in a further examination of the same data, whether behavioral or linguistic. What is required is a theoretical model for ethics, whose adequacy to the data is to be judged only after it has been worked out to a sufficient degree of complexity.

The call for a theoretical model may seem inconsistent with this book's avowed intention to base ethics on experience. This is where the example of the sciences will prove helpful. For the history of science is a history of collaboration between empirical data (that is, reports of what has been experienced as factual) and theoretical conjecture (that is, ideas thought up to make sense of the data). The job of moral theory is to think how the human world might best be ordered in order to reconcile desires and behavior in such a way as to minimize injustice and unhappiness, for everyone and over the short and the long term.

14. Hypothetical Principles

The principles on which such a theory rests will be hypothetical, but the hypotheses can be quite simple ones. The assertion of the hypotheses cannot help but appear dogmatic, yet the dogmatism is relative. The principles are *a priori* with respect to the theoretical model—that is, they cannot be challenged or justified within it but must be taken as given, prior to and as a condition of the development of the model. But the model as a whole is *a posteriori* with respect to empirical evidence. In other words, the evidence takes priority and the fate of the model follows after; if it is incompatible with the evidence, the theory has to be abandoned or modified—unless some way can be found to reinterpret the evidence.

Hypothetical: A hypothesis is a statement advanced provisionally for the purposes of argument; it may or may not be confirmed by evidence. The term is from Greek *hypo-*, "under" (as in "hypodermic," under the skin), and *thesis*, "a placing or situating": something laid down, as it were, under the argument, to provide it with a (temporary) basis. The structure of the term is exactly parallel to English "understand," the sense of which, however, is normally quite different. "Coming to an understanding" prior to further debate, when the agreement is provisional, catches part of the meaning of "hypothesis."

A priori, a posteriori: Prior and *posterior,* although they have become English words, are pure Latin. *Prior* means "former" or "first": *posterior* means "following after" or "later." The particle *a* means "from." So a statement is true *a priori* if it can be asserted before the question of evidence is even raised, but true *a posteriori* if its only claim to truth rests on evidence. "It is raining" can only be known *a posteriori*; "either it is raining or it isn't" can be known *a priori*.

A distinction is to be drawn, however, between a priori principles necessary for the development of any theoretical system, which are incorrigible in the light of empirical evidence because they are empirically empty, and functionally a priori principles necessary for the development of a particular system. These are corrigible in the light of empirical evidence, when such evidence is brought to bear on the adequacy or inadequacy to experience of the system as a whole. The principle of contradiction, which says that a proposition and its denial cannot be simultaneously true, is an a priori principle of the former type. The principle of the conservation of energy, which says that in any closed physical system the total quantity of energy in all its forms remains constant over time, is a functionally a priori principle of physics.

Among functionally a priori principles a further distinction is drawn between two types: elementary and transcendent. *Elementary principles* are hypotheses about the elements of the world to which a given theory applies. They have empirical content, in that they refer to actual events and specify how these must occur, but they apply to such events distributively, that is, one at a time. The system is built up by considering what follows if events that take place according to the principles occur serially or simultaneously, under more or less complex conditions, and so on. The principles of science, for example, of quantum mechanics or of genetics, are of this type. The inclusion of such principles is a condition of the empirical relevance of any system.

Transcendent principles also purport to refer to actual events, but they apply (and one of their characteristics is that the manner of this application is generally obscure) to the totality of events, often overlooking distinctions between *kinds* of event. Instead of resting upon the principles as hypotheses, the system is constrained by them as requirements. In a system built up on the basis of elementary principles, a statement is admitted as true if it can be shown to follow from the principles. In a system developed in the light of transcendent principles, a statement is rejected as false if it cannot be reconciled with the principles. Most principles of metaphysics and religion—for example, the existence and goodness of God, the infallibility of the scriptures, or the purpose of history—are of this second type.

Transcendent: From Latin *transcendo,* "to climb over" (*trans,* "across," and *scando,* "to climb"), hence what lies beyond some boundary or obstacle. A transcendent principle is one that appeals to something beyond possible experience.

As these examples show, the logical form of transcendent principles is often existential. That is, they posit the existence of a particular entity (God, the inspired Word, History), which dominates everything to which the theory applies. In contrast, the logical form of elementary principles is always universal; that is, they treat actual or postulated objects or events as

The Seven Deadly Sins: Pride (1953; director Claude Autant-Lara)

Michèle Morgan is too proud to admit her family's poverty; she continues to play the role of the socialite—even though doing so deprives her and her mother of the necessities of life—with eventually tragic consequences.

examples of types, bringing them under general headings according to their properties or other characteristics.

Some elementary principles have customary expressions that are apparently existential—for example, the postulation of an absolute zero of temperature or an absolute limit of velocity. But the velocity of light and the zero point of the Kelvin scale do not exist as God is alleged to exist; they limit actual processes distributively and can be formulated so as to avoid all reference to existence. All objects whatever have definite temperatures and velocities. To say that there is a lowest possible temperature or a highest possible velocity is not to say that such a thing concretely exists, but only that of all the things that do exist, none can move faster or be colder than these limits allow. When put in this way, such principles cannot be confused with transcendent ones.

> *Kelvin scale:* A temperature scale (named for the Scottish physicist Lord Kelvin, 1824–1907) in which the unit is the degree Celsius but zero is at minus 273°C, the theoretical lowest limit of temperature, at which all the motion of particles, which represents the energy of heat, has ceased.

This distinction is introduced only to clarify the nature of the system to be developed in the following chapters. Many ethical theories appeal to transcendent principles, but these tend to conflict with one another. The resulting uncertainty about the warrant for ethical recommendations, together with a tendency on the part of moralists to shift ground from one justification to another in the course of argument, has weakened the force and intellectual interest of the theories in question, and indirectly of ethics in general. The principles appealed to have not always been explicit. Often the best critical intentions are not enough to prevent a covert appeal to principles whose personal or cultural roots are too deep to make their overt recognition possible. I must in honesty admit that this remark may very well apply to the argument of this book.

Usually, however, the function of transcendent principles has been consciously to universalize conclusions based on local evidence, although with no sense of philosophical impropriety. Such principles have been useful in stabilizing the local situations from which the evidence was drawn, but they have generally been disastrous when exported by well-meaning missionaries, and even their local use has frequently been repressive. Moreover, although I have included transcendent principles among functionally a priori principles capable of indirect empirical test, they have customarily been employed in a way that excludes the possibility of empirical refutation. For example, the principle that God is good and desires the happiness of created beings appears inconsistent with the prevalence of misery in the world, but this argument may be effectively disposed of by reference to God's ineffable purpose. *Ineffable* means unspeakable or unutterable, and so beyond any possibility of our comprehension; using the term thus blocks discussion altogether.

15. The Rejection of Transcendence

For these and other reasons, transcendent principles are best avoided in the construction of a theory of morals. One person's orthodoxy is another's heresy. If conflicts are to be resolved, the reaffirmation of such principles is not the way to go about it. The motivation for much work in ethics is to be found in personal, institutional, or national conflicts, which is why so many ethical theories are rationalizations of a status quo, ennobled by an appeal to the appropriate transcendent principle: democracy, the church, tradition, the revolution. None of these will do for resolving the conflicts that now confront the world, because each is the apotheosis of a localized belief and none carries universal conviction. We must have either universally shared transcendent principles or none at all. In the present circumstances we have no hope of arriving at shared transcendent principles, so the only available option is to dispense with them altogether. Accordingly we are left with elementary principles alone for the construction of our theory. The foundation of this theory must lie in what is immediately accessible to, or testable by, every individual, no matter what his or her situation in the world; assumptions that transcend this must be resolutely excluded.

This recommendation appears to conflict with the declared intention of proceeding hypothetically. Two things should be said here. First, antecedently plausible principles may be put forward hypothetically, in the sense that the theory stands ready to discard them, even though it does not expect to be called upon to do so. Second, hypothetical principles stand a better chance of leading to fruitful systems if they are antecedently plausible. The example of science is again useful.

Although some modern scientific hypotheses—of quantum mechanics and of relativity, for example—seem implausible to nonscientists, so that science has often been represented to them as an affair of marvels and mysteries, the elementary principles through which you will be introduced to science as a student are familiar and convincing in the light of ordinary experience. The components of the universe referred to by the principles may be smaller or larger than everyday objects and their properties may be unusual, but they are objects or regions in space and time and their properties can be exhibited in simple phenomena. If you ever held a sufficiently strong magnet in each hand and felt the force of magnetic interaction at a distance, you should be ready for anything modern physics has to offer. The stability of science lies to a great degree in this accessibility of its basic hypotheses, from which by a series of steps you may be led to the most remote or surprising of its truths.

This condition is of recent origin. Science got nowhere in its animistic and theological stages because it lacked conceptual precision and because the elements of experience on which it rested were mysterious and implausible. What set in motion the appetite for explanation was the abnormal, the pathological, the fearful. The principles invoked to explain them were more bizarre than the experiences themselves, so that credulity became a virtue without which orthodoxy was impossible. Something like this is still true in moral theory at the popular level. For example, many people think that morality is impossible without religion. This doctrine often has an effect exactly opposite to what was intended; it has weakened morality rather than strengthened it. Religion is now far less plausible to educated people than morality is in its own right, so that if morality is made to depend on religion, people may suppose that if religious belief declines, the grounds of moral behavior have also been eroded. If right behavior is no more important than ritual behavior, then morality stands on a weak footing indeed.

Another popular view is that the way to approach moral problems is to try to understand human nature, whatever that may mean. This hampers the work at hand. If science had insisted on understanding the nature of matter, or of space, or of time, before tackling its other problems, we would still believe that the earth was at rest in the center of the universe. Human nature may be the last thing we understand. One of the most useful contemporary philosophical contributions to the debate about human nature has been the existentialists' assertion that there is no such thing—nothing compels me to be one way or another just because I am human. I still want to know what being the kind of animal I am makes it likely that I will become in the absence of self-determination, so the work of psychologists and sociobiologists is essential. But we do not have to wait for it to be finished before we get on with the work of moral philosophy.

Sociobiology: A theory according to which social behavior generally, including moral behavior, is largely determined by our biological endowment, so that light can be thrown on it by studies of animal behavior. Its principal exponent has been the American E. O. Wilson (1929–).

Do not conclude, from the polemical tone of these remarks, that the position advocated here is necessarily antireligious or antihumanistic. The foregoing critique has no bearing on the value of religion in its own sphere. Religion has its place, but that place is not in the discussion of moral theory, because, in order to achieve universality, special assumptions belonging to one religious tradition or another must be excluded *even if they are right.* Starting from what you happen to believe to be true is not good enough. The starting point must be something *generally agreed* to be true, at least for the purposes of argument.

The widest agreement will be commanded by the smallest set of principles, so that the rule is to reduce the number of functionally a priori principles to a minimum. In some ideal future everyone might agree, after persuasive argument, on one set of transcendent principles, and they might prove to be the principles of a currently popular religion. But this cannot be assumed in advance, and you will have gathered that I think such a possibility an idle dream. To count on it and use the expectation as a reason for forcing one religious view or another would be oppressively immoral.

16. Doubts about Human Rationality

One condition for the utility of moral argument is independent of and indeed prior to any principles whatever in the sense just discussed: namely, the shared conviction that argument is an acceptable mode of procedure. If philosophy is motivated by any single conviction, it is surely that human beings ought to have reasons for acting as they act and for believing what they believe, and that these reasons ought to be the best they can find. An underlying assumption here is that the beliefs and actions in question are not trivial. If people are not persuaded by reasons, arguing with them makes little sense. Even under the minimal view of rationality given earlier (see section 9), many people are not in the habit of weighing alternatives rationally; under special circumstances, such as times of emergency, reasoning has always had to be supplemented by coercion. History shows that this has happened far too often, even if it has occasionally been unavoidable. An unquestioned following of the orders of the airline captain or the fire marshal while the emergency lasts makes sense. An unquestioned following of the orders of the drill sergeant has a more dubious justification, though as long as the idea of the military is accepted then so is that of military discipline. An unquestioned following of the orders of academic or religious officials has no justification at all—they should not be *giving* orders. An exception to this last claim is the religious community freely entered on condition of obedience; as in the military case, we may have our doubts about the institution, but we cannot deny the cogency of its internal rules.

> *Reason, rationality:* Both from Latin *ratio,* "reckoning," "account," in its turn from *reor,* "to reckon, be of opinion, judge." *Ratio* translates one of the senses of the Greek *logos,* so that "rational" and "logical" largely overlap in meaning. The demand that individuals be reasonable is sometimes seen as heavy and limiting, as though reason were the enemy of more spontaneous

values. But in the end all human values require an undergirding of rationality. The story is told of the philosopher Epictetus (Greek, 50–138), who was challenged by one of his students to prove that logic was necessary. What kind of proof did the student want? asked Epictetus, who then added, "You see that logic is necessary, since without it you cannot tell whether it is necessary or not." In a similar way, no challenge to reason can hope to stand up unless it is presented rationally.

Without going into the question of political freedom, we may agree that, if people are to be induced to behave in one way rather than another—morally rather than immorally, let us say—the chief alternative to coercion is rational persuasion. Nonrational persuasion, such as propaganda or high-pressure advertising, counts as a form of coercion. Moral argument is a key form of rational persuasion, and its utility will be seriously curtailed if rationality is not widespread.

Defining humans as rational (as is suggested, for example, by calling the species *homo sapiens*) does not offer reassurance on this point. Rationality in the sense of being *able* to reason, even in the minimal sense specified earlier, is in any case not enough; we must have a disposition to *use* the ability, a habitual recourse to it in situations that call for decision. The confidence with which philosophers have sometimes assumed that this was the case, at least whenever it really mattered, has been badly shaken in recent decades. Think of who gets elected, what wars are fought, or even of how most people live their lives, what they buy, how they choose to be entertained. People speak of a crisis of values. We can make as good a case for a crisis of rationality itself. If things are really as bad as they are sometimes made to appear, philosophy cannot possibly be of any help. Philosophy cannot help in any case if those who appeal to it do not know what the problems are that need to be solved. For both these reasons let us, before we go any further, make a brief assessment of the contemporary situation.

Homo sapiens: The name given to our species in the Linnaean system of classification (named for the Swedish botanist Carolus Linnaeus, 1707–1778) is *Homo sapiens sapiens. Sapiens* in Latin meant "wise, sensible, judicious," but the root verb *sapio* meant "to taste." The metaphor therefore stresses the human capacity for discrimination rather than calculation.

Notes

1. Samuel Johnson, *The History of Rasselas, Prince of Abyssinia* (New York: Home Books Co., n.d.), p. 90.
2. C. D. Broad, *Five Types of Ethical Theory* (London: Routledge and Kegan Paul, 1930), p. 285.
3. The negative formulation has been ascribed to Rabbi Hillel the Elder. See Karen Armstrong, *A History of God* (New York: Alfred A. Knopf, 1993), p. 72.

III

The Contemporary Crisis of Values

17. Strains in the System of Values

Every age is considered by many of its contemporaries to be an age of crisis, if only because the stable world in which fortunate children grow up turns out on mature inspection to be full of changes. No doubt some of the current anxiety can be attributed to this perennial discomfort, but, even when the most generous allowance has been made for it, the present age still seems to suffer from a more acute crisis than its predecessors. Our century might be said to have been in chronic crisis, which is not the contradiction in terms it appears to be. In this chapter we will look at two crises, one in cultural attitudes generally and one in the profession of philosophy. They have much in common.

Crisis is a transliteration of the Greek for "decision." Crises go on until decisions are arrived at that change the situation. Our chronic condition is one of indecision. Many questions that were once thought to have been finally decided, about humanity, nature, society, and God, have been reopened. The bases for decisions about more recent problems, such as nuclear proliferation, population growth, environmental overload, the gap between rich and poor, urban violence, ethnic strife, and new viral epidemics (such as AIDS), have hardly yet been established. We have learned to live with crisis, because fundamental decisions can nearly always be put off. But the longer they are put off, the more unpleasant the available alternatives may become.

Crisis: The root verb in Greek is *krino*, "to distinguish, choose, decide"; it leads to Latin *cerno*, from which we get "discern." The derivative *krites*, "a judge or umpire," gives us "critic" and "criterion."

The trouble is that we wish to be sure that our decisions are right, and this requires a degree of certainty we have not attained about the aims and the consequences of action. The old certainty has gone. Its demise was a long-drawn-out process that came to a foreseeable climax in the middle of this century. What was not foreseen was the eruption, at the same historical juncture, of grave new uncertainties. In the circumstances, we can hardly be surprised if the structure of values shows signs of strain, since value is an indispensable ingredient of decision, and any uncertainty about it spoils the whole decision-making process.

18. The Effect of the Popularization of Science

Once again this state of affairs manifests itself differently at the level of popular understanding and the level of professional analysis. In the previous chapter I maintained that these levels ought to be intimately connected where ethical questions are concerned, but that such a connection is not necessary in the case of scientific questions. Paradoxically, the connection has been established far more successfully in science than in ethics, and this fact itself contributes to the crisis.

For the popular understanding of science, which is often accurate enough, has rendered far more difficult than formerly the acceptance of the principles on which values depended for so long. Technology, the form in which science presents itself most dramatically to the public, has transformed the environment to which those values were appropriate. The coincidence referred to above, of new uncertainties with the decline of the old values, was not so fortuitous after all. And yet the attitude of science has been consistently benign. It did not set out to destroy faith, but to improve the conditions of human life. With respect to material well-being, the success of science has been spectacular. But the claims of the optimists at the turn of the century, who saw in science the final answer to all human problems, no longer seem even remotely valid.

I do not wish to exaggerate the seriousness of this critical situation. Nevertheless, impartial observers from another planet, reading only bestselling novels and the periodical press, would probably come to an extremely pessimistic conclusion about the human condition, the continued advance of science notwithstanding. Some characteristic symptoms of the malaise of our age, they might conclude, are fear, anguish, loss of identity, alienation, and boredom. Fear and boredom are directly attributable to technological change, and loss of identity to scientific developments; anguish and alienation are produced indirectly, as quasi-philosophical responses to scientific and technological stimuli.

The crisis of identity in a scientific age is an old problem. It is a problem of contrasts, arising uniquely in a Western civilization brought up on Christianity. Human beings were viewed, in the Christian West, as the children of God, specially created as the apotheosis of the natural order, compound of body and spirit, to whom the earth had been given as a central habitation and the heavens as a covering. They have been shown, by Copernicus and later astronomers, to be clinging to a speck of matter, suspended in an infinite abyss, which is not near the center of anything and provides only accidentally and temporarily an environment friendly to life. Darwin showed in his turn that nothing is special about human origins; we are an accidental, and again probably temporary, terminus of a random and unintelligent process. Freud and the anthropologists have added that our personal and social behavior is largely determined by internal and external conditions whose origins we cannot remember and that we cannot control.

Nicholas Copernicus (1473–1543), Polish astronomer. He concluded that it made more sense to take a heliocentric view (Greek *helios*, "sun"), according to which the sun is at rest in the center of the solar system and the earth moves around it, than to adhere to the old geocentric view, according to which the earth was at rest in the center of the universe.

Charles Darwin (1809–1882), English naturalist. On the basis of observations of wild and domestic animal and plant life, he developed a theory of variation and selection that, applied to nature over long periods of time, could account for the origin of species—including the human species.

Sigmund Freud (1856–1939), Austrian neurologist and the founder of psychoanalysis. His theories of mental structure and drive, and especially of the role of the unconscious, have had a dominant influence in all fields of culture in the West.

Pascal acknowledged that he was frightened by "the eternal silence of the infinite spaces"; although less humble representatives of the established order met the doctrines of evolution and psychoanalysis with indignation, they were clearly frightened too.

> *Blaise Pascal* (1623–1662), French mathematician, scientist, phi-
> losopher, and theologian. His *Pensées* ("Thoughts") include,
> among many other things, existential meditations and applica-
> tions of probability theory to belief in God.

19. The Effect of Technology

Such fear was misplaced, or premature. Nothing is inherently pessimistic
about the view of human beings presented by modern science. To argue
from the new view of our circumstances and origins to a lessening of our
stature is to succumb to the genetic fallacy: the fallacy of attributing to
mature individuals or finished works the shortcomings and the virtues of
their parents or creators. Intellectually, science put humankind at an un-
precedented advantage with respect to nature, and at first it promised to do
so practically as well. Only quite recently has the possibility had to be taken
seriously that the insertion of scientific determinations into a complex
network of human and natural causes and effects may have started chains
of events that cannot be controlled.

> *Technology:* Greek *techne* meant "an art" or "a system of making
> or doing." The usual sense of words ending in "-logy" (from
> *logos* [see p. 38]) is roughly "theory of" or "discourse about," as
> in the case of "biology," from *bios*, "life." An exception to this rule
> is "ideology," which began as a theory of ideas but came to mean
> a system in which the ideas are incorporated. "Technology"
> follows this pattern: it has come to mean a culturally developed
> apparatus that amplifies human power by means of machines.
> As such it is extremely ancient. Technology captures our atten-
> tion now mainly because the available power is so great, and so
> disproportionate to the wisdom of those who wield it.

The two most familiar cases of this danger are the existence of nuclear
weapons and the difficulty of preventing their use by irresponsible governments, and the lowering of the death rate by successful attacks on disease

without a corresponding lowering of the birth rate. The human race may eventually destroy itself by one method or the other if controls are not devised. But these dangers, serious as they are, are for the immediate future less pressing and less difficult to avert than a series of others that have arisen as indirect consequences of the application of science and technology to human affairs.

The rise of technology has had two effects on individuals. One has to do with their control of their world and the other with their enjoyment of it. Both raise the question of value in a fundamental way. First, technology has transformed the production of material goods. In preindustrial society consumers were not far removed from the source of their material supplies. If they themselves did not control that source, then somebody like them did, somebody with greater powers and privileges, perhaps, but somebody who could be met, and on occasion even conquered, at the level of person to person. Industrialization changed the situation irreversibly; social and political structures became for the first time genuinely inhuman, and human beings became alienated from these structures.

The term "alienation" has become familiar in thoughtful conversation, and it is often assumed to be a special mark of our age, but the term's philosophical history justifies this view only partially. Alienation, according to Hegel, is a necessary condition of consciousness. The object of consciousness must be different from, and over against, the conscious subject. The emergence of consciousness and its ultimate reconciliation with its object is therefore a dialectical process of self-alienation. Every individual, in whatever age, goes through the process, so it is not remarkable that contemporary human beings do so. The alienation of the individual takes place within a larger framework, which is not thereby deprived of its unity.

Alienation: The root is Latin *alius,* "other" in general (not, like *alter* [see p. 23], the other of just two), hence "different." "Alien" came to have the meanings of "foreign" and "insane"—psychiatrists used to be called alienists—for obvious reasons: foreigners and mental patients are different from the rest of us. So alienation can involve both separation and estrangement; I can be alienated from my society by being excluded from it or by failing to recognize myself in it.

Georg Wilhelm Friedrich Hegel (1770–1831), German philosopher. He is known for his Absolute Idealism, according to which the

> history of the universe is the history of Mind coming to know itself by the dialectical overcoming of contradictions.

But Marx raised the possibility that the object, which originally depended on consciousness for its constitution as an object, might become autonomous and turn on its creator. Social and political institutions—certainly human constructions—may enter on careers that human intervention, at the individual level or even in some cases collectively, is powerless to stop or influence. This state of affairs is most characteristic of institutions that have a strong material base: industries, armies, governments, and also churches and universities in their organizational, as opposed to their human, aspects. These are the dominant institutions in contemporary society. Alienation in this sense, the separation of the individual from any genuine involvement in the control of the conditions of his or her existence, is a prominent feature of the crisis of values. It attacks the structure of value because the locus of the activity of value is precisely in the attitude of the individual to the conditions of that existence, and to the change or perpetuation of those conditions.

> *Karl Marx* (1818–1883), German philosopher. He adopted Hegel's historicism and his dialectic but put them on a materialist basis. History becomes the history of class struggle, and religion and morality tools of oppression by a dominant class.

This active employment of value is accompanied by a more passive one in which the world acts on the individual instead of the reverse. Every true action is preceded by an assessment of the state of the world, in which the world acts on the individual in the form of perception. In the passive case, however, perception is followed by no overt action on the individual's part. What perception stimulates is purely internal and is a matter of enjoyment rather than involvement. Here too technological advances have changed the customary relationship between the individual and the world. Mass transport and mass communication, the development of smart appliances on the domestic side and of automated processes on the industrial side, have increased the time available for enjoyment but weakened the appeal of traditional means of providing it.

Enjoyment, like need, is relative to prevailing social norms, so that people who might once have been content with parlor games or amateur musical entertainments may find such amusements insipid when they have been exposed to video arcades and rock concerts. The general point here is expressed in the lyrics of a once-popular song, "How're you going to keep them down on the farm after they've seen Paree?" But even Paris may seem jaded after a while, and boredom, the insipidity of a life of idleness or the mere repetition of activity, has become a characteristic mark of the affluent society (though less of society is affluent than was predicted a few decades ago; indeed, many people have less leisure than ever, and those who have more are all too often unemployed).

Men and women all of whose wants are provided for, so that they are free from the necessity of devoting the major part of their attention to satisfying basic needs—really free, as few people in the history of the world have ever been—find that taking significant action is a good deal harder than they expected. Technology has partly offset this problem with the invention of distractions, from the Sony Walkman through interactive video games all the way up to virtual reality, together with means of transportation that enable those who can afford it to change the scenery at will. Some individuals have always known how to make good use of wealth and leisure, but until now they have been in the minority. One question for the future is whether the majority could possibly do so.

20. The Problem of Relevance in the Recent History of Ethics

Our security as human beings is threatened; our identity as producers of useful work is threatened; our ability to derive satisfaction from leisure is threatened. While these pressing problems of value have been developing on the plane of daily human involvement, what have the philosophers been up to?

The nineteenth century was a period of intense philosophical activity in the field of value. On the one hand, the utilitarians, the evolutionists, and the self-realizationists concerned themselves passionately with the systematic consequences of intellectual assumptions and individual action. On the other, Marx and his followers explored the consequences of material assumptions and collective action. Kierkegaard and, later, Nietzsche explored the moral and aesthetic predicament of the individual who is outside any system. The intellectual consequences of the scientific and technological changes described above were not felt seriously until early in the present century.

Søren Kierkegaard (1813–1855), Danish philosopher, was the first modern existentialist. He reacted against Hegel's idealistic system, pointing out that the one person who cannot possibly be included in any system is the thinker whose system it is. His chosen epitaph was "That Individual."

Friedrich Nietzsche (1844–1900), German philosopher. His lyrical work *Thus Spake Zarathustra* represented the philosopher as a dancer, enjoying the freedom of the heights above the "slave morality" of the herd that in his view marked Western—especially Christian—culture.

Just at that time philosophy in the English-speaking world underwent a profound change, largely due to the influence of G. E. Moore. The result was that a dominant part of the field became virtually irrelevant to daily human life. Elsewhere, philosophy continued to be relevant, but on the whole it was unreliable. With the exception of the development of phenomenological value theory in the early twentieth century by thinkers like Max Scheler, and the version of existentialist value theory developed by Jean-Paul Sartre under the pressure of the German occupation of France in the early 1940s, not much occurred in European philosophy that offered an advance on nineteenth-century concepts of value. In American philosophy the exception was John Dewey, whose theory of democracy was as much educational as ethical. The position taken in this book has affinities with Dewey's instrumentalism.

G. E. Moore (1873–1958), English philosopher. Moore thought that many philosophical theories, especially those of the idealists, were far more puzzling than the puzzles they claimed to solve, so he came to direct his interest more to the odd things philosophers said than to the world they were trying to understand.

Phenomenology: The root verb is Greek *phaino*, "to appear." Hegel's *Phenomenology of Mind* is a discourse (*logos*, see p. 38) about the progressive appearance of Mind in the development of human thought. Twentieth-century phenomenology, whose chief exponent was Edmund Husserl (1859–1938), has had a different focus. It is a theoretical approach to appearances as such, freed from the prejudgments to which language and culture unthinkingly subject them in experience.

Max Scheler (1872–1928), German philosopher, was known chiefly for his work on the concept of sympathy.

Jean-Paul Sartre (1905–1980), French philosopher and writer. Sartre's existentialism dominated French philosophy immediately after World War II, when the breakdown of old values made a form of heroic individualism briefly possible; "man being condemned to be free bears the weight of the whole world on his shoulders."[1] His later work was a sympathetic critique of Marxism.

John Dewey (1859–1952), American philosopher and educator. He stressed the importance of inquiry as a problem-solving activity and held that democracy was a prime value.

Instrumentalism: The Latin *instruo* literally means "instruct," though not in the usual sense of that word in English; *struo* is "to put together" (in some kind of order) and gives us "structure" and all its compounds. An "instrument" then is an agent of order, of construction—a tool or implement. Instrumentalism regards truths and values not as fixed or given but as tools for the construction of desired outcomes.

The critique of moral philosophy on the grounds of its relevance or irrelevance to pressing contemporary issues is not new. The early twentieth century saw the end of a long period of stability, which was undermined by World War I and the economic chaos that followed it. The structure of Western values was put to a severe test. If philosophers had merely retreated into their studies, keeping up, if only in private, the standards of their intellectual calling, they might have been forgiven. Some did so, but many sold themselves to the dominant political forces. Even among those who maintained their independence, some publicly bemoaned the futility of philosophy, while others took refuge in otherworldly speculation of an uncritical kind.

In the case of French philosophers, these charges were leveled by the critic Julien Benda, whose book *The Treason of the Intellectuals* was one of the first expressions of a widespread disillusionment with the role of scholars in a world of social and political unrest. Benda had in mind especially those scholars who embraced nationalism and racism, and later on communism or fascism, putting their talents at the service of domination or repression. He lamented the fact that a class of people once devoted to values that were independent of material ambition should have betrayed those values in the interest of personal or group enrichment and aggrandizement.

The issue here is a delicate one. Benda did not insist that intellectuals ignore the practical. On the contrary, he thought that, while some of them ought to be completely above the battle, many, if not most, should be at work in the real world. But he thought they should maintain their own standards there and not relax them in response to the demands of money or power. The two extremes in the relations between thinkers and the world appear to be scholarly aloofness on one side, corrupt involvement on the other. Honest involvement would be fine, but it has been rare, because those in power will generally not listen to truths that are not in their interest.

Between retreat into scholarship and compromise with the world of politics, I recommend a position closer to the first. Philosophy requires detachment if it is to be intellectually rigorous, although to be detached from human concerns and to think them uninteresting or unimportant are two different things. Even Kant, than whom few philosophers have been more detached or more rigorous, remarked toward the end of his *Critique of Pure Reason* that the "supreme end" of philosophy was "the happiness of all mankind."[2] Kant also enunciated, in another text called *On the Common Saying: "This May Be True in Theory, but It Does Not Apply in Practice"*, the principle that "whatever reason shows to be valid in theory, is also valid in practice."[3] This suggests that if we get the moral principles right, their application will be straightforward.

I began this section with G. E. Moore and must now return to him. Moore's friend Bertrand Russell went to jail during World War I to protest England's involvement in the conflict, thus giving evidence of a lively and courageous moral conviction. Nobody can legislate for others when it comes to the application of moral principles in personal life. My concern at this point is to stress that a theoretical interest in ethics is not a substitute for the moral life. The two need to be kept in balance, in the profession of philosophy as well as in individuals.

21. The Naturalistic Fallacy

Moore's contribution to philosophy was to shift professional attention from the world to language. The main concern thus became a second-order one. Although this diminished the relevance of the subject to the most pressing human problems of the day, it provided an environment in which the reliability of philosophical argument could be worked on dispassionately and without haste. The shift was therefore, from that point of view, all to the good.

Moore's reflections on the language of ethics led him to formulate and expose what he called the "naturalistic fallacy."[4] The term "good," Moore thought, must mean *something*, but he believed that he had shown, by a series of arguments, that it could not mean any natural property or indeed anything at all that could be made the basis of a definition for it. "Good" must therefore stand for a non-natural, directly apprehended thing or property, and every attempt to define it in terms of something else must be fallacious.

Some of Moore's arguments have acquired classical status. One in particular, the "open-question argument," is of general philosophical application. This argument showed that the question of what the good is must always remain open, because it always makes sense to ask, if "good" is defined as some X, whether X really *is* good. We might say that philosophy just *is* the domain of open questions. But the doctrine of the naturalistic fallacy had an unfortunate effect on the subsequent development of ethics.

Moore's approach made the problem of the *meaning* of "good" (or "right") the fundamental problem of ethics. But many terms have more basic meanings. For example, the teleological tradition emphasizes ends that are good—that is, that ought to be realized—and the deontological tradition emphasizes actions that are right—that is, that ought to be done. If this formulation is acceptable then in both cases "ought" functions as a more fundamental concept than either "good" or "right," because they can be expressed in its terms.

Further, nobody would think, or could think, that anything ought to be done or striven for unless it *mattered*. If our concern is with the ordinary language of ethics, it must, I am convinced, focus first on the notion of *mattering*. Moore compared "good" to "yellow": "yellow" cannot be defined linguistically, and yet we know directly what things are yellow. But although whether things are yellow or not does not generally matter (except in cases where aesthetic considerations come into play), whether they are good or not always matters. This is an essential part of the meaning of "good," and it is by no means unanalyzable. To put it differently, yellow things remain yellow whether it matters or not, and the meaning of "yellow" does not depend in any way on this distinction. So "yellow" is not the sort of property that can sustain an analogy to "good."

The assumption that "good" stood for something indefinable led to the view that it could not be reached in any indirect empirical fashion, but had to be intuited directly. The trouble with intuitions is that they themselves may turn out to be learned from nonphilosophical sources. Many of the prima facie duties intuited by Ross,[5] another representative of the intuitionist view, embodied principles of behavior suitable to educated English gentlemen; this, like the fact that men and not women were the preferred models, was hardly accidental.

The greatest weakness of any philosophy that derives its raw material mainly from language is that a language always reflects the social attitudes of the people who use it. The analysis of language is an indispensable part of philosophical method, but in questions of value it can play at most an auxiliary role. The intuitionists were right in insisting that all knowledge must be expressed in terms that reduce, in the end, to a set of terms that refer directly to elements of immediate experience and are incapable of further analysis. Their mistake was to set much too high the level at which the process of analysis reached this point. The more complex the term whose meaning is to be intuited, the greater the likelihood of overlooking distinctions that on closer examination would take inquiry to a more fundamental level.

Alfred Jules Ayer (1910–1989), English philosopher, whose early book *Language, Truth, and Logic* was influential in bringing the doctrines of logical empiricism (see p. 67) to the attention of the English-speaking world.

Finally, the doctrine of indefinability of "good" paved the way for the positivist conclusion that since the meaning of ethical terms was so elusive and so difficult to confirm they had no cognitive meaning at all. The emotive theory of A. J. Ayer[6] and C. L. Stevenson[7] held that the use of ethical language is simply the expression of attitudes. Although other terms might acquire emotive meaning along with sense meaning (given by ostensive definitions, that is, by pointing at something in the world) and linguistic meaning (given by verbal definitions), ethical and aesthetic terms have *only* emotive meaning, and are characteristically defined by *persuasive* definitions. According to this view, "X is good" means something like "I approve of X; do so too."

Cognitive, emotive: "Cognitive" stands for what belongs to the domain of knowledge or cognition, as opposed to "emotive," which stands for what belongs to the domain of feeling or emotion. The "kn" of "knowledge" and the "gn" of "cognition" both derive from Greek *gnosis*, originally "a judicial inquiry" but then "knowledge" or "acquaintance." Other members of this family of derivatives are "cunning" and "king." "Emotion" is from Latin *emoveo*, "to move out or away," and thence "to shake" (as applied to the foundations of the city walls); "emotion" in English originally had the connotations of agitation or tumult.

In the following decades, this analysis of the meaning of ethical terms was superseded by even more refined analyses of the structure and function of ethical language: J. O. Urmson's work on grading,[8] R. M. Hare's on the logic of commands,[9] P. H. Nowell-Smith's on the multiple functions of ethical expressions,[10] and Stuart Hampshire's on the segmentation of language.[11] Nobody could deny that these were valuable contributions to philosophy regarded as a professional activity for which, among professionals, no excuse needs to be made. But hardly anybody would claim either that these efforts had anything to do with the object of moral philosophy as outlined in the previous chapter.

22. Ethics as Practical Reason

Since the 1960s the tide has turned. Moral philosophy began to revert to an earlier conception of its task as that of *practical reason*. Works like those of Stephen Toulmin[12] and Kurt Baier[13] held that ethics provides reasons for moral action, and not merely criticisms of moral judgments or analyses of moral language. Second, the work of Rawls on justice,[14] Ronald Dworkin and Virginia Held on rights,[15] and of Alasdair MacIntyre on virtue,[16] revived the great tradition of normative ethics. Mention should also be made of significant developments in practical ethics (in relation to medicine and business, for example),[17] of the controversial extension of ethics to deal with the rights of animals,[18] and of a growing body of distinguished work on feminist ethics.[19] In spite of a few recent articles, however, consequentialism is still under- (or mis-)represented,[20] and ethics generally lacks any empirical anchor. These are the deficiencies this book aims to remedy.

Practical reason: Reasoning, the construction of logical arguments, normally produces a conclusion in the form of a declarative proposition. But the idea that it might issue in action, or at any rate in an imperative to action, goes back to Aristotle. "Practical" derives from Greek *praxis*, "doing" (as opposed to

> *pathos,* "suffering," and contrasted with *poiesis,* "making," and *theoria,* "contemplating").

The parochial development of professional philosophy in the mid twentieth century was not necessarily a symptom of the malaise that infected the structure of value in society at large. But it is fair to suggest that the choice of ethical problems tackled by philosophy in that period was influenced by the difficulty and complexity of the genuine problems of value confronting the modern world. The retirement of most philosophical concern from those problems did not lessen the gravity of the crisis, which may be seen as compounded of popular bewilderment and professional indifference. The account given above simplifies both, but the picture it paints of the predicament of contemporary men and women and the implicit criticism it levels at contemporary philosophy are accurate enough.

This brings us back to the question posed at the end of the previous chapter, on which the utility of moral argument was said ultimately to depend. The question at this point is not whether human beings ought to be rational, but whether they are rational. We must have confidence in an everyday function of reason before we can appeal to it in everyday affairs. Only when confidence is justified can moral argument go on to insist that reason should cultivate its powers for moral ends.

23. Grounds for Confidence in Rationality

Here is found the first direct contribution of science to ethics. The science in question is admittedly one of the more controversial, but it is one that has contributed as much as any other to the current crisis, and an appeal to it at this point is appropriate.

Psychoanalytic theory advances the hypothesis that the basic drives that characterize the *id,* under the pleasure principle, are deflected and controlled by the *ego,* under the reality principle. A critical stage in the development of the individual consists in the discovery by the ego that the id is self-destructive when left to its own devices. The id demands immediate satisfaction, in primitive forms, mostly involving food or sex, which can easily lead to conflict or danger. The ego cannot allow this, and represses or redirects instinctual energy in search of less risky gratifications. Discovery is a rational process, even when it is not fully conscious. That the reality principle is able to make any headway at all against instinctual drives is evidence of rationality, at least in the minimal sense, not as something to be striven for but as something normally provided. Pain or retribution following action constitutes data on the basis of which the ego makes a choice, the outcome of which is a prescription for an altered line of action.

Id, ego, superego: These Latin terms are the *English* translations of German *Es*, "it," *Ich*, "I," and *Ueberich*, literally "over-I." It was presumably the informality or awkwardness of these expressions that led the translators, with their English classical education, to fall back on a more elegant (and to them more familiar) Latin rendering.

This is not yet conscious argument. It is not even a *conscious* choice between alternatives: the painful alternative is rejected without any pause for deliberation. In moral situations things are more complicated. Freud located traditional morality in the *superego*, the internalized code of a society that has accumulated the experience of many egos and that communicates its standards by means of parental authority. But this makes morality as irrational, from the viewpoint of the individual, as instinct. The id tries to coerce the ego from within, while the superego tries to coerce the ego from without. This view of morality is in agreement with the received doctrine in all ages prior to ours: original sin needs to be redeemed by grace from above, hence morality requires a religious warrant.

All this makes for the impression that I am a helpless spectator of a struggle whose battleground is my own body. In this struggle the rational ego finds no part to play, so that for many people the conscious subject remains in utter moral perplexity, assailed in turn by libidinal drives and by automatic—that is, perfectly learned—responses of guilt. The root of our crisis lies here, in the fact that society has relied so long on external standards of morality that most people are no longer able to formulate their own morality, or to furnish independent corroboration of the morality of others.

Moral argument is located, as all genuine argument must be, in the ego, not in the superego. Its true function is to enable the individual to follow rules and also to know when not to follow them, to repress instincts and also to know when to indulge them. The ego has to learn to outwit not only the id but also the superego. Because it has independent access to reality, it is able to do this—that is the reassuring part. But if, in so doing, the ego is to be moral and not merely realistic, it must be guided by rational principles of a different order from those associated with traditional moralities. These principles form the subject matter of moral philosophy properly conceived.

Notes

1. Jean-Paul Sartre, trans. Hazel Barnes, *Being and Nothingness* (New York: Philosophical Library, 1956), p. 553.
2. Immanuel Kant, trans. Norman Kemp Smith, *Critique of Pure Reason* (London: Macmillan, 1933), p. 665.
3. Immanuel Kant, trans. H. B. Nisbet, *Political Writings,* 2nd enlarged ed. (Cambridge: Cambridge University Press, 1991), p. 92.
4. G. E. Moore, *Principia Ethica* (Cambridge: Cambridge University Press, 1903), p. 10.
5. W. D. Ross, *The Right and the Good* (Oxford: Oxford University Press, 1930).
6. A. J. Ayer, *Language, Truth, and Logic* (London: Victor Gollancz, 1936), Chapter 8.
7. C. L. Stevenson, *Ethics and Language* (New Haven, Conn.: Yale University Press, 1944).
8. J. O. Urmson, "On Grading," *Mind* 59 (1950), p. 145.
9. R. M. Hare, *The Language of Morals* (Oxford: Oxford University Press, 1952)
10. P. H. Nowell-Smith, *Ethics* (Harmondsworth: Pelican Books, 1954).
11. Stuart Hampshire, *Thought and Action* (London: Chatto and Windus, 1960).
12. S. E. Toulmin, *The Place of Reason in Ethics* (Cambridge: Cambridge University Press, 1950).
13. Kurt Baier, *The Moral Point of View* (New York: Random House, 1965)
14. John Rawls, *A Theory of Justice* (Cambridge: Harvard University Press, 1971).
15. Ronald Dworkin, *Taking Rights Seriously* (Cambridge: Harvard University Press, 1977); Virginia Held, *Rights and Goods: Justifying Social Action* (New York: Free Press, 1984).
16. Alasdair MacIntyre, *After Virtue: A Study in Moral Theory,* 2nd ed., corrected and with postscript (London: Duckworth, 1985).
17. For medical ethics, see, for example, Tom L. Beauchamp and James F. Childress, *Principles of Biomedical Ethics,* 3rd ed. (New York: Oxford University Press, 1989); for business ethics, see, for example, Richard T. DeGeorge, *Business Ethics,* 3rd ed. (London: Collier Macmillan, 1990).
18. See, for example, Tom Regan, *The Case for Animal Rights* (Berkeley and Los Angeles: University of California Press, 1984).
19. See, for example, Virginia Held, *Feminist Morality: Transforming Culture, Society, and Politics* (Chicago: University of Chicago Press, 1993).
20. For a representative collection see Philip Pettit, ed., *Consequentialism* (Aldershot: Dartmouth Publishing Co., 1993).

IV

The Role of Authority

24. Proper and Improper Uses of Authority

So far the argument is leading toward a utopian vision of a population guided by rational principles on the basis of which its members construct moral arguments and thereby obtain ready solutions to their moral problems. We can safely assume that this state of affairs will never be realized. Hardly anyone is prepared to tackle every problem by going back to principles in this sense.

What most people call their "principles" are rules of thumb to which they are emotionally attached, the violation of which makes them feel guilty or uncomfortable. These may have been acquired directly from parents or teachers, or indirectly by a kind of social osmosis. At some time or other some thought may have been devoted to the status and implications of such principles, but if challenged they will probably be at a loss to defend them articulately. As far as most moral agents are concerned, all principles whatever, in our sense, are transcendent. They come from elsewhere, if not from above; the agent commands evidence for none of them, but accepts them, as almost everyone always has, on authority. To believe something, it is enough for most people to know that it is believed by other people they respect, as long as it does not strike them as utterly implausible.

But allowing for differences between the cases, the same thing could be said of most people's knowledge of the external world. Both science and morality appeal more frequently to authority than to experience. This has always been so and it probably always will be. Yet the nature of the authority in the two cases is not the same. They offer an illuminating comparison, epitomized in the contrast between the doctor and the minister or priest. For the purposes of argument I shall oversimplify this contrast considerably; doctors are far more vulnerable to criticism, and priests perhaps far less so, than will appear in what follows.

Authority: Latin *auctoritas* came from *augeo,* "to increase," which is the root of our word "augment." Another English cognate is "auction," a sale at which bids keep increasing until a price is reached. *Auctoritas* meant originally "the giving of increase," hence supplying, supporting, being the source of sustenance, exerting power and command.

Doctors and priests both occupy positions of powerful authority over persons committed to their care. According to the principles by which they operate, individuals who refuse to comply with their edicts run life-threatening risks, although they have as a rule no way of making an independent assessment of the accuracy of those edicts. But, compared to the situation a few generations ago, the proportion of the population guided by priests is growing smaller, while most people continue to rely on doctors.

The difference between the two is not only in the ground of their authority but also in the manner of its application. Ordinary people understand that the ground of the doctor's authority is experimental, and they understand, or can be brought to understand, the principles on which experimental science rests. The doctor will try to explain the patient's situation, about which the patient can seek a second opinion, and the doctor is required to obtain the patient's consent for invasive procedures. What patients cannot do, and what they are willing to pay doctors to do for them, is to work out the consequences of the body of experimental knowledge as these apply to their own condition, or perhaps even to understand their condition as it must be understood if that knowledge is to apply to it.

But the ground of the priest's authority is another authority, and so on in a chain of authority terminating in a divinely authoritative revelation of some kind. In comparison with the previous case, the application of it is simple, and ordinary people can generally follow the argument that leads from the goodness of God to their own sinful state. The authority of the priest, however, is needed not only to apply but also to reinforce the principles of religion. By contrast, the authority of the doctor is needed to ensure the rational application of the principles of medicine, which themselves require no reinforcement.

That is the difference. Obedience to the doctor need not involve individuals in any abdication of their responsibility for themselves; they are simply making use of the division of specialized labor in a complex society. But obedience to the priest does involve such an abdication, even though, as Sartre has shown, it is an abdication that can never really be successful.

But if you seek counsel—from a priest, for example—you have selected
that priest, and at bottom you already knew, more or less, what he would
advise. In other words, to choose an adviser is already to commit oneself
by that choice.[1]

You did not know, we may suppose, what the doctor would advise. But if
you had chosen to seek advice from a philosophy professor, the same
problem would have arisen: the responsibility for that choice would have
been just as much yours as the choice of the priest was in the case envisaged
by Sartre. This inescapable responsibility of individuals for their own
behavior makes the question of authority a crucial one.

25. The Emergence of Science as Authoritative

Moral authority has so far been closer to the priest than to the doctor. I do
not maintain that the theory of morals can now be made scientific, but I do
want to inquire how nearly morals can be brought to rest on elementary
principles of truth and falsity, how far they can be removed from transcendent principles of good and evil. Scientists have managed to arrive at a basis
for agreement that transcends ideological, religious, and national differences, and they form a community of genuinely international scope. They
have tacitly suppressed considerations of morality, political or otherwise.
The ground of their agreement is not a common understanding of what is
right and wrong, but a common understanding of what is true and false:
what is testable, confirmable, demonstrable.

Good and Evil: Here are the root meanings of the main value terms
used in everyday moral language, which throw light on the
human preoccupations that lead to moral concern.

Our word	*Comes from a root meaning*
good	fitting
better	a remedy
evil	excess
bad	a hermaphrodite
worse	confused, stirred up
right	straight
wrong	twisted

A hermaphrodite (from Hermes and Aphrodite, male and female gods) is a birth combining male and female characteristics,
and thus undesirable from the conventional point of view.

Viewed historically, this represents a remarkable inversion of doubt and certainty. In some earlier periods—like the late Middle Ages—general agreement prevailed about right and wrong, but fierce philosophical arguments surrounded truth and falsity. Judgments of truth were held to rest on transcendent principles, and the reconciliation of doctrinal differences was impossible in the absence of such principles held in common. On the practical side, doctors formed a kind of priesthood, and traced their authority to Hippocrates and Galen; the alchemists looked back to the half-mythical Hermes Trismegistus, the physicists to the all too historical Aristotle, though the use they made of his authority was not his fault.

Hippocrates, Galen, Hermes Trismegistus: Hippocrates (c. 460–c. 377 B.C.E.) and Galen (c. 131–c. 201) were Greek physicians. The Hippocratic oath, a code of conduct for the practice of medicine, still influences medical education. Galen treated several Roman emperors, made important discoveries, and wrote many books that, like those of Aristotle (see p. 97), were treated for centuries as definitive, hampering the advance of medicine. "Hermes Trismegistus" (the "thrice-mighty") was the Greek name of the Egyptian god of knowledge, Thot, who is represented with the head of an ibis.

The history of science since the Middle Ages is the history of the resolution of the conflict about truth and falsity, not by the establishment of one transcendent principle rather than another, but by the elimination of such principles altogether—a step already recommended for the theory of morals in Chapter I. With the development of science people began to realize that no principle was compelling if not assented to by individual judgment, and this made individual judgment superior to the principle. Giordano Bruno, one of the first philosophers of the new scientific attitude, puts the point bluntly in an exchange between a traditionalist and one of the moderns. When the perplexed Burchio asks, "Well, who is going to decide what the truth is?," Fracastoro replies, "That is the prerogative of every careful and wide-awake intelligence, of everybody who is as judicious and free from obstinacy as he can be. . . ."[2]

Giordano Bruno (1548–1600), Italian philosopher, the last major figure to be put to death by the Inquisition for his beliefs. He

> broke with Aristotelian doctrine, defending the idea of an infinite universe and the importance of free inquiry.

Bruno's death at the stake in 1600 showed that he was ahead of his time. Such a bold reliance on private discernment seemed to many of his contemporaries blasphemous and foolhardy, an option for relativism and chaos in preference to order and absolute assurance. This was just as true of Protestants as of Catholics. The Reformation, while it changed the individual's relationship to authority by removing the intermediacy of the priesthood, left the *concept* of authority as it was. The warrant for the principles was now biblical rather than ecclesiastical, but that was a political change as much as a religious one.

The reliance on individual judgment for which Bruno stood, foolhardy as it may have appeared, turned out to be the condition for intellectual progress. The edifice of science has been so constructed that it rests on principles to the evaluation of which a careful and wide-awake intelligence is entirely adequate. This democratization of knowledge has not hampered the task of science, which is the explanation and control of nature. Intelligence alone did not complete the construction; imagination and evidence were also required. But the resolution that intelligence was not to be subverted by authority was worth dying for, as the evidence itself was not. Karl Jaspers points out, in defense of Galileo, who retracted his support of the Copernican theory rather than suffer the fate of Bruno, that truth cannot suffer by retraction;[3] what took courage was not the recognition of truth, but the insistence that everyone had a right to it.

Karl Jaspers (1883–1969), German psychiatrist and philosopher who spent the last part of his life in Switzerland. Jaspers took an existentialist view according to which individuals encounter what he called "the Encompassing" in "limit-situations" such as loss, pain, and death.

Galileo Galilei (1564–1642), Italian scientist. He made some of the earliest telescopes and discovered Jupiter's moons, and also put terrestrial mechanics on a sound experimental and mathematical basis. In 1663 he was brought before the Inquisition and forced to recant publicly his support of the Copernican doctrine, which involved the motion of the traditionally immovable earth. It was reported that at the end of the trial he said under his breath *"eppur si muove!"* (nevertheless it does move!).

The Seven Capital Sins: Anger (1963; director Eduardo de Filippo)
Marie-José Nat prepares to throw a pitcher and a bottle in a fit of anger. The anger, provoked by flies in soup, spreads through the population until its eventual consequence is the destruction of the entire country in a nuclear holocaust.

26. Science as Imagination Controlled by Evidence

The combination of evidence and imagination is worth further attention. If we reject the hypothesis of supernatural origins—as we must to avoid futile conflict, if we care about the accessibility of the argument to all—all authority springs from the human imagination. Science, no less than religion, began as a speculative account of some of the more noticeable regularities in human experience. Science dealt originally with natural, as opposed to human, events. Although they were anticipated by Aristotle, the human sciences developed late. The province of the earliest science included the stars and the seasons, the elements, the generation and decay of plants and animals, health and disease. The imagination of the early scientists constructed original and often extravagant accounts of the way the world must be if these things and processes are to behave as they do.

Religion dealt with some of the same things, regarding them, however, in their special capacity as determinants of human security and welfare— as needed or feared—and with other phenomena such as joy and terror, love and hatred, death and the hope of immortality. Striking similarities sometimes obtained between the imaginative production of what would become a scientific theory and the imaginative production of what would become a religious dogma. Either might be marked by a heightened quality of some experience of intellectual conviction that led to its being taken for a vision or a revelation, by a compulsion to write or recite what had been seen or revealed, often in the special literary form appropriate to stories that were to be remembered by the initiated but kept from the masses, and by the censoring or digesting of the esoteric (or secret) doctrine for exoteric (or public) purposes.

Often the scientific and religious elements were combined in a single traditional story, a myth whose purpose was the explanation of widely accepted beliefs about the world and about human affairs. What distinguished the later development of science from the later development of religion was that in science the imagination was brought under control without being suppressed. As time went on, both kinds of imaginative construction encountered limitations. Once a myth had been generally accepted, an alternative myth stood little chance of establishing itself unless it could be used as the emotional platform for some political change.

Most of the new religions grew up in periods of political ferment. Strict religious traditions did not allow much room for the free exercise of the imagination, at least where the explanation of phenomena or behavior was concerned. This may have been one reason why art flourished, since it offered the main outlet for imaginative construction of a noncontroversial sort. But the history of science, when it managed to disentangle itself from religion, has been the history of *imagination controlled by evidence*. Even if it takes imagination to see that something *is* evidence for a given view, once it acquires that status it becomes independent of the imagination.

This arrangement has the great virtue that it specifies an acceptable procedure for the *rejection* of an earlier imaginative account, which leaves the contemporary imagination (that is, at the time of the rejection) free to replace the old account with a new one. Changes in the scientific tradition can therefore come about peaceably, as changes in the religious tradition rarely can. In both cases there are vested interests, but only in the scientific case can those entrenched in them be expected to yield in the face of evidence, even if they refuse to do so in practice.

The upshot of all this has been that science, which is seen to conduct its affairs in a reasonably open manner and to treat its principles as corrigible in the light of further evidence, has come to be generally trusted as a guide to practical action in the physical world, and to some extent in the human one. Again the point is oversimplified. We could cite plenty of examples of stubbornness and prejudice among scientists, and many cases in which scientific advice turned out to be disastrous. It has been suggested, for example, that it was not until the beginning of the twentieth century that medicine cured more people than it killed. Such cases, however, do not detract from the general success of science in arriving at a mode of operation that requires no transcendent assumptions, is generally plausible, has obvious advantages, and reflects the advance of knowledge.

27. A Distinction between Applied Science and Applied Morality

As has already been remarked, ordinary people do not become involved with science directly. For them science is mediated by engineers, whose task is to take principles (such as the generation of electricity) worked out on a small scale and apply them on a large scale, or to adapt sensitive reactions (such as those involved in photography) to processes that will work under the challenging conditions of everyday use. Perhaps what the second chapter called for was moral engineering, a similar adaptation of refined philosophical principles to daily moral problems. But the analogy cannot be pushed too far. The man or woman who uses the device provided by the engineer need have no understanding at all of the laws by which it operates. When you press the button that turns on the air conditioner, you do need practical knowledge of a constant physical relationship, that is, the relationship between room temperature and the position of air-conditioner buttons, but you need no acquaintance with thermodynamics. From the lay person's point of view, the relationship in question is a strictly magical one, like the relationship between people's sticking pins in effigies and the suffering of their enemies. We are certainly not looking for push-button morality. That would not count as morality at all, since for an action to be moral the agent must be aware of the relationship between the action and its consequences, not merely as a reliable coincidence but as a case of a more general relationship between an intention and its achievement.

All this accords with the difference discussed in Chapter II between our everyday relations to science and to morality. The laws of science stand at a distance from daily experience of the world, and it requires work to get to them, while moral rules are immediately relevant to daily experience. The logical parallel, however, need not be given up. From the hypothetical principles of science, laws are deduced that can be trusted to apply to physical events, and that are therefore authoritative for the determination of such events. By the same token, rules may be deduced from the hypothetical principles of morality, which will be similarly authoritative for the determination of human actions. Obedience to such laws will not constitute the abdication of individual responsibility spoken of earlier in this chapter.

In view of this parallel, why not simply make morality a science? To answer that question we must investigate the limitations as well as the potentialities of the scientific approach. For the next four chapters, then, the argument will concentrate on what science can and cannot contribute to the theory of value, and on various philosophical issues raised by this inquiry, before returning to morality proper in Chapter IX.

Notes

1. Jean-Paul Sartre, "Existentialism Is a Humanism," in Walter Kaufman, ed., *Existentialism from Dostoievsky to Sartre* (New York: Meridian Books, 1956), p. 297.
2. Quoted in G. de Santillana, ed., *The Age of Adventure* (New York: Mentor Books, 1956), p. 268.
3. Karl Jaspers, *The Perennial Scope of Philosophy*, trans. R. Manheim (London: Routledge and Kegan Paul, 1950), p. 10.

V

The Nature and Limitations of Science

28. The Elements of Scientific Theory

The function of science is the explanation of nature in nature's own terms;[1] the method of science is imagination controlled by evidence. Science *exists*, however, as overlapping sets of universal propositions affirmed and agreed to by individual scientists, in the light of which particular propositions about matters of fact can be grouped together and explained. A proposition is what is asserted by a declarative sentence. The same proposition can be asserted by different sentences: "it's raining," "*il pleut*," "you'll need your umbrella," and "the weather forecast really got it right this time" can all under appropriate conditions assert the proposition that it is raining. Similarly, the same sentence can assert different propositions: "I'll take five" can assert that I would like to buy five items, or that I choose the number five in a game or competition, or that I am going to take a short break.

"Universal" and "particular" here have the meanings they have in elementary logic: universal propositions assert something about *all* members of some class, and particular propositions assert something about *some* members of the class, or about *this* member. The terms "some" and "all" do not have to occur explicitly in the assertion of a proposition. For example, "AIDS is a disease of the immune system" is a universal proposition; it says in effect that all AIDS sufferers have something wrong with their immune systems. Similarly, "Tom tests negative for HIV" is a particular proposition, though not about a member of the class of AIDS sufferers.

Explanation in the philosophy of science is a logical relation between a universal proposition and some particular propositions, the latter following from the former when appropriate local conditions are inserted. Also one universal proposition may be said to explain others if the required logical relation holds between them. The precise nature of the explanatory relation can become very complex, since in practice propositions form large networks, from highest-level universals to lowest-level particulars via many layers of intermediate generality. However, in this context we do not need to go into the complexities of explanation in specific sciences, since the role of science in our argument is as an analogy. For this purpose a simplified logical structure will do.

Explanation: Literally a "flattening out," from Latin *ex-*, "out," and *planus,* "flat"; hence the removal of obstacles to understanding, a making plain.

The lowest-level propositions will express facts about the world and will be expressed by observation sentences. Facts may be unobserved or even unobservable, but in the first instance the world we want to explain is the world we can observe, and according to the definition that opened this chapter the material for the explanation must be drawn from that world too.

In the logical empiricist language of the 1930s to the 1950s, observation sentences were called "protocol sentences," because they represented something everyone could formally agree on. The propositional content of such a sentence or set of such sentences is a factual description. In science as it is practiced today, only a small part of the scientist's effort is devoted to recording observations; far more is devoted to interpreting observations and carrying out calculations based on them. In purely theoretical branches of science no observations will be made at all. But we must always remember that the world science deals with is *this* world, the one we live in and depend on and care about; for every scientific claim, somebody somewhere will have been in direct observational contact with something in the world.

Logical empiricism: A movement of thought that originated in Vienna between the wars and spread, mainly to America, because of the emigration of its exponents. The leading figure in this group was Rudolf Carnap (1891–1970). The logical empiricists held that meaningful expressions must be true or false and that truth-claims must rest either on logical or on empirical grounds. This led to the dismissal of value language as cognitively meaningless.

Part of the furniture of this world consists of instruments designed to produce observable facts of a highly artificial kind: blots on electrophoresis columns, peaks in spectra, meter readings, computer printouts. These, however, are the basis for observations as genuine as those made directly in nature "with the naked eye." The fact that some sciences are experimental is sometimes cited against the view that the basis of science is observational. But an experiment is only a way of enabling the researcher to make an observation that could not have been made without preparation. It forces nature to do what it would have done anyway, but while we are watching. Much of the activity in many experiments consists of making sure that something *else* does not happen; the event to be observed has to be protected from the influence of other events. That is why laboratories have to be sterile, and why one of the most characteristic sounds in many laboratories is the vacuum pump.

Protocol sentences: The origins of this expression are curious. The "-col" of "protocol" comes down from Greek *kolla,* "glue" (as in "collage," an artwork produced by sticking shapes or objects to a surface); a protocol was originally a sheet stuck in front of an order of ceremony, which showed who took precedence over whom in a procession or at table. From this it came to stand for diplomatic propriety in general, and especially the agreed-upon text of a treaty. The use of "protocol sentence" in logical empiricism thus carried rich associations, but these were for the most part lost as the movement crossed the Atlantic in the 1940s, and the term fell into disuse. The concepts of research protocol and treatment protocol survive in medicine as detailed specifications of steps to be taken in a given order.

Every observation is particular and individual. Individual observations may be lumped together in reporting a repeated experiment, but no such thing as a generalized observation can be made. Each encounter with the world involves a unique observer and a unique event in a limited region of space and time. Everybody knows, and it is probably true because he spent a lot of time in an orchard in 1666, that Isaac Newton watched apples falling when he was thinking about the theory of gravitation; he wondered whether the moon might be a falling body, just like the apple. (It is.) Falling apples are part of the informal observation basis of Newtonian physics; things falling in general clue us all in to the fact that we live in a gravitational field. Observation sentences reporting the behavior of an apple in free fall would each refer to a different point in its descent; they would say that it had reached a specific distance at a specific time after starting to fall.

> *Sir Isaac Newton* (1642–1727), English mathematician and physicist, inventor (with Leibniz) of the calculus. His merging of celestial and terrestrial mechanics opened one of the most fruitful periods of development in the history of science. He was also a mystical theologian; having been born prematurely and posthumously (after his father's death) on Christmas Day, he seems to have been confident that his work was destined to show mankind God's design for the universe.[2]

Actually this would be terribly difficult to do with an apple, owing to the impracticality of noting its position and looking at a stopwatch simultaneously. So the formal observation basis of Newtonian physics depends on other strategies, such as diluting gravity by rolling balls down inclined planes, or using it at full strength in conjunction with high-speed photography. The acceptance of such observations as valid for scientific purposes depends as a rule on their being agreed upon by more than one observer; when this happens, they are said be *intersubjectively corroborated*. Exceptions to this rule may be made for rare events, but here we would need to examine closely the credentials of the observer, and if possible to look for others' observations of comparable events.

> *Intersubjective corroboration:* "Subject" here means the individual observer as knower and agent in a world of objects. "Subject" and "object" both derive from Latin *iacio*, "to lay" or "to throw"; since *sub-* means "under" and *ob-* means "over against," we have the idea of an individual who happens to have landed where he or she is, confronting things that happen to be located in the vicinity and events that happen to be transpiring there. That is indeed a fair description of the human condition. Latin *roboro* is "to strengthen" (it is connected to our "robust"); corroboration in this context means that if another subject feels or notices what I as a subject have felt or noticed, both of us have stronger reasons for trusting our experiences.

Observation sentences describe events or states of affairs. They depend on our perceiving that the event is occurring or that the state of affairs is the case. This in turn rests on sensation, the activation of the organs of sense by external stimuli. In their most primitive form sensory data may be simply impressions of heat or cold, light or darkness. The corresponding perceptions may be as elementary as the recognition that one spot is larger or brighter than another, that a pointer coincides with a mark on a scale. The discrimination of the fine structure of the field of appearance that characterizes the observations of expert scientists represents a degree of sophistication that they have acquired through years of training.

Perception: Latin *capio* is "to take or seize," so perception is "seizing-through"—through the senses, that is. What is perceived is thus not given but rather taken, which implies an activity of the subject; we interpret sensory inputs as evidence of the presence of perceived objects, but this interpretation may be biased by our fears or interests.

The rendering as a description of what appears perceptually calls not only for discrimination, but also for the command of a language whose terms are precisely defined and apply to *classes* of perceived states of affairs. Training in science consists, among other things, in giving students the opportunity to observe and describe typical states of affairs, on the basis of which they can interpret what other scientists are talking about. In developing the parallel with the theory of value, we should remember that the step from the sensory data of observation to a description may be a long one. The step from the casual observer's description of some state of affairs (which will probably omit most of the relevant data) to the scientist's description may be equally long.

29. Generalizations and Hypotheses

The universal propositions that constitute the main body of science are of two principal kinds: *generalizations* and *hypotheses*. Hypotheses contain terms not found in the vocabulary of description; generalizations (which are generalizations *of* particular factual descriptions) contain only descriptive—or *observational*—terms, apart from grammatical or logical connectives. For example, the generalization covering the falling apple referred to above is a formula that relates distance fallen to elapsed time; this formula says that the distance is proportional to the square of the time, and uses a constant of proportionality g that stands for the acceleration of gravity near the surface of the earth. The hypothesis that accounts for this generalization is Newton's formula for universal gravitational attraction, which relates the force between any two objects to their masses and their distance from one another. This formula says that the force is proportional to the product of the masses of the bodies divided by the square of the distance between them, and uses a constant of proportionality G called the universal gravitational constant. In our case the two bodies are the apple and the earth. The force acting between them is not observed directly but through its effect on their movements. In this case this means the movement of the apple only, since the earth, although it also moves, does not do so perceptibly.

The formula for the falling apple is a generalization; the formula for the universal gravitational relation is a hypothesis. The relation between sentences that express hypotheses, sentences that express generalizations, and observation sentences is as follows: observation sentences are *instances* of generalizations, and generalizations are *consequences* of hypotheses. Hypotheses, however, always need to be taken in sets, or to be supplemented by other sentences, before generalizations can be derived from them, since they contain terms that do not occur in the generalizations. The formula about the falling body follows from the universal formula only if, in addition to the necessary values for the constant of gravitation and the mass and radius of the earth, the definition known as Newton's second law is provided. This says that the acceleration produced in a body of a given mass by a given force satisfies the relation

$$\text{force} = \text{mass} \times \text{acceleration}.$$

This allows us to express the local constant g in terms of the universal constant G and vice versa. But no theoretical entities such as force enter into the definition or understanding of the local constant, which can be calculated directly on the basis of observations.

Generalizations and hypotheses are so called because of their logical form and their relation to observation sentences, not because they are true. Generalizations that have been shown to the satisfaction of scientists to be true—that is, that have been *accepted* as true—are called *laws*. In a similar way, hypotheses that satisfy this condition are sometimes called *principles*. But showing truth in the two cases involves two different sets of considerations. To return to the example of falling bodies: one of the generalizations implicit in it is that whenever a heavy object is released from rest and allowed to fall freely near the surface of the earth, its acceleration will be g. The trouble with establishing the truth of this is that most heavy bodies in the universe never have been, never will be, and never could be released from rest and allowed to fall freely near the surface of the earth, so that to assert what *would* happen if they *were* so released (which is what the generalization amounts to) goes far beyond the evidence, which is merely an accumulation of observation sentences like the ones given.

This is a logical pitfall from which no satisfactory escape has been discovered, but philosophers have often skirted it by appealing to transcendent principles like the Principle of the Uniformity of Nature. This says that, subject to local conditions, things behave in the same way always and everywhere. We have no grounds for asserting any such principle. But all that is required to overcome this difficulty is to agree that, while the generalization cannot be finally known to be true, we still resolve to accept it as true until evidence presents itself to the contrary. This admits the generalization as a law according to the convention stated above. A sufficient number of observations of heavy objects accelerating at the required rate predisposes the observer, in the absence of contrary instances, to accept such a law.

Universal forces, on the other hand, are never observed. The hypothesis always says: "If the world were constructed in the way proposed by hypothesis H, and the relation between its construction and its behavior were expressed by the conditional 'if H, then O,' then behavior O would be observed. It *is* observed. Therefore it is not unlikely that the world is constructed in that way." This cautious formulation is required because the inference from observations of the hypotheses from which they follow is illegitimate—alternative hypotheses are always possible. The inference commits what is known as the "fallacy of affirming the consequent."

In the conditional sentence "if A then B," A is known as the *antecedent* and B as the *consequent*. If the conditional is true, then affirming the antecedent A allows me to affirm also the consequent B (see Table 5-1). But affirming the consequent does not allow me to affirm the antecedent; such a move would be fallacious, because any number of other conditionals with the same consequent might be true at the same time. If Jill fails the course, she will be sad. I meet her later and she is sad. But I cannot conclude that she failed the course. On the contrary, she did brilliantly in the course; she says she is sad because her grandmother just died. I might have thought of this alternative hypothesis, which would have explained her sadness just as well. Might she be using the grandmother story as an excuse? Another hypothesis occurs to me: that she may have quarrelled with her boyfriend. And so on.

Inference, implication: An inference is a carrying (Latin *fero*, to bear or carry) of truth from one proposition to another; I infer that something is the case (for example, that this remark is about a word or a person) because I already know that something else is

> the case (it's in a box). (I also need to know a rule relating the two.) Note that an inference is something that somebody does; it should not be confused with implication, which is a relation that holds between propositions whether anybody draws the corresponding inference or not. If one proposition implies another, it is as if the second is already present in the first, metaphorically "folded" into it (Latin *plico*, "to fold"—compare "explicate," to unfold the meaning of something).

In the scientific case we may reasonably say that the truth of the hypothesis is "not unlikely," because scientific theories have been worked on for so long that most of the alternative hypotheses have been entertained and refuted. Does this "not-unlikelihood" ever turn into a likelihood great enough to justify the acceptance of the hypothesis as true? The answer to this question has to be in the negative. But the coherence of the sentences derived from the hypotheses with sentences generalized from observations, their usefulness in prediction, and their fitting in with everything else we know, enable us to make a resolve similar to the one for laws: we hang on to our principles until the evidence compels us to change them.

The nature of the evidence that would compel such a change is not as obvious for principles, however, as it is for laws. The refutation of a law involves the observation of factual situations that are directly incompatible with it: heavy objects remaining suspended in mid air, for example. The relation between antecedent and consequent has another useful feature:

Table 5-1 Relations between Antecedent and Consequent in Conditional Statements

Valid	I. *modus ponens* ("the mode of putting") If A then B A therefore B	II. *fallacy of affirming the consequent* If A then B B therefore A	**Not Valid**
Valid	III. *modus tollens* ("the mode of taking") If A then B not B therefore not A	IV. complex *modus tollens* If A and C, then B not B therefore either not A or not C	**Valid**

from the denial of the consequent we can conclude the denial of the antecedent. This was the basis of Karl Popper's doctrine of falsification: if we can't verify laws no matter how many confirming observations we make, he said, we can at least falsify them by making contrary observations; if we can't find any contrary observations, then the law will remain unfalsified, and that is as good as it gets.

Sir Karl Popper (1902–1994), Anglo-Austrian philosopher. He pointed out that a proposition that cannot be falsified makes no empirical claim; the theories that deserve our respect will be those that have offered themselves to falsification but have so far remained unrefuted. Something similar happens in the moral realm: Popper also argued that social and political arrangements not open to criticism are oppressive and that only those systems that offer themselves to opposition deserve our respect.[3]

Refuting a principle is not so easy. Because principles, being hypothetical, contain nonobservational elements, observational consequences can be drawn from them only if they are taken together with other propositions. Let us call these "additional assumptions." If from a principle together with additional assumptions an observational conclusion follows, and if the contrary observation is made, the principle is not necessarily falsified; the additional assumptions may be at fault. In this way favored principles can always be protected. The philosophical doctrine known as *conventionalism* maintains that scientific principles are not to be regarded as truths about the world, but as propositions everyone has agreed to protect in this way. We have adopted the convention of looking at the world in their terms, but we might have looked at it in other terms.

30. The Relevance of Theory to the World

Remember that the word "theory" just means a way of looking at the world (see Introduction). The existence of a theory, complete with principles and laws, enables scientists to make assertions that seem quite implausible to ordinary people in the light of their experience. Scientists may say, for example, that electromagnetic waves and other forms of radiation are constantly passing through people's bodies, or that chairs and tables are composed of tiny particles in violent motion. Scientists start out with observations not much more complex than other people's, but when they feed their observations into theories conclusions follow that are apparently at variance with the plain evidence of the senses.

Nobody would tolerate this state of affairs if not for the fact that entertaining such hypotheses makes it possible to predict what the plain evidence of the senses will be at some future time—a feat that, apart from its usefulness, is impressive enough to render implausibilities acceptable. In most cases the prediction is less than perfect, and its outcome is highly probable rather than certain, but since this probability is usually computable with accuracy we can tell how much reliance can wisely be placed on the prediction. This is the next best thing to certainty.

One of the great puzzles of the philosophy of science has always been the *origin* of the hypotheses that, by standing apart from experience, enable thought to leave the plane of experience and return to it elsewhere or in the future. One popular view has been that the hypotheses are arrived at by *induction* from particular experiences. Induction is a mode of argument that draws conclusions about classes from information about their members; in the language of the previous section, it infers universal propositions from sets of particular ones. Induction is therefore an appropriate way of getting from observations to generalizations, though, for reasons similar to those that apply to the fallacy of affirming the consequent, the conclusion of an inductive argument can only be probable, never certain. However many members of a class we may have observed, it is always possible that the next one will have anomalous properties.

Induction: Latin *duco,* "to draw or lead," gives us a whole family of words: production, reduction, deduction, induction. The last two are of special interest, having been adopted as technical terms by logicians. "Deduction" leads from something already established; "induction" leads toward something to be established. So deduction is from a generalization to its instances, induction from instances to a generalization; deduction from laws to observations, induction from observations to laws; and so on for parallel cases. Peirce (see p. 76) added the notion of "retroduction," leading from observations directly to hypotheses.

In the case of hypotheses induction will not work, since, as we have seen, hypotheses make reference to things that are not encountered in experience. Hypotheses must rest in some way on experience, but they cannot do so in the simple inductive way. The most satisfactory account makes them the products of the scientific imagination; in C. S. Peirce's words they are "the spontaneous conjectures of instinctive reason."[4] Reason does not make its conjectures at random. An intuitive notion of relevance to experience can be formalized in logical terms by means of the set of relationships between observation sentences, generalizations, and hypotheses given above. Hypotheses have potential connections with experience through their joint logical consequences. Whether these consequences, when worked out in detail, will be correct descriptions of experience remains to be seen. If they are not, the hypotheses need modification. But for a hypothesis to count in the first place its consequences will have to be descriptions of possible experiences.

Charles Sanders Peirce (1838–1914), American philosopher and the founder of pragmatism. Peirce anticipated many of the main developments in contemporary philosophy, including phenomenology and semiotics.

The logical connections between hypotheses and observation sentences, and those between one observation sentence and another, by means of which predictions are made, are assumed to reflect causal connections between the things to which the sentences refer. In the first case, unobservable events (for example, the transitions between atomic states postulated by quantum physicists) must, if science is to have any standing at all as an account of the real world, play a part in the causal determination of observable events (for example, the emission of light). In the second case, a prediction is a logical movement, via the theory, from a set of observation sentences describing events previously observed (the *data*) to an observation sentence describing the predicted event. If the prediction is to be useful, this movement must anticipate the causal movement, via the physical world, from the events previously observed to the predicted event. If the data describe vibrations in an aircraft wing, and if when plugged into mechanical and aerodynamical theory they lead to the prediction that the wing will fail, it would be a good thing for the prediction to be made and acted upon before the real vibrations lead to the failure of the real wing and the loss of the aircraft.

The assumption of parallelism between the logical structure of theory and the causal structure of the world is itself a metascientific hypothesis whose confirmation is provided in a rough way by the success of science in making predictions. But we would know nothing of the causal structure, and could not begin to construct a theory, if we were not somehow involved in the physical world—if we did not have bodies equipped with sense organs. The perceptions on the basis of which we enunciate observation sentences are themselves the end points of causal chains.

Figure 5-1 shows how causality enters into the picture in a dual sense. The unbroken arrows in the diagram represent causal connections. Their direction is significant. If A is the cause of B, B cannot be the cause of A; furthermore, according to the standard analysis of causality, if A is the cause of B, A must *precede* B in time. The causal process is unidirectional. Since, however, the perception of A, on which knowledge of A rests, is a causal consequence of A itself, it follows that *knowledge is always retrospective*. If description means the direct result of observation, then an event cannot be described—that is, no eyewitness account can be given—until it has happened. Eyewitness accounts of complex events are themselves often unreliable; the point of starting from elementary observations is to secure reliable agreement. Although it seems to contradict this claim, prediction is not the same as knowledge. The broken line in the diagram, which leads from the description of A to the description of B, and which must produce the description of B before B happens if it is to represent a prediction, is broken because the outcome is always in doubt until it is confirmed by the actual occurrence of B. The description and the perception confront one another, and it cannot be *known* that they will agree until the comparison is made. The anticipation of nature is always hypothetical and cannot be otherwise. But time continually passes, and, as predictions continue to be fulfilled, our confidence in science increases. No logical reason can be offered for this increase in confidence, but confidence is a psychological and not a logical matter. This view of the relation between the observed past and the anticipated future was stated in the eighteenth century by David Hume and has not been improved upon.

David Hume (1711–1776), Scottish philosopher. A skeptical empiricist, Hume realized that experience is always limited to the appearances of the moment, from which nothing can be inferred for sure about the future or the ultimate constitution of things. But he held that our intellectual and moral habits can be relied upon for practical purposes.

Figure 5-1 Causal and Predictive Relations

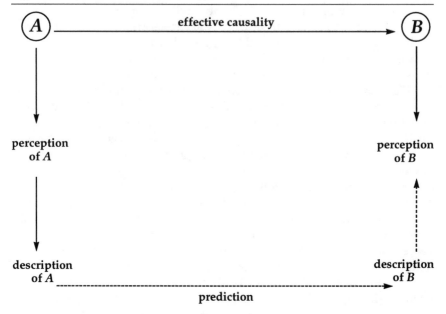

Notes

1. Peter Caws, *The Philosophy of Science: A Systematic Account* (Princeton, N.J.: Van Nostrand, 1965), p. 11.
2. See Frank Manuel, *A Portrait of Sir Isaac Newton* (Cambridge: The Belknap Press of Harvard University Press, 1968).

VI

Science and the Theory of Value

31. The Analogy between Scientific Theory and the Theory of Value

Science, then, although it cannot provide us with certain knowledge of the underlying and unobservable structure of the world that surrounds us or of the future course of events, does organize such knowledge as we have in the way most likely to be useful in dealing with future contingencies. It makes the most of our situation as human beings with finite intelligence and powers, so that our judgments about matters of fact in everyday life can be informed and rational. Judgments of value, on the other hand, are still largely *ad hoc*, made up afresh for each occasion, or based on authority or prejudice. Our task, then, is to learn what can be learned from the experience of science as it applies to the theory of value.

The first step is to look for analogues in the theory of value for the various elements listed above as indispensable to the structure of science: sensory data, observation sentences, generalizations and laws, hypotheses and principles, together with the logical relations that link these elements and the causal relations that these links reflect. Such analogues can be found, but when we examine them it proves impossible to transfer the logical structure of science to the theory of value in any simple way.

To start at the most elementary level, what statements about value correspond to observation sentences? Observation sentences express factual descriptions, and we might be tempted to make the empirical basis of value theory a set of such sentences describing attitudes or preferences: "Susan reports that she prefers tea to coffee," or "George expresses disgust when he tastes mayonnaise." But these are just ordinary observation sentences with nothing particularly value-laden about them. On the basis of such sentences a science of preferential behavior might be constructed, which would be a legitimate part of psychology. It would be a scientific theory about what people do, or say, or think (that is, say they think) in situations appropriately described by value terms, but it would not be a theory of value.

The trouble with such a theory as a possible theory of value is that the observer is treating someone else—George or Susan—as the object of inquiry. This situation is significantly different from what obtains in the scientific case. If Susan is a seismologist, nobody needs to say, "Susan reports a tremor of 5.5 on the Richter scale"; Susan just reports a tremor of 5.5 on the Richter scale. Until the observer enunciates the observation sentence, nobody else knows what it is going to say. If we get rid of the intermediary and ask what kind of value sentences have the same particularity, immediacy, and privacy as observation sentences, we have to conclude that they are sentences that express not factual *descriptions*, but factual *prescriptions*.

Before the psychologist can report that Susan prefers tea to coffee, Susan has to prefer tea to coffee. Unless she is making a deliberate effort at detachment (making a psychological report about herself), she will not just express her preference in comparative terms but will make an assertion of a more direct kind. If, for example, tea and coffee are served after dinner, she will not normally say, "I prefer tea to coffee," but will just ask for tea; what matters to her is not her preference of tea to coffee but her actually having tea. (In special cases she might be expected to draw attention to the preference: for example, if only coffee is being served but the host expresses a willingness to make tea if anyone prefers it.)

The paradigm of a factual prescription is "A should be B" or "A ought to be B"—"he ought not to drink so much," "you ought to protest against the war," "she should have told me the truth." These ordinary-language expressions refer to states of the world, not to states of the agent's mind, which is why "I wish that A were B," or even "Would that A were B!," are unsuitable formulations. What the new expressions say about the world, however, is not empirical in the ordinary sense. They could be brought into an impersonal form to make them more like the observation sentences of science, but there would be a fundamental difference between the two types even so. This leads me to call the new examples *virtual observation sentences*. Their propositional content will accordingly be *virtual descriptions*. By this I mean that, in the expressions involving value, *the facts the sentences describe need not be the case.* Value attaches to his abstention, your protest, her truthfulness, whereas in fact he is an alcoholic, you acquiesce in an unjust foreign policy, she lied. These facts form an essential part of the situation; they cannot be left out. Virtual descriptions alone are therefore incomplete. We need something more complex. The lowest-level propositions of the theory of value have two parts, which we may call, borrowing an expression from mathematics, a real part and an imaginary or virtual part, or, in the language of this chapter, a factual part and a prescriptive part.

Virtual: This term has become familiar because of the development of what has been called "virtual reality," but it has a well-established scientific use ("virtual displacements" in mechanics, "virtual images" in optics, more recently "virtual machines" in computer science). The root idea is that something is exercising the function or exerting the power that would belong to a real object in a corresponding position, even though it does not in fact have physical existence. For the root (and for reflections on its significance) see p. 21.

As in the case of the scientific theories discussed above, you do not have to master the mathematics of complex number theory in order to understand the analogy I wish to draw from it. Complex numbers are expressed in the form

$$x + iy,$$

where x and y are real numbers but the i prefixed to y indicates that it enters into the expression with a special modality. i stands for the square root of -1: $i^2 = -1$. Hence $(iy)^2 = -(y^2)$, although no real solution exists to any equation of the form $a^2 = -b$. In the theory of value, in an analogous way, the complex description has two parts. It asserts, by implication, that something is the case and, explicitly, that something (usually, although not necessarily, something different) ought to be the case.

The prefix "it is the case that" and its variants can be employed as a standard form, rather as the logician Arthur Prior[1] employed them in his logic of tenses. The standard form of a straightforward factual description will be "it is the case that x," and the standard form of a complex description will be "it is the case that x, and it ought to be the case that y." If we take x in the straightforward way to stand for "it is the case that x," and borrow "i" (for "imperative") as a modal prefix, so that iy stands for "it ought to be the case that y," the standard form will again be

$$x + iy.$$

The mathematical analogy is not to be taken too seriously; its significance is as a reminder that some ideas cannot be expressed in simple form even when part of what is involved in them has a simple customary expression.

Although the possibility is allowed for that x and y may be identical ($x + ix$ is not inconsistent)—that things may be all right as they are—y always has a different temporal reference from x. *It is always future.* Even in constructions like "it ought to have been the case that y," this rule holds; the point of reference shifts to a time at which *y* was future, and the sentence translates into "it was the case that (it ought to be the case that *y*)," to borrow Prior's technique once more. This difference lies at the root of the distinction between science and the theory of value.

32. Positive and Negative Features of the Analogy

Science is a kind of knowledge, and as such it must always be retrospective. But values are different from knowledge. They do not come to us from the world; they go from us to the world. They refer not to what is or was the case, but to what will or may be the case. They are, therefore, always *prospective* or *future referential*. The difference between science and the theory of value turns out to be as fundamental as the difference between past and future. This being so, there can be no surprise in the discovery that values are not easy to find in the world with which science deals, a fact that has disturbed many people in search of a science of value. Values are not easy to find in the world because they are not yet there.

This point cannot be stressed too strongly, and it will be referred to again. For the moment we may complete the list of analogies. Principles have already been dealt with; they are just as hypothetical in the theory of value as they are in science, and their origin too is to be found in the human imagination, not elsewhere. The principles required for the system of this book will be introduced as they become relevant. Since principles of the theory of value are to lead, eventually, to prescriptions for action, their validation will follow a different pattern from the validation of scientific principles. In science we say: if the world operated according to such-and-such principles, then such-and-such phenomena would be observed. To test the principles, we ask whether the phenomena are in fact observed. If they are, that gives us reason to think that the principles are true, in the always conditional sense specified above, in which remaining unfalsified and having no serious competitors leads to acceptance as true for the time being. This has been called the "hypothetico-deductive" strategy. First we float a hypothesis, then we deduce consequences from it; as long as these encounter no contradiction in observation, we are justified in keeping the hypothesis.

But in the theory of value we say: if such-and-such principles were acted upon, then such-and-such a world would result. To test these principles we ask not only whether such a world really would result, but also whether this is the kind of world we want. If it would and is, that gives us reason to think that the principles are right, in a similarly conditional sense: remaining unchallenged and having no satisfactory alternative leads to acceptance as right for the time being. This might be called the "hypothetico-deductive-imperative" strategy. First we float a hypothesis, next we deduce consequences from it, then we affirm that these ought to be the case. The term "imperative," as you will remember, comes from a Latin root meaning "to command."

Laws in science correspond to rules in value theory. The rules have the same dual nature as the laws, being on the one hand acceptable generalizations of complex descriptions and on the other the deductive consequences of hypothetical principles. The difference between rules and laws is like the difference between virtual observation sentences and straightforward ones. Rules look like laws with an imperative modal prefix, which must also be attached to at least one of the principles from which the rule is derived. A rule specifies a way of doing something, but it also says that that is the way it must be done. This "must" may be conditional, as in the case of Kant's hypothetical imperative. If you want to be playing chess, then you must move the bishop on the diagonal; if you don't care about playing chess, then you can do anything you like with the bishop.

Generalizing on the factual part of complex descriptions raises the following problem. Many states of affairs x may obtain in which we wish to assert that "it ought to be the case that y"—including, as we have seen, the case in which x and y are identical. The point of having a descriptive part there at all is that it makes a difference in the application of the rule. If x is identical with y, no action is called for. If not, the action called for depends on the relation between x and y. At the other end of the scale, we may encounter states of affairs in which if x were the case y could never be the case, so that to say it ought to be the case would be practically empty (though it might still be morally necessary to say it).

One way of handling this problem is to let the descriptive part drop out on generalizing, leaving only the imperative part. The logical relations between principles, rules, and prescriptions are then strictly analogous to those between principles, laws, and descriptions in science; the relations hold between the indicative contents of the sentences in question, and the modal prefix is carried through unchanged.

The foregoing account of the structure of science, on which the analogy with the theory of value is based, has been schematic in the extreme; it is an example of what has sometimes been called "formal reconstruction," which was characteristic of the work of the logical empiricists between the 1930s and the 1950s. Since that time the philosophy of science has paid more attention to areas of science that might be called *frontiers, superstructure,* and *context* than to its robust and workaday central elements.

By "frontiers" I mean those areas of inquiry remote from daily experience that require the greatest experimental investment and the most advanced resources of the mathematical imagination: basic particle physics, the cosmology of the earliest moments of the universe, the neurochemistry of transmitters and receptors. By "superstructure" I mean the layers of inquiry that correspond to higher-level complexes such as those involved in the biomedical and social sciences, where methodology becomes more statistical, observations may themselves be aggregates, and generalizations may be local in scope. By "context" I mean the social and psychological setting of the scientific enterprise and its practitioners, the dominant research programs and paradigms, and second-order questions of convergence and cultural relativity. I use the term "paradigm" here in the sense given to it by Thomas Kuhn—that is, an exemplary model of how science is done—rather than in its older meaning as a representative case of some grammatical or other form.[2]

For present purposes most of these considerations are marginal. None of them makes an essential difference to the structure of theory and its relation to observation. What has been called the "hypothetico-deductive" or "covering-law" model (which might have been called the "umbrella model," where a higher-level law covers a whole class of generalizations and their instances), although admittedly too simple to deal by itself with all developments in scientific theory or all aspects of scientific practice, has not been improved upon as a first approximation to the logical and epistemological status of science in what I have sometimes called the "flat region" (see Introduction).

As has been emphasized in the preceding sections, moral values need simple formulation if they are to be useful, and introducing too much technical rigor into the theory of morals does little good. As Aristotle remarks, "It is the mark of one who is educated to look for precision in each class of things just so far as the nature of the subject admits."[3] The situation of the moral agent is always approximate. What is wanted, therefore, is a robust theory that will correspond to the longest-standing and most thoroughly worked-over findings of the empirical sciences.

33. A Phenomenological Distinction: Knowing and Willing

A scheme of analogies between science and the theory of value is given in Table 6-1. (The term "nomological" covers cases of lawlike behavior or empirical regularity; the rest of the diagram is self-explanatory.) The chief difficulty with this scheme arises at the level in the theory of value that corresponds to raw sensory data in scientific theory. What, on the side of value, corresponds to seeing blue or hearing a loud noise? Here it seems useful to revive a classical usage in philosophy and speak of conation as an analogue of perception. By "conative data" I mean the intuitively felt tendencies of an individual to accept some things or circumstances and

Table 6-1 The Analogy between Science and the Theory of Value

Levels	Types of Sentence	Elements of Scientific Theory	Elements of Theory of Value
Theoretical	hypothesis	principle	principle
Nomological	generalization	law	rule
Descriptive	observation sentence (may be virtual)	factual description	complex description
Phenomenological	–	perceptual data	conative data

reject others, to try to acquire some and get rid of others. "Data" is perhaps misleading but is worth keeping for the analogy. I do not mean that we discover such tendencies in ourselves and make the fact that they are there the basis for prescriptive utterances; the tendencies themselves are the basis. But the rendering of the tendencies as an articulate prescription calls for the same degree of experience and sophistication that is required for the rendering of raw perceptual data as an articulate description.

Nomological: Greek *nemo* meant "to deal out, distribute"; *nomos* meant "something allotted or assigned," including living space, and came to mean law generally.

Conation: As it occurs in Spinoza, *conatus* is "the effort by which each thing endeavors to persevere in its own being."[4] The root verb in Latin is *conor*, "to undertake, exert oneself, strive." But *conatus* also means "an impulse or inclination." In both senses, active and passive, it has the direction toward the future that we have identified as the fundamental characteristic of value.

Baruch (or Benedict) Spinoza (1632–1677), Dutch philosopher. His *Ethics* was an attempt to set out philosophical truths in a deductive system *more geometrico* ("in a geometric fashion"). For Spinoza the whole universe is one, being God in one aspect and nature in another. He encourages us to be guided by an "intellectual love of God" and to view things "under the aspect of eternity" (*sub specie aeternitatis*).

The point is that the relation of human beings to the world is not just a static relation of knowledge. It is at the same time a dynamic relation of will. Science is equipped to deal only with the part that belongs to knowledge. The way in which values are constituted out of conations requires elaboration. Something may be learned from the way in which facts are constituted out of sensations.

"Fact" is still a useful category in spite of the attacks that have been made on it by relativists and postmodernists, who think that a general or comprehensive account of the human situation is no longer possible. Let me repeat in different terms a point made in the Introduction. As its root suggests (see p. 5), the word "fact" stands for something finished or accomplished, that has come to be what it is, recognizably and reliably. Check on a factual conclusion again, and it's still as it was. The claim here is not (as some critics may think) that facts are things observers can never be wrong about, though there is what might be called an "apodictic certainty" about them; as the saying goes, they "stare us in the face." But after suitable inquiry on our part, making as sure as we can, by double-checking and consulting other observers, that they are not illusions or mere subjective impressions or mirages, facts make a robust basis for the edifice of science, the only empirical basis available.

The claim that facts have apodictic certainty is controversial and needs explanation. The term "apodictic," as used by Kant for example, has been taken to mean *necessarily* certain, but it need not mean this and is most useful when it does not. Kant thought that some things, such as the three-dimensionality of space, had necessarily to be the case because they so obviously were the case. Perceived space cannot have more than three dimensions; he was right about that. But apodictic certainty must not be confounded with mathematical necessity. In the late eighteenth century, just as Kant was claiming a necessary three-dimensionality for space, mathematicians like Gauss were showing that geometries of four or more dimensions were consistently possible. That such geometries are formally consistent does not mean that we could live in one perceptually. The three semicircular canals in the inner ear are accurately aligned in the three orthogonal planes of Euclidean space, to whose local structure we are precisely adapted and which is therefore apodictically certain in our perceptual world.

Apodictic: An *apodeixis* in Greek is a "pointing out"; the *-deixis* part is cognate with the *-dex* in "index," the index finger being the one that does the pointing out (and an ordinary index pointing out where to find things in a book).

> *Carl Friedrich Gauss* (1777–1855), a German mathematician and astronomer who made fundamental advances in number theory and many other fields.

Nobody supposes that facts exist in some strange way apart from the objects and events that constitute them. Nor are they insulated from considerations of value; some facts (not all!) are "value-laden," especially in the context of the human sciences. But values are often thought to be a special kind of entity that we might find embedded in the world—put there, perhaps, by God—if only we knew where to look. One of the most celebrated of these hidden values is "meaning." People search endlessly for meaning as though they expected it to turn up one day, whole and perfect and recognizable, putting everything in perspective and making the course of future action clear and attainable. As long as this kind of illusion persists, no theory of value can provide the rational control of our aesthetic and moral circumstances that science provides for our material circumstances. What the theory applies to, and the mode of being it enjoys, must be clearly understood, and not only in technical terms but in its everyday embodiment. To this task of understanding we now turn.

Notes

1. A. N. Prior, *Changes in Events and Changes in Things* (Lawrence: Department of Philosophy, University of Kansas, 1962).
2. T. S. Kuhn, *The Structure of Scientific Revolutions* (Chicago: University of Chicago Press, 1962).
3. Aristotle, *Nicomachean Ethics* 1094^{b}25.
4. Benedict de Spinoza, *Ethics*, trans. James Gutmann (New York: Hafner, 1949), p. 135. This is Part III, Proposition VII; "effort" is a translation of "*conatus.*"

VII

Fact and Value

34. The Temporal Asymmetry of Fact and Value

Fact looks to the past, to what is already established; value looks to the future, to the realization or avoidance of our hopes and fears. That is the fundamental difference between them. For purposes of argument I paint this opposition more sharply than ordinary English does. "Value" is not a technical term for most people. Like many familiar and frequently encountered words it has a broad spectrum of usage, part of which covers economic rather than moral or aesthetic matters. Values in the marketplace rise and fall, are compared and contrasted with prices, are unexpectedly found in neglected stock issues, and so on. My intention is not to legislate linguistic use, but to draw attention to, and focus on, a feature of the concept of value that will help in the construction of a robust moral theory.

Fact and value meet in the present—not in any arbitrarily selected present but in *this* present, which divides what is already part of my cumulative experience from all the future possibilities that await me. This egocentricity is unavoidable. All knowledge is somebody's knowledge, every value is somebody's value, but my world is circumscribed by my knowledge, and my action in that world is determined by my values. My being as a knower and as an agent is located here and now, at a point in space and time on which the whole past of the universe converges and from which its whole future originates. True, much of that future will be determined by causal processes that do not pass through me; I shall always be surrounded by a world over which I have little or no control. But my agency, if I really am an agent, will affect the future course of things to some degree and make the world as a whole different from what it would have been without me.

We have seen that knowledge is the result of a causal process, and action is in some sense the beginning of another such process. A crucial question, which must sooner or later be faced, is whether processes that do pass through me en route from past to future are fully causal or not, whether action really is the causal beginning of something—whether, in short, I am truly an agent. Although it does not affect the temporal asymmetry discussed above, a negative answer to that question changes the relationship between fact and value so that it no longer depends on the asymmetry except in an academic way.

If we were not truly agents, then facts, whether past or future, would be what they are, while values would be merely the attitudes we adopt toward them. We would be powerless to influence the facts; the future would differ from the past in only one respect, namely that we did not yet know it. We could entertain hopes and fears about it, thus investing it with value. But the values we held could not affect the outcome of the causal process. This point has nothing to do with the issue between chance and determinism. In a fully determined universe even the most accurate predictions suffer from practical limitations that prevent their ever being complete. From our point of view it would make very little difference whether things were determined and we just happened to be ignorant of them, or whether chance played a part in the universe, in which case our ignorance would be a necessary condition. Either way we could do nothing about it.

Determinism: The view that everything that happens does so because of what has happened before, and could in principle be predicted down to the last detail. According to this view, desires and intentions must themselves be determined by antecedent conditions. No subject, therefore, could be said to participate effectively in a free choice.

One of the difficulties with values as mere attitudes is that they become factual, in their own way, as soon as they are reflected upon. The advice of the Stoics (and of Descartes, who made it one of his provisional maxims in the *Discourse on Method*) was "change your desires rather than the order of the world." But many people find that it is easier to change the order of the world than to change their desires. What passes for a change of desire is often a rearrangement of the order of the world that removes the stimulus of desire—retreating into a monastery, for example. Desires are part of the order of the world, and the fact that they belong to an interior world makes them, if anything, harder to manipulate.

The Stoics originally took their name from the *Stoa*, a porch or colonnade in Athens where Zeno of Citium (fl. 300 B.C.E.) used to lecture. Well-known Stoics in later periods were the former slave Epictetus (see p. 39) and the emperor Marcus Aurelius (121–180). Their basic doctrine held that the world will be as it will be but that it is governed by divine principles of order and reason. Wisdom consists therefore in accepting one's lot and living in harmony with nature.

Rene Descartes (1596–1650), French philosopher and mathematician, the inventor of analytic geometry. Descartes set the tone for modern philosophy by practicing his method of radical doubt on earlier views as well as on commonsense beliefs. He is famous for his conclusion that one's own existence in the moment is the only thing of which one can have certain knowledge (*cogito, ergo sum,* "I think, therefore I am"). However he soon supplemented this with certain knowledge of God, thus rehabilitating many of his old beliefs.

A regress is possible: I observe the state of the world, which I cannot change; I find in myself an attitude toward it, let us say one of discontent. At the same time I find myself taking up a second-order attitude, perhaps of disapproval, to my attitude of discontent, and so on. But these successive levels are all factual: that is the way the world is, this is the way I am. Value involves at least the potentiality of choice, and it therefore attaches much more plausibly to future states of the world than to states of my mind. A value is a future fact, selected from among a set of alternative, and mutually exclusive, future facts, and marked with an imperative. The chosen fact may not come about; in such a case, we speak of the value as unrealized.

At first sight ordinary usage identifies value with some characteristic of the future fact, by virtue of which it is marked with an imperative. We speak of pleasure, beauty, honor, and so on as values, and consider that these abstract qualities confer value on the facts that embody them. But this puts the cart before the horse. We would not know that the abstract qualities were values if we had not first attached value to their concrete embodiments. Pleasurable experiences, beautiful objects, and honorable actions constitute the empirical basis for generalizations about pleasure, beauty, and honor, and we know them for what they are without the generalizations. Also, the generalizations have exceptions. This is one reason why theories of value developed at the abstract level so often appear irrelevant to the experience of value in everyday life. The wise move is to begin with the unit of value in experience—namely the future fact itself—rather than with a conventional abstraction.

35. The Concept of the Open Future

The use of the term "future" in this connection requires clarification. In ordinary language the term automatically connotes contingency, the possibility that things may be other than they are, so that it is not necessary to insist that future facts are only probable. Philosophers are less tolerant. You may argue that when I say "future fact," I mean "fact that will be the case," and that if I really mean "fact that may or may not be the case," I ought to say "possible fact." I do not wish to become involved in an argument about subjunctives, but "possible" will not do, for two reasons. First, "possible fact" can mean "fact that may now be the case although it is not known to be," or "fact that might now be the case although it happens not to be," neither of which allows the fact as a value. Second, people may well attach value to impossible facts.

The objection to "future" rests in part on a metaphysical assumption about determinism, according to which the existence of future facts is implicit in the existence of present ones. This assumption is inconsistent with the view that the conscious subject plays an efficacious role in the determination of events, and it is therefore rejected. I defer the argument for this rejection until the next chapter, on freedom. The alternative to the assumption that future facts are implicit in present ones is to assume that statements about the future cannot now be said either to be true or to be false, which, although it is awkward for logic, is in no way inconsistent with the ordinary use of future-referential statements. As Aristotle insisted, the following two assertions differ significantly from one another:

1. It is now the case that either there will be a sea fight tomorrow or there will not be a sea fight tomorrow.
2. Either it is now the case that there will be a sea fight tomorrow or it is now the case that there will not be a sea fight tomorrow.

The second pins down future facts now; the first leaves them open in the sense required by the proposed definition of value.

36. Difficulties in the Elimination of Subjectivity

Although the contrast between past and future is the basic element in the distinction between fact and value, it does not do justice to the distinction as it affects our daily experience. The present, after all, is not a simple cut on

The Seven Deadly Sins: Envy (1953; director Roberto Rossellini)

Orfeo Tamburi is a painter whose wife (Andrée Debar) is envious of his model's role in his life. She transfers her affection to the family cat, with unhappy consequences for her marriage.

the continuum of time that serves no other purpose than to separate the past from the future. It has a finite, though brief, duration in time (what some philosophers have called the "specious present"), and an internal structure of its own in which fact and value overlap. What we are prepared to recognize as fact depends to a large extent on the values we hold. The way we perceive the world to be is in some respects a function of the way we would like it to be.

Science has virtually eliminated this element of subjectivity from its description of the world by its insistence on *intersubjectivity* in its observations. We can never say that the world finally *is* a certain way. *Saying* introduces a possibility of error that cannot ultimately be averted, and requires a vocabulary that may already be colored by theory. But the evidence from centuries of scientific experience suggests that experienced observers under normal conditions can reach a high degree of concurrence in their reports. This leaves open the possibility that what we all intuitively believe may be true, namely, that underlying appearances is an objective and enduring reality whose structure is reflected accurately, if not completely, in scientific theory.

Might we find a way of eliminating subjectivity from value judgments by similar techniques? For example, we might insist on intersubjective corroboration for assertions that the world *ought* to be a certain way. As a rule we can always find another person to agree with any imperative we may formulate. But the evidence from centuries of dispute about value suggests that in most cases we can just as easily find somebody who disagrees, which lends no support at all to the view that the world objectively ought to be a certain way. Facts coerce us from without, and sometimes there is nothing we can do about them. Some people may experience value as coercion from within, and we saw earlier that the conscience or superego may be determined from without, but the situations are not parallel. That I happen to have been influenced by the parents or culture I happen to have been born to and into, and that I happen to be unable to resist this influence, are accidental facts about me and give no ground for thinking that the values I have thus internalized belong in the objective world.

Even if cherished values make us reluctant to admit that some unwelcome fact is the case, we can generally be convinced by the evidence of independent observers. In this way people discover that they are colorblind, tone-deaf, and so forth, or are unbuttoned, or repeat themselves. Independent observers are not so helpful, though, when it comes to questions of value. I may be interested to know what others think, but I have to decide for myself where my values lie. Sometimes a lone dissenter will insist that a disastrous course of action is wrong when everybody else says it is right; we would not wish this voice to be silenced by the majority. But somebody who insisted that squares had three sides or horses three legs would not be commended for this dissenting stand.

I dwell at this length on the fact-value distinction because it is controversial, and the controversy is of general philosophical interest. The contrast between fact and value is analogous to the contrast between observation and theory; many philosophers find it obvious that facts are *always* contaminated by values, observations always colored by theory. That this is *often* the case I freely admit. Yet in any observation of fact we sooner or later come up against something in the world that we cannot change by changing our theory or our values. In the end, the way the world is decides what we must accept.

People who deny the possibility of value-free facts or theory-free observations usually wish to defend one or both of two valid claims. The first claim is that values determine which facts we bother to attend to, while theories determine which observations we take the trouble to make. The second claim is that many so-called facts are inextricably bound up with values, and many observations are essentially dependent on theory. What uncritical folk take to be facts about society or politics or religion may be not only interpreted but described differently by people from a different culture or with different convictions. In a similar way some observations in the social or biomedical sciences, or in the more complex parts of the physical sciences, could not be made at all if the data to be gathered were not already conceptualized in terms of a definite theory. All true—but this does not invalidate the claim that we are connected to some facts in the world in a pretheoretical way and below the threshold of value, originally and whenever we choose to be, as long as we have not lost the knack.

This last point may be the crux of the matter: most people grow up learning to jump to the conclusions of their local culture and its historical moment, and come to see everything through the lenses of convention and prejudice. When they become philosophical and realize this, they conclude that it must be true of everyone always. But this is too hasty. Once we are aware of the influence of culture and history, we can compensate for and transcend it. Two good avenues toward this end are the study of phenomenology—that is, the analysis of what presents itself to us in appearance while we consciously suspend all our usual assumptions about it—and an experimental acquaintance with the basic physical sciences in which we encounter the stubbornness of the data.

Apart from deluded persons, everybody can in principle be brought into a community of agreement about matters of fact, given evidence and a willingness to confront it. What would be needed to create a similar community of agreement for judgments of value? Evidence will not do, at least not by itself. Such a community of agreement can only be constructed on a basis of argument. That is why the problem of value is at bottom a philosophical one, while the problem of fact is at bottom a scientific one. The resolution of a scientific disagreement always rests, in the end, on evidence; the resolution of a philosophical disagreement rests, in the end, on argument.

This distinction is too clear-cut, since scientists argue and philosophers cite cases, but it embodies the main point of difference. Science consists of the accumulation and explanation of evidence about the past, with all that this implies for our knowledge of the future. The theory of value consists of the formulation and justification of arguments about the future, with all that this implies for our attitude toward the past. The apparent future reference of science, in prediction, involves a hypothetical shift of perspective to a point from which the predicted event is seen as past. The apparent reference of value to the past, in approval or regret, involves a hypothetical shift of perspective to a point from which the approved or regretted event is seen as future. "In his circumstances I would have done the same thing" is a form of approbation that puts the speaker temporarily in a position where the decision is yet to be taken. "If I had known then what I know now, I would never have done it" is to be construed in a similar way. Past actions or events are not approved or regretted merely as facts, but as facts *that might have been otherwise.*

This shift of perspective introduces some distortion into the ordinary meaning of "regret" and "approval." We might want to claim that some merely present attitudes—for example, horror at the behavior of Hitler—involve value and lend themselves to emotive analysis. Even here I think that the horror lies in the fact that at some point in the past the "final solution" had *not yet* been decided upon and that the decision was an apparently free choice of an apparently human being. But granting a present feeling of (perhaps retrospective) moral or aesthetic disapproval of a past fact, with no future-referential component at all, not even a displaced one, we have to admit that the role of value in this feeling is merely passive, except as it is accompanied by a resolve not to let the same thing happen again. In the absence of such a resolve we often use expressions like "pious horror" to indicate that in some way the attitude is not to be taken seriously.

One object of this book is the clarification of moral judgment as *active*, that is, as contributing to the determination of action on the part of the person making the judgment. From this point of view, the detached assessment of the actions of others, the debate about what should be called "good" or "right" after the fact, about what "virtue" means, and so on, is of secondary interest. What is crucial is what people decide to do, the process by which they arrive at the decision, and the arguments that enter into the process. Only in such considerations does value take on its full significance.

37. Theory as the Rectification of Experience

Some imperatives leave little room for argument: for example, food and drink for people at the extremes of hunger and thirst, or relief for those in extreme pain. This can lead to the misunderstanding that underlies all hedonistic theories of value, those that make the simple equation of pleasure with good and pain with evil. On the most primitive level conative tendencies away from pain and toward pleasure are indeed factual and inescapable; we have no choice in the matter. But these overriding tendencies, instilled by the evolutionary process as necessities of survival, have no more to do with the theory of value than mechanisms of perception with a similar origin, such as the dilation and contraction of the pupil of the eye, have to do with the theory of knowledge. They are not activities consciously engaged in, even though the conscious activities of knowing and valuing depend on them or on processes like them.

Valuing bears to such raw feeling the relationship that knowing bears to untrained seeing. Just as science must be suspicious of what is superficially seen, such as moving stars and bent sticks, so also the theory of value must be suspicious of what is superficially felt, such as a desire for pleasure and a dislike of pain. The function of the theory is precisely to render the intellect independent of ephemeral considerations like these, to rectify experience by making possible a move away from the immediacy of experience in thought, so as to bring the outcome of this thought to bear on future experience.

Naive perception comes to naive conclusions about the world. Science starts from the fact that we have some knowledge, even if it is crude, and goes on to determine as best it can what we really know and do not know. Naive conation, in a similar way, comes to naive conclusions about action; the theory of value starts from the fact that we have some desires, even if they are clumsy, and goes on to determine as best it can what we really want and do not want. The community of agreement that we seek comes about only if individual values are rectified by a theory of value held in common.

Looking more closely at four special cases of the interaction of fact and value may help clarify the relations between them.

1. Facts as such may be regarded as values.
2. Values may be regarded as facts.
3. Facts by themselves always fall short of value.
4. Value goes beyond any fact or set of facts.

I will deal with these in the immediately following sections.

38. Facts as Values, Values as Facts

(1) *Facts as such may be regarded as values,* for example, in the pursuit of historical or scientific truth. The search for evidence about the past is an attempt to arrive at a future state of fuller knowledge of the past; the search for scientific law is an attempt to bring about conditions, again in the future, in which our understanding of or control over our world will be greater than it is now. The sciences cannot be considered coldly objective, in contrast, for example, with literature or the arts. If science had not engaged the passions, it would never have been invented. At the same time science requires a disciplined separation of the values it serves from the objects it studies.

(2) *Values may be regarded as facts.* This case comes in two versions, the first classical, the second modern. For Plato the highest value resides in a real object that really exists and is therefore fully factual, namely, the Form of the Good. For Aristotle the highest good is that to which the universe tends, whose actualization is the goal of every rational activity, including the activities of nature itself. The value of fact in Plato is reflected in his view that knowledge is better than opinion. He does not mean knowledge of a commonplace factual kind—for example, the fact that Athens is to the east of Syracuse—but knowledge of that special class of fact that determines the relation of human beings to their world.

Plato (c. 427–347 B.C.E.), the most famous pupil of Socrates. In Plato's *Dialogues* most of the significant problems of philosophy are stated, which led Alfred North Whitehead (see p. 155) to characterize the history of Western philosophy as a series of footnotes to Plato.

Aristotle (384–322 B.C.E.), Greek philosopher, the most famous pupil of Plato. He wrote systematic treatises on virtually every aspect of the philosophy and science of his day, and was known for almost two millennia as "the Philosopher" or "the Master of Those Who Know."

The second sense in which values may be regarded as factual is of more recent origin. It is that of the social scientist. The values that human beings hold determine their behavior, insofar as that behavior is determined by them at all. We might therefore conclude that a science of behavior is the only true science of value. Accordingly, analyses of preference and choice are offered as guides to the nature of value. If introspective accounts are to be ruled out as inherently untrustworthy, then the only way to find out about values is to observe preferences. Behaviorism brings evaluation into the realm of science by insisting that it should be looked at only from the outside.

If we want an account of human conduct that can be fully assimilated into the natural sciences, then this strategy makes sense. The logical thing for rational beings to do, if they are trying to explain events, is to follow the methods of science as far as they can be pushed, so behaviorism needs to make no excuses for itself. But to insist on a natural science of the human begs a large question about the relations between human beings and the natural world. "We thought we were dealing with sociologists," said Sartre; "our mistake: they were entomologists."[1] Human beings are not ants. We have no evidence that individual ants have values that guide their behavior, but we know that human beings do. And the assumption that preferences expressed in actions are straightforward reflections of values actually held cannot safely be made for human subjects.

Behaviorism: A movement in psychology founded by John B. Watson (American, 1878–1958) and developed by B. F. Skinner (American, 1904–90), in which subjective states were rejected as

> meaningful objects of scientific attention, which was focused instead on elements of overt behavior. Behaviorism was thus a form of positivism (see p. 23).

Preferential behavior involves a choice between available alternatives. These may not include the valued alternative at all, but this does not mean that no preference will be expressed. The strongest desire that a given state of affairs should come about is wholly compatible with the realization that it will never do so. In such a situation, behavior, whether action or description—for example, in a structured interview—may not provide any clues at all to the values involved. Without data the scientist is lost, but massive changes may take place in values without any change in the data for anybody except the person whose subjectivity is the locus of the values in question. Such a dissonance between value and preferential behavior might lead to a charge of bad faith against the person concerned, but that is no excuse for behavioristic oversimplification.

Further, even if in the individual case expressed preferences reflect values accurately, disagreement can still arise between individuals in a way that is unknown in the case of perception. Figure 7-1 shows schematically some different ways in which preferential behavior, and hence value, may be distributed in individual persons. The shaded area I call the *range of indifference*; the area above it marked "+" I call the *range of positive value*; and the area below it marked "−" is the *range of negative value*. The individual A is one to whom few things matter very much; he has a wide range of indifference flanked by narrow ranges of value. B, on the other hand, is extremely sensitive to everything, so that for her the reverse is true. C is hypercritical, let us say, and D too easily satisfied; their ranges are therefore skewed. The event x, represented by a broken line crossing all four individuals, does not matter at all to A; it has a negative value for C, but a positive one for B and D. Agreement is therefore impossible.

All this is not to be taken as meaning that social scientists are wasting their time. Science does what it must; it engages in the search for regularities in experience and for theories to account for them. Values may, and indeed must, enter into the explanation of human behavior. If there were no other analytical approach to them, they might take their place alongside electromagnetic and gravitational fields as theoretical entities required for the systematic completion of the human sciences, as fields are required for the completion of the natural sciences. But the matter need not end there. Because we are the source of the imperatives that create them, we have much more direct access to the structure of values than to the structure of the physical world.

Figure 7-1 Individual Ranges of Value

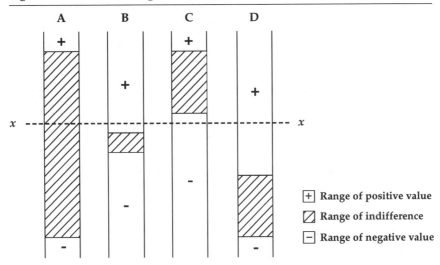

39. Facts as Inadequate to Values

By showing that facts may be made the object of concern and that values may enter into the scientific explanation of facts, the two relationships between fact and value dealt with so far might seem to mute the contrast of fact with value. But, as we have seen, the distinction is preserved even in these cases. The two relationships remaining to be discussed have the effect rather of sharpening the contrast. (3) *Facts by themselves always fall short of value*. The contemplation of fact as fact can, as we have seen, yield a kind of satisfaction, but the satisfaction lies not so much in the fact being what it factually is as in its being known, or having been successfully established, or relating in some meaningful way to other facts. Satisfaction, again, cannot be equated with value. It represents the enjoyment of value, but the value is *what is enjoyed,* not the enjoyment. You might look forward to enjoying something and thus constitute the enjoyment itself as a second-order value, and this series might continue with anticipating the pleasures of anticipation and so on. Satisfaction arises from the realization of a state of the world to which an imperative has been attached.

Facts must therefore have been future for somebody, at least implicitly, if they are to count as values. An unanticipated fact may be a value if an imperative would have been attached to it had it been thought of before the event. The fact that it *was* unanticipated may be a value: consider, for example, the disappointment of a child who says, "I wanted it to be a surprise." Apart from these modalities, the facts themselves lack any value whatever. This is profoundly significant in understanding the special flatness and boredom that characterizes lives full of material possessions but without imagination and without hope. The understanding of the factual situation helps, but it may not be enough by itself to remove a sense of incompleteness and dissatisfaction. The life of value requires participation in the emergence of new facts, a sense of involvement in the situation as something more than a mere onlooker.

The story of Socrates' disappointment with the philosophy of Anaxagoras is worth repeating. Socrates tells it in the *Phaedo*; he has been condemned to death by the Athenians and is explaining to his friends what he thinks about mortality and why he will not leave Athens to escape his sentence. Anaxagoras, says Socrates, talks about *noûs*, or mind, as the principle according to which the world moves purposively from one state to another, but when it comes to explaining particular facts he forgets all about *noûs* and refers instead only to "air, and ether, and water and other eccentricities." Socrates insists that what gives direction to his actions is not his bones and muscles but his conception of what is best, and this in quite concrete form, namely, his determination to stay in Athens and endure the punishment the state is to inflict. Action requires an antecedent factual basis, but it is not to be explained fully in terms of factual antecedents; that is Socrates' contention. Facts, once they have transpired, die and become immortal, and at this point they cease to be relevant to the determination of future facts, which is the province of action and therefore of value.

Anaxagoras (c. 500–428 B.C.E.), Greek philosopher, possibly the teacher of Socrates. He accounted for the surface variety of things by postulating large numbers of seedlike particles, corresponding to basic stuffs, all to be found everywhere, the preponderance of one type in a given object giving it the appearance of that stuff. He also thought there was a smaller number of particles of noûs or mind, whence the dictum: "In everything there is a portion of everything, but in some things there is mind also."

---

40. Values as Outreaching Facts

The inverse of this relationship is provided by the observation that (4) *value goes beyond any fact or set of facts* that may have been established. Taking account only of the factual state of affairs is not enough for action. A commitment is required, to securing that state of affairs against change or to realizing a new state of affairs. To avoid lapsing into futility or boredom,

I must involve myself, become engaged in some project, seize the future. How can I do this with confidence when the future is so uncertain? It will be a leap into the unknown, or what some people have called a leap of faith.

Religious faith, in the West, has been on the whole a poor illustration of this concept; for most believers it has become domesticated and comfortable and unadventurous. The philosopher who revived this leap beyond fact to value and made it especially his own was Kierkegaard. Faith for Kierkegaard is the election of a future state of the world that is by no means likely to come about in the ordinary course of events, and the attachment to it of the imperative. If I do this, my situation comes alive; I may experience anguish, dread, and fear and trembling, but I will not be bored. Faith is an extreme version of the situation of value, in which the stakes are high and the possibility of failure correspondingly great. Kierkegaard himself could not attain to it, he says; he was not the Knight of Faith but the Knight of Infinite Resignation, for he saw the hopelessness of what he had chosen as a value.[2] We do not have to conduct our lives in terms quite as melodramatic as Kierkegaard's, but without some commitment to the chosen value it is not truly constituted as a value at all.

We constitute our values from the range of possible future facts, or even impossible ones, by an act of choice. Values are not discovered in the world; they are made and projected into the world. The term "project" is used by Sartre to distinguish the mode of being of human beings from the mode of being of physical objects: human beings *are* nothing more than physical objects, but they *undertake to be* something more. One of the most fundamental ways of achieving this human mode of being is negation, and Sartre's analysis of this is instructive for the present purpose.[3]

If I enter a restaurant looking for my friend Pierre, the restaurant is as it is, with its tables, customers, waiters, wine bottles, and so forth. But all this *being* is of no interest to me if my friend is not here. From my point of view, all this affirmation can be summed up as a simple negation: he is not here. If I am eager to find him, I must exchange this world for another in which he is more likely to be found, since that is the world to which I attach value. Objectively speaking, the world contains no negative facts and no values; it can be fully described, as it is, without resorting to either. What this conclusion overlooks is that my world is incomplete without me; indeed, it would not exist without me. If I choose to inject into it negations and values, then no argument to the effect that these are unnecessary to a full description can prevent me from doing so. That is why every reductive account of the world that denies freedom, or subjectivity, or value fails on the grounds of irrelevance. Everything such an account asserts about the world may be true, but what is true of *the* world is not necessarily true of *my* world. *My* world is the product of the temporal involvement of my subjectivity with *the* world, and it is to my world that values belong.

No inconsistency follows if I add that values often belong in my world as phenomenologically *given*. The fact that something matters may not be evident to a detached observer, who will be satisfied that the objective account is exhaustive, but it stands as an indubitable datum to the subject whose involvement in the situation makes it matter. Values are not given by the agency of sense perception, as facts are. If I am to get a grasp on my situation as a whole, the concept of *data* has to be enlarged to take account not only of the retrospective aspect of the world presently apprehended as fact, but also of its prospective aspect presently apprehended as value.

This leaves an unresolved ambiguity between value as datum and value as project, between the given and the chosen. But precisely this ambiguity makes possible the emergence of rational long-range projects. The first true experience of value may lie in a fear of imminent pain or of the imminent removal of immediate pleasure. Once I have understood, however, that the feared outcome does not *necessarily* ensue, a sense of possibility develops. This enables me to see beyond the overriding probabilities that are *given* as values (either positive or negative) to less likely alternatives that may be *chosen* as values and also, with a little effort, attained. A value once chosen and habitually pursued will gradually assume the character of the given, but it remains a matter of habit ("second nature") nevertheless. The same thing happens with facts: we become habituated to configurations, ensembles, and sequences, which then appear given as wholes even when what is perceived is only a fragment of the whole. Nothing is wrong with the process in either case. On the contrary, it is a necessary simplification of the complexity of experience, provided we are aware that it takes place.

Notes

1. Jean-Paul Sartre, *The Communists and Peace,* trans. Martha H. Fletcher with the assistance of John R. Kleinschmidt (New York: George Braziller, 1968), p. 91.
2. Søren Kierkegaard, *Fear and Trembling* (with *The Sickness unto Death*), trans. Walter Lowrie (New York: Doubleday Anchor Books, 1954), pp. 38–64, passim.
3. Jean-Paul Sartre, *Being and Nothingness,* trans. Hazel Barnes (New York: Philosophical Library, 1956), pp. 9–10.

VIII

Freedom

41. The Pervasiveness of the Question of Freedom

If values are future facts to which human subjects attach imperatives, we are naturally interested in whether or not these facts come about. Science can tell us, within limits, what future facts are probable, assuming that there is no unexpected interference with the course of events. We could, therefore, inquire what was most likely to happen and resolve to attach an imperative to that. The best way of being sure of getting what we want is to want what we are probably going to get. And this would be the only rational thing to do if the course of future events were already determined, that is, if, given total knowledge, unexpected interference were to prove inconsistent with firmly established scientific discoveries.

The Stoics believed that an immanent reason controlled the fate of the world and of human beings along with it, so that human actions were powerless to effect real change. The Stoics therefore recommended the willing acceptance of the inevitable as the only means of achieving internal harmony. In a similar argument, Hegel arrived at the conclusion that true freedom consisted in the voluntary acceptance of necessity. But most human beings think that what they as conscious subjects freely decide to do has a genuine effect on the future state of affairs. Considerations of probability do not stop them from trying to bring about events that are not probable at all but only possible, and sometimes not even that.

The admission that we have conscious subjectivity—an admission that is difficult for a conscious subject not to make—raises all the old questions of the relation between that subjectivity and the world it experiences. Most of these questions fall under the heading of the so-called mind-body problem. The mind-body problem is old and difficult and has many facets: is mind-stuff different from body-stuff? If so, how is the mind lodged in the body? How does it affect what the body does? If not, how do mental functions arise in the body? And why do we want to distinguish so sharply between them and physical functions? Whatever solution may be proposed to the mind-body problem—the identity of mind and body or a dualism that holds them to be distinct, two-way interaction between them or epiphenomenalism (the view that mind is a by-product that has no effect on what happens in the body)—the point of departure for an examination of it must lie in the subjectivity of the individual. Whatever I may have come to know or to assert about the mechanisms of perception or of action must have been preceded by my consciousness of perceiving and of acting, which is simply given before any analysis or inquiry.

Epiphenomenon: A phenomenon is something that appears, from Greek *phaino* (as in "phenomenology"); *epi-* suggests (among many other meanings) "accompanying" or "depending on." An epiphenomenon then is a secondary appearance in relation to some primary event or activity that is indifferent to the epiphenomenon and would be unchanged if it did not occur.

Consciousness: Latin *scio* is "to know"; from its present participle *sciens* comes our word "science." *Conscio* meant "to know oneself to be guilty," which we have in "conscience." "Consciousness" is a variant (the French for "consciousness" is *conscience*). *Conscientia* meant originally "knowing something jointly with someone else" (*cum,* "with," which shows up in some compounds as *co-* or *con-*), but came to mean inner knowledge—as though the other person in question might be oneself. No doubt because consciousness is a precondition of our engaging knowingly in any activity (including definition or explanation), it is hard to define and even harder to explain. But it clearly involves the idea that, when I think or act, I not only know what is being thought or done but I also know that it is I who am thinking or doing it.

Arguments against the involvement of consciousness in action on the grounds that perception is only a complex chain of physiological causation forget that the apprehension and setting forth of the argument require such an involvement. But the scientific account of action does not, in itself, require any acknowledgment of this subjective involvement. From a vantage point outside the events dealt with, the argument for determinism can be carried through consistently, while the argument for freedom is clumsy and inconclusive. Determinism views our actions, like all other events, as the inevitable and unalterable outcome of earlier events, and hence not freely initiated by us. But it views them from outside, and as agents we are not outside these events: we are participants in them. From that internal perspective the maxim holds good that *even if human beings are not free, we cannot help behaving as if we were.* This conclusion echoes Kant's; for him freedom was a regulative concept, one we can choose to make use of in ordering our lives even though it cannot be conclusively shown to apply to any specific state of affairs.

Once the question takes on this personal aspect—and it would be odd, in discussing the freedom of persons, to leave it out—the two sides are better balanced. For in spite of differences in philosophical conviction, people have some overriding similarities of behavior, among them a tendency to try to do something about things if they go wrong. The spectacle of a hard-boiled determinist struggling to change the world may be dismissed by the determinist in question as just another ironic episode in the necessary unfolding of events. This argument might be correct; clearly it cannot be refuted. But how much energy do we want to spend on trying to refute it? Treating ourselves as free—that is, as able to make a difference and being responsible for the differences we make—is not something that need put us on the defensive; according to all criteria of plausibility and common sense, the burden of proof really belongs on the determinist side. That volition, the exercise of the will, should be efficacious is no more or less intelligible than that perception should be informative.

Burden-of-proof arguments: In arguments where no definitive conclusion can be reached on the basis of the available premises it is sometimes useful to ask a second-order question about the urgency of the issue or the plausibility of the alternatives. For example, if the members of some cult claim that my house occupies the site of the first Martian landing on earth, and argue that it should be torn down to make room for a temple, I don't have to go to elaborate lengths to refute them even though I have no definite evidence to the contrary—the burden of proof is definitely on them.

42. No Demonstration Is Possible

The mere denial of determinism is not adequate as a guarantee of genuine freedom. It is a necessary but not a sufficient condition. That is, we cannot sustain the argument for freedom unless we deny that our acts are fully determined in advance, but denying this will not clinch the argument for freedom. If the world were totally chaotic, or partly determinate and partly probabilistic, human beings might be as helpless as if it were wholly determinate. To provide the sufficient condition, to clinch the argument for freedom, we would have to show with scientific rigor that conscious human subjects, as agents, can make a genuine difference to the course of events.

The character of scientific investigation works against the possibility of such a demonstration. Science is devoted to the establishment of invariable or statistically probable causal connections between states of affairs. Where human action is concerned science systematically bypasses the agent, as indeed for its own purposes it must. One feature of science that makes this bypassing easy is the habit of expressing predictions, based on causal laws, in the form of probabilities.

Suppose the situation A obtains at a time that we will call t_1, and suppose we are interested in knowing whether as a result a situation B will obtain at a later time t_2. Science may express the probability that B will obtain as p (B/A), "the probability of B, given A." But this makes no reference to intermediate times, and what may be happening at those times. If time is continuous, then any stretch of it, however short, that is defined by an initial t_1 and a terminal t_2 contains in principle infinitely many times, later than t_1 but earlier than t_2, that must be passed over in establishing causal connections between A and B. In a case involving human action, we can always choose an A *before* the action takes place and a B *after* it takes place. Repeated trials will serve to establish a statistical connection between the class of As and the class of Bs that takes no account of the struggles and indecisions the action in question may have involved. The action will become just another event in the pattern of events, rather than the free project of a human agent.

According to the position advocated here, the agent occupies an inaccessible region of subjectivity into which the causal processes of perception disappear and from which the causal processes of action emerge. Science jumps the gap and preserves the causal continuity, as Figure 8-1 shows. A and B may be pushed closer and closer together by refined techniques of psychological investigation—they do not have to be external to the physical person—without affecting the analysis. They can never be brought into coincidence; that would altogether destroy the notion of causal relatedness. But this applies in other cases as well. The fact that A and B are always separated by a finite interval of time means that every causal connection

Figure 8-1 How Causality Bypasses Subjectivity

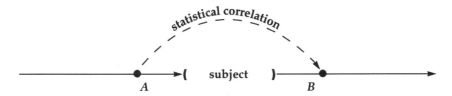

must jump over a discontinuity of this sort, not only connections between the antecedents and consequences of human action. Indeed every causal connection must jump over infinitely many such discontinuities.

This conclusion is implicit in the work of Hume. We see, he said, what we call causes and what we call effects. But no matter how finely we penetrate into the intermediate region, we discover only other events of the same kind that are effects of the original causes or causes of the original effects. The connections themselves can never be discovered, but are always read into the situation by us after the fact. A genuine connection in thought (a psychological connection) holds between the idea of the cause and the idea of the effect, but the assumption that this reflects an objective connection is unjustified. We may reasonably suppose that such a connection exists, since the world presumably hangs together somehow independently of its being *thought* together—though an idealist would maintain that its being thought together is precisely the mechanism of its hanging together. What is unreasonable is the conclusion that the objective connection must be like the connection in thought—for example, that if the second is invariable the first must be so too.

Idealism: The view that the substance of the world is thought rather than matter. Idealism has a distinguished history, going back to Plato; its most influential modern advocate was Hegel (see p. 45). Its appeal lies in the fact that we know that worlds are thought—you are thinking yours right now —and we don't know in the same way that material objects exist independently of thought. But getting independently-thought worlds together into a collectively-thought or divinely-thought one proves to be just as problematic as postulating a material world, and a good deal less helpful in throwing light on the interconnectedness of things.

Yet the validity of this parallel between the causal and the logical is one of the fundamental assumptions of science, as was pointed out earlier. In science we have no reason to doubt the parallel; on the contrary, it is extremely useful. It remains an assumption nevertheless. In the analysis of free action, on the other hand, we have every reason to doubt it, but people persist in carrying it over from science and using it to demonstrate that free action is impossible.

Even in science invariable connections are the exception, though they are the ones seized upon as examples in introductory philosophy of science courses. By a simple extension of a familiar analysis of probability, the possibility of free action can be reintroduced without abandoning the causal-logical parallel. Consider once again the relation between an event A and an event B expressed by the probability $p\ (B/A)$. If we adopt a subjective view of probability, this represents an *expectation* that B will follow upon A, whose strength is measured by a willingness to stake more or less on the outcome. Now one of the marks of freedom on the part of the agent is the ability to do something wholly unexpected, unexpected not by the agent, but by an outside observer equipped with a complete history of the agent's previous behavior. A wholly unexpected event would have a probability of zero, and we ordinarily assume that a probability of zero on the logical side corresponds to physical impossibility on the causal side.

However, as I have argued,[1] this interpretation rests on a misunderstanding of the axioms of probability. Nothing is inconsistent in the notion that an event with a logical probability of zero might nevertheless happen. This is certainly provided for in ordinary language ("I would *never* have expected her to do that"), and it reflects our intuitive conviction that action can genuinely be the beginning of a finite causal chain and not simply an element somewhere along an infinite one.

The question of the agent's ability to do the unexpected brings into focus what I take to be the central difficulty in the philosophical dispute about freedom and determinism. Serious philosophical work has been devoted to showing that the dispute is unnecessary—that no inconsistency arises between the language of freedom in moral discourse and the language of determinism in scientific discourse, that the problems of philosophical ethics would not be affected one way or the other by a decision about determinism, that free (uncoerced) actions make sense in a physically determined world while free (uncaused) actions do not make sense at all.

In particular, the ingenious thesis of D. M. McKay[2] has moved the debate to a new imaginative level. McKay's thesis offers a means of reconciling an agent's insistence that the outcome of his or her actions cannot be known, with an observer's insistence that it can. But a cardinal difficulty remains, which has to do not with the possibility of a reconciliation of freedom and determinism in objective terms—that is, for human agents in general, or for some anonymous agent—but with my own involvement in my own action. If I say of an action, "I did it," or "I was in full control of myself when I did it," as a way of accepting responsibility or claiming credit, I cannot at the same time say that the action was uncaused. Nor, however, can I admit that it was wholly caused by some antecedent set of circumstances and could in principle have been expected by a sufficiently well-informed observer, as any determinist account would require. For this would involve the paradoxical assertion that events that were not under my control (and such events would be arrived at if the causal chain were pushed back far enough) had fully determined an action that was under my control.

Compatibilists, who think that the agent's freedom is compatible with rigid determinism in the natural world, would retort that the earlier events had determined me, and that I then determined the outcome of my action, which was therefore under my control. But on this account I am an agent only by courtesy. I could not have chosen to do otherwise. The awkwardness of this position comes to light if we apply it to the case of philosophical argument. We cannot exempt argument from the determinist scheme, since argument involves brain states and movements of the vocal cords that have to be accounted for in the determinist balance sheet.

Suppose that I have been determined by earlier events to be an advocate of nondeterministic free agency, and that you have been determined by earlier events to be an advocate of compatibilism. As we argue the point, something is happening, but neither of us can be said to be *doing* anything: if you convince me, I can't help being convinced; if I stick to my guns, I can't help doing that either. So it won't be much of an argument—not the sort of thing we can enter into with argumentative relish and get right or wrong. How we feel about it, and how it comes out, will simply be parts of a script read off from the determining conditions. *We* aren't in it as philosophers, arguers, or agents. We are only in it as spectators—participant spectators, since we've been programmed to *feel* like agents, but spectators nonetheless. The whole exercise is meaningless. Meaning requires freedom—not surprisingly, since it is one of our highest values.

43. Some Preanalytical Considerations

The alternatives offered above (actions as uncaused, actions as wholly caused by physical antecedents) cannot be considered exhaustive if we are to find a way to escape this difficulty. As Kant rightly saw, the route of escape lies in another dimension, out of the plane of causal relations between observed events. We can take this route only by acting, not by arguing, and we all do take it, as a matter of course, every time we say, "I did it." Determinism can never establish itself in the face of that assertion, for its establishment would require the demonstration of tight causal relations between the antecedents and consequences of action, every step in which would have to be physically self-contained. The conscious subject, which cannot be said to be physical (it is conscious *of* the physical), persists in intruding itself between these antecedents and consequences and spoiling the whole program. It is not so much that the conscious subject is undetermined, nonmaterial, and unintelligible, as that it is prior to the concepts of determination, materiality, and intelligibility.

The aim of defending the freedom of human agents will be satisfied as long as the issue is not settled in favor of determinism, and the foregoing remarks may be sufficient for this end. We must insist upon that much because many people feel uncomfortable about their control over their actions in a world that they believe has been shown to be determined, at least in principle and with respect to events in the flat region, among which human actions must certainly be counted. But this negative conclusion is not the only one we can draw. Some nonphilosophical arguments provide more reasons for asserting the possibility of causality outside the domain of observed events, and are worth a moment's attention.

The actions of some living organisms are straightforward responses to the stimuli that impinge upon them, the connection between stimulus and response being linear and determinate. As far as that is concerned, many actions performed by human agents appear to fall into this class: blinking, knee jerks, and so on, as well as more complicated learned responses. But such reflex or habitual actions, whose causal mechanism does not involve consciousness or decision, do not count as actions at all in the sense in which the term will be used here. Etymologically speaking, the use of "action" to refer to the behavior of inanimate objects or to involuntary bodily mechanisms is secondary. The evolutionary origins of genuine action lie in the development of a cortical brain from a diencephalic one. The diencephalon, or brain stem, channels neural energy directly from stimulus to response. The cortex, on the other hand, diverts the energy from the stimulus and temporarily absorbs it, feeding it into the mechanism of response after a period of delay that represents the activity of choice, or sometimes suppressing the response altogether. Conscious deliberation, leading to the delayed and selective action that we call voluntary, appears to be associated with the advanced development of the cortex, especially the frontal cortex, found only in humans and some of the higher mammals.

Evolution: From Latin *evolvo,* "to unroll," from *volvo,* "to roll, to turn," with the prefix *ex-,* "out" (the "x" drops out before many consonants). One meaning of *evolutio* was "reading (a book)," because books came rolled up. So evolution means simply the unrolling of things, how they turn out—not a very sinister idea. The difficulty that religious thinkers have had with evolution in the last century or so has been with the claim that organisms just happen to turn out the way they do naturally, rather than being products of intelligent design.

From the point of view of evolution, the interesting question is: why should the animal be conscious? If we reject the view, held by Descartes among others, that consciousness is a superaddition in the case of humans that distinguishes them absolutely from the animals, we must assign to it an effective role in the preservation of the species and assume that it makes a genuine difference to the outcome of action. Any theory that implies that the history of the conscious animal is just what it would have been if it had happened not to be conscious makes consciousness a mystery and opens the way to metaphysical nonsense. The admission that consciousness has an evolutionary origin and significance does not mean the advocacy of a so-called "evolutionary ethics," such as that developed by Herbert Spencer, for example, or by Nietzsche. The evolutionary argument points to the efficacy of conscious volition but does not indicate the ends that volition should seek.

Herbert Spencer (1820–1903), an English philosopher who extended principles of evolution learned from Darwin to the universe in general. Evolution he characterized as a passage "from a relatively indefinite, incoherent homogeneity to a relatively definite, coherent heterogeneity." The expression "the survival of the fittest" is due to Spencer.

The exact nature of the free subject remains obscure, but perhaps this is just as well. The notion of the subject's understanding itself completely leads to an infinite regress: if I understand myself, am I identical with that which I understand, or do I make a separate movement of understanding-myself-as-understood? As Sartre points out, my consciousness of the world is at the same time consciousness of my being as a knower. He might have added that my action in the world is at the same time consciousness of my own being as an agent. Sartre called the awareness of self that accompanies the self's awareness of the world the "prereflective *cogito* (I think)";[3] it is matched by a "prereflective *ago* (I do)," the "I" in each case being implicit in the knowing or the acting.

Understanding or *explaining* my own being or action is a different matter, and cannot have this prereflective unity, since it requires three terms: the thing explained, the explanation, and the person to whom the explanation explains the thing, in my case, me. A consequence of this analysis is that we have to acknowledge three ultimately unexplainable concepts: the self, the world as a whole, and the relation between the two (that is, the apprehension by the self of the world as a whole, together with its inverse, the action of the self on the world as a whole). An adequate analysis of free agency would involve the explanation of these unexplainable concepts. This makes the task not merely difficult but incoherent.

44. Free Agency Retained as an Unrefuted Hypothesis

If rational justification of human freedom is futile, practical demonstration is equally so. Freedom has no function unless it enables people to achieve what they set out to achieve, but the antecedent intention to achieve it can always be pointed to as determining the action in question, which may then be said not to have been free after all. This difficulty cannot be sidestepped by a so-called "gratuitous act," an act imagined by the French novelist André Gide as wholly unprovoked and undetermined. Such an act would not count as free either, because its effect was not intended or desired. In order to show myself to be free, I would have to do something I both wished and at the same time did not wish to do.

All these contortions are unnecessary. Our conscious subjectivity confronts the world. Within the limits of our apprehension we seek to understand the world, and within the limits of our freedom we seek to change it: to understand it correctly, and to change it for the better. At these limits, as Kant points out in his characteristic manner, the intellect is forced to admit its own inadequacy:

> Two things fill the mind with ever new and increasing admiration and awe, the oftener and more steadily they are reflected on: the starry heavens above me and the moral law within me.[4]

But both dimensions are given in experience. Whatever difficulties their reconciliation may present, no solution that eliminates one altogether can be acceptable in the long run.

The admission of limitations on the intellect need not be construed as a hint that something greater lies beyond the intellect. People often suppose that human rationality argues a Rationality of the Universe, as though the fact that every case of rationality as we know it is the product of an extremely complicated physical organization—a central nervous system—were evidence that this extremely complicated physical organization was a product of rationality. This is fallacious; that guacamole is a product of the blender does not mean that the blender is a product of guacamole. But one of the most persuasive cases against freedom rests on a similar argument. The argument, a variation on the Stoic position, maintains that rational action may be free in relation to the physical world and yet determined in a larger setting as the working out of a purpose higher than ourselves. If this is a conscious purpose, the problem simply emerges on a higher level, since the limitations referred to are logically inherent in the very notion of subjectivity and must attach themselves to any consciousness whatever. If the higher purpose is unconscious, what can we make of it? The idea of an unconscious force at work in the world is familiar. The classic references are Adam Smith's "invisible hand" and Friedrich Engels's "power which works as a whole, unconsciously and without volition."[5] A similar concept surfaces in the late work of Sartre as "totalization without a totalizer." None of these cases gives us a reason to accept the notion of a blind intelligence directing events in spite of anything we can do. Accepting such a notion prematurely works against efforts to find more cogent explanations. In any case, for the individual, being manipulated by a hidden force is no improvement over purely physical determination, and cannot subjectively be distinguished from it.

> *Friedrich Engels* (1820–1895), German philosopher. Engels had first-hand experience of capitalism as manager of a factory in Manchester. He wrote *The Condition of the Working-Class in England in 1844*, and collaborated with Marx on the *Communist Manifesto*. He developed a dialectics of nature according to which natural history, not only social history, proceeds by overcoming contradictions, a position difficult to maintain without the risk of falling back into idealism.

The most fundamental objection to the efficacy of free action springs from the dualism of mind and body that it seems to require. In the above quotation from Kant, the inner being to which the moral law appeals is of a different order from the outer being of the starry heavens, and yet the realm of freedom governed by the moral law must somehow interact with the realm of nature symbolized by the starry heavens. In Kant the inner form

The Seven Deadly Sins: Lust (1953; director Yves Allegret)
The affair between her mother (Viviane Romance) and a lover (Frank Villard) destroys the innocence of a young girl (Francette Vernillat). As a consequence the security of her family is shaken and she leaves home.

of intuition is time, and the location of the moral law within provides an incidental reinforcement of the connection between time and value. None of the monistic devices for the reconciliation of freedom with determinism has disposed convincingly of the fact that I am not the world on which I exert my action and that my freedom is merely illusory if it cannot introduce genuine novelty into that world. This point has to be faced honestly.

A dualism does come into play here, but it need not be the old mind-body dualism, according to which mind and body are different sorts of thing, different substances, one material and the other spiritual. Distinguishing two mind-body problems, the mind–live body problem and the mind–dead body problem, clarifies our thought about the issue. If, as I hold, mental activities are natural functions of complex live bodies with central nervous systems and sufficiently developed brains, then the mind–live body problem dissolves. As a parallel example, suppose we invented what we called the "wetness-water" problem, and asked how water could possibly be wet, as some people still ask how bodies can possibly think. This would be regarded as an odd way to do philosophy. We might reasonably ask chemists to tell us everything they could about the molecular structure of water, which would inform us about the mechanism of its wetness, but we would not keep asking whether the wetness and the water were one thing or two, or whether the water produced the wetness, or whether it would still be water if it were not wet.

If the foregoing view of the mind–live body problem is accepted, then the mind–dead body problem reduces to the live body–dead body problem. To that problem we now have the main outline of an answer, in terms of self-replicating and self-regulating systems exchanging material and energy with their environment. The ascent in complexity from atoms to molecules to macromolecules like proteins, and eventually to DNA and the regulation of growth and reproduction, begins to look more and more continuous and plausible as research continues. Once mind has emerged at the top of this ascent, it can turn its attention not only to the world of bodies that sustains it but also to its own mental contents.

This self-referential turn complicates the puzzle about freedom. Inquiry into the workings of the physical world on the part of many embodied minds reaches the conclusion that processes in that world are deterministic, *as long as they do not involve minds*. But the universe manifestly does include minds: ours, and no doubt those of many animals as well. There is no evidence that it remains causally tight all the way up from fundamental particles to poems or symphonies. The idea of strict deterministic causality was learned in the special case of mechanics, especially celestial mechanics, where the interacting elements are few and isolated. Physics managed to extend the domain of determinism down to microscopic, but not to quantum, levels, and the breakdown of strict causality in the direction of the very small may be mirrored by a breakdown in the direction of the very complex.

This is a point that cannot be argued a priori; we cannot baldly assert that everything is tightly deterministic when this has been shown only for the middle region between the very small and the very complex. Pierre Simon Laplace made such an assertion, rather excitedly, in 1814:

> An intelligence that could know, at a given instant, all the forces governing the natural world, and the respective positions of the entities that compose it, if in addition it was great enough to analyze all this information, would be able to embrace in a single formula the movements of the largest bodies in the universe and those of the lightest atom: nothing would be uncertain for it, and the future, like the past, would be directly present to its observation.[6]

But he thought everything in the world was a Newtonian particle, and we know that this is not the case. If we wished to make a similar claim, we would have to ground it afresh empirically. That would be a daunting task, given the known complexity of the world beyond the flat region. Yet surprisingly many people still take such a view of determinism for granted.

> *Pierre Simon Laplace,* Marquis de Laplace (1749–1827), French mathematician and astronomer. He is celebrated for having remarked to Napoleon, who commented on the fact that his Celestial Mechanics made no mention of God, "Sire, I have no need of that hypothesis."

For the moment we can safely say that determinism has not been demonstrated at the level of human action. It is only an insistence on a causally tight universe that makes the problem of free action so vexing and places such an unbridgeable chasm between the subject and his or her world. A shift in the burden of proof, so that it is the causal tightness rather than the freedom that must be demonstrated, will provide ample leisure for exploring the consequences of the hypothesis of efficacious subjective volition.

Notes

1. Peter Caws, "Three Logics, or the Possibility of the Improbable," *Philosophy and Phenomenological Research* 25 (4) (June 1965), pp. 615–26.
2. D. M. McKay, "Information and Prediction in Human Sciences," in S. Dockx and P. Bernays, eds., *Information and Prediction in Science* (New York and London: Academic Press, 1965), p. 255.
3. Jean-Paul Sartre, *Being and Nothingness,* trans. H. Barnes (New York: Philosophical Library, 1956), p. liii.
4. Immanuel Kant, *Critique of Practical Reason,* trans. L. W. Beck (Chicago: University of Chicago Press, 1949), p. 258.
5. Friedrich Engels, letter to Joseph Bloch, 21–22 September 1890, in Robert C. Tucker, ed., *The Marx-Engels Reader,* 2nd ed. (New York: W. W. Norton, 1978), p. 761.
6. Pierre Simon Laplace, *Essai philosophique sur les probabilités* (Paris: Gauthier-Villars, 1921), p. 3.

IX

Order

45. Order as Relative to Human Interest

The rational exercise of my freedom consists in changing my world (or protecting it against change) in a way that realizes my values. The world can be counted on to change even if I do nothing; it obeys its own laws of development and decay. My intervention is called for if I conclude that a future state of the world to which I attach an imperative will not come about naturally, or that a present state to whose maintenance I attach an imperative is in danger of dissolution. This means constant intervention, since every situation, left to itself, changes by slow degrees into something else, and few situations that occur naturally are likely to be those I want. Any particular state of the world is antecedently improbable, since the natural course of things on a macroscopic scale is determined, as far as we can tell, wholly at random. The chances that the state that happens to be realized at a given moment in the history of the universe will meet the exigent specifications of individual human desire are therefore vanishingly small.

This fact is generally concealed from us by two circumstances.

(1) The evolution of animal species, of which the human is one, takes place in such a way that any population that survives finds itself in an environment to which it is reasonably well adapted. The probability that physical conditions suitable to life as we know it should be realized in any given region of space and time is very low, and if the life had been created independently and then sought the conditions, the conjunction of the two would be nothing short of miraculous. But in fact the conditions determined the nature of the life. Cosmically speaking, the biosphere is a thin shell on a microscopic particle, but it required no intelligence on our part to locate it and make our home in it.

(2) Nature, even when the animal species is well adapted to it, is on the whole hostile to the individual. But herd living and its subsequent develop-

ment into civilization have provided a collective defense against this hostility, so that nowadays many individuals in developed countries have to expend little effort on securing and maintaining conditions of reasonable comfort. That subsistence is now easy in many parts of the world is in itself one of the determinants of the crisis of value. An animal equipped by a long history of necessity to make frequent adjustments in its environment tends to go on making adjustments even when the necessity is removed. If no change is obviously called for, this may lead to the invention of novelty, but it is more likely to end in frustration. Food and shelter are the obvious values of people who are hungry and cold, but the values of those who are satisfied and comfortable are not quite so easily discovered.

What civilization helps to guarantee is a degree of order, domestic, social, civil, and international. Order in these senses is something to be striven for and something that, once achieved, must be actively maintained. It therefore has precisely the character of value, and the realization of a value is always equivalent to the achievement and maintenance of an order (though not necessarily of the public variety): the disposition of the elements of a situation in a satisfactory or acceptable way. The term "order" seems originally to have applied to things organized in rows, for example, citizens in order of rank or precedence, but it soon came to mean any regular arrangement, social or otherwise, extending eventually even to the regularities of nature.

Order: Latin *orior* means "to rise" (*oriens* means "rising," so the Orient is where the sun rises and orientation originally meant taking one's direction from the sunrise). From *orior* are derived *origo,* "origin," but also *ordo,* "a series, line, row, order." The connection may be through the successive points on the horizon at which the sun rises as the seasons progress, or through a habit of lining things and people up with reference to a distant point, perhaps on the horizon.

Nature seems ordered to us because we are adapted to its regularities. But the expression "the order of nature," taken as descriptive of the physical universe, is vacuous. No matter what may be the case, no matter how chaotic or disorganized the behavior of the elements of the world, at every moment each thing is where it is, standing in a definite and, in principle, describable relation to each other thing. After the explosion the pieces fall where they do (and human lives are or are not snuffed out); this is the factual outcome according to the laws of physics and biology. It can be thought of as disorder only by contrast to other situations that, under the circumstances, might be expected or preferred. The notions of expectation and preference introduce the now familiar syndrome of temporality and value. The dying man in T. S. Eliot's "Animula," "Leaving disordered papers in a dusty room," may regret his failure to achieve some value or other, but in a sense the room is fully ordered, every paper and every particle of dust occupying its fixed and proper place. The word "proper" is appropriate only if we have an interest in preserving that room in that state, a plausible objective for an artist working with assemblages, for example, or for pious literary enthusiasts if it happens to be Eliot's own room, which they wish to keep as it was in his memory (and open to visitors for a fee). Here the conventional notions of order and disorder are reversed, and the unsuspecting janitor who comes in and dusts, putting the papers in neat piles, will be accused of having destroyed something of irreplaceable value.

These considerations point to a definition of order in such everyday contexts. We shall say that a state of affairs is ordered in some way if a change in it matters, and that it is maximally ordered if any change would be a change for the worse. In a library in which everything is out of order, it does not matter if the positions of two books on a shelf are interchanged, but if the books are in alphabetical order it does matter. Again, if the books are out of order but it matters that they should be in order—if their being in order is a desired state of the world—a process of ordering can be carried out, starting from a situation approaching chaos in which arbitrary changes make no difference and ending with a fully ordered situation in which an arbitrary change would be destructive. Libraries are a special case; more generally, any action that seeks to realize a value amounts to the imposition of some order on the world, or to the safeguarding of an existing order against the threat of disorder.

46. The Thermodynamic Concept of Order

The achievement of order requires the expenditure of energy, and it can therefore be attempted only when energy is available. Even the maintenance of order requires available energy. The natural tendency of ordered situations is to become disordered if care is not taken to preserve them—as ruins, neglected gardens, untidy apartments, littered streets, and wrinkled clothes all testify. Human energy spends itself in a series of orderings against a series of natural tendencies toward disorder, and the series manifests itself on every scale of existence, from the daily routine of personal habit to the rise and fall of civilizations.

> *Thermodynamics:* From Greek *thermos,* "hot," and *dynamis,* "power, force"; a branch of physics dealing with the energy associated with heat, the work done by heat engines. Thermodynamics is philosophically interesting because it deals with random microscopic motions that sum into lawlike macroscopic ones, thus challenging the idea that the behavior of complex entities can be explained in any simple way by the behavior of their constituent parts.

The improbability of the emergence of useful order without the expenditure of energy is expressed in the second law of thermodynamics. Strictly speaking, the laws of thermodynamics apply only to expenditures and transfers of energy in the form of heat, but some of the concepts involved have proved irresistibly suggestive to workers in other disciplines and have acquired a much more general currency. Chief among these is the concept of entropy.

> *Entropy:* Greek *trepo* is "to turn"; *trope* is "a turning" (compare English "trope," a turn or figure of speech). *Entropia* in Homer is "a trick or dodge," but *entrope* in general is "a turning toward or into," hence "a transformation," the sense for which Clausius chose it, with the comment: "I prefer going to the ancient languages for the names of important scientific quantities, so that they may mean the same thing in all living tongues."[1] Entropy in physics measures the transformation of energy from available to unavailable for the purpose of doing work; in information theory it measures transformation of message content from more to less certain, that is, a loss of information. So negative entropy or "negentropy" stands for an increase in available energy or an increase in information.

Entropy, roughly speaking, is a measure of disorder, a measure of the randomness of the distribution of energy in a physical system. A closed system, one that receives no energy from outside, will if left to itself gradually lose whatever order it had. If its elements are carefully organized at the beginning, so that their energy is concentrated locally and not generally distributed, the entropy of the system is at a minimum. But as time goes on, the elements will gradually lose their definite relationships to one another, the coherence of energy will disappear, and the entropy will eventually rise to a maximum. This will happen even more rapidly if the organized energy is made available to perform external work.

In an automobile engine the explosion touched off by the spark briefly organizes the energy of the reacting particles, by causing them to move rapidly away from one another. Those that happen to be moving in the direction of the piston perform work upon it, while the others waste their energy on the walls of the cylinder. When this brief episode is over and the piston has moved, the particles continue to move about in the cylinder with great speed, but now they move at random, some in one direction and some in another, some toward other particles, some away from them. They are therefore good for nothing but to be swept out as exhaust and replaced by another population of temporarily organized particles. The temporary organization is conferred upon the new set of particles, as upon the old set, by the chemical energy whose release is triggered by the process of ignition. During the chemical reaction that releases this energy, the system of particles is not closed but open, receiving energy from the process of combustion and expending it in moving the piston. Only after the chemical process is over do the contents of the cylinder function briefly as a closed system, subject to the second law of thermodynamics and therefore to a rapid increase in entropy and a rapid decrease in useful order.

The second law does not say that order in a system can never increase; it says this only of closed systems. Therefore, whenever we find a noticeable concentration of order in the natural world, we may reasonably expect to find an open system, one that enjoys a supply of energy from some external source. The biosphere, in which animals (including human beings) have evolved, civilizations grown up, and works of art been produced, is such a system; it receives daily from the sun great quantities of energy in the form of radiation. The presence of matter anywhere in the universe represents a concentration of enormous amounts of energy, an idea that has become familiar in an age of nuclear weapons, submarines, and power plants. The sun represents the concentration of a vast amount of matter, according to our standards (as stars go, it is rather small). This matter is continually being augmented as the sun's gravitational attraction sweeps up a great tubular region of interstellar dust in its progress through space, but it is also continually being attenuated by radiation, and the reserves are steadily, although quite slowly, decreasing.

This radiation, of which the earth collects only a minute fraction (since radiation leaves the sun in all directions, whereas the earth is to be found only in one direction at any given time), has been going on for a long time and will continue for an even longer time. The time scale dwarfs anything that we can have any real conception of, but the situation of cosmic privilege that we now enjoy was not always the case and will not always be so. In the last few billion years, which are the only ones that really count for our purposes, the earth has stored much of the energy it has received from the sun in chemical and biological traps that we know as vegetation, animal life, and mineral deposits (not including the heavy elements, such as metals, which come from a different process at an earlier stage in the earth's formation). As might be expected, this trapped energy shows up not merely as matter in motion, but as ordered matter, the order being an inevitable consequence of the constant influx of new energy.

The concentration of higher levels of order in cities, libraries, and museums reflects in its turn the availability of surplus energy in intermediate forms—food, fuel, hydroelectric power, and so on. Virtually all this available energy can be traced back to the sun, although we are now learning to be independent of the sun by turning the material of the earth itself into energy.

47. Human Agents as Sources of Order

The definition of order in terms of what matters has apparently been forgotten in all this discussion of thermodynamics. But the thermodynamic concept of order is shot through with implicit references to value. "Available energy" and "useful work" hardly require comment, but even the classical formulations of the second law of thermodynamics reveal a preoccupation with the achievement of particular ends. The second law asserts the impossibility of devising an engine that will effect the transfer of heat from a cooler body to a warmer one unless it is provided with an external source of energy. This statement has been referred to by scientists themselves as "a confession of our helplessness in making molecules do what we wish."[2] The law is formulated in terms of impossibility only because what it excludes was once thought possible.

Although its rigorous formulation is due to Rudolf Clausius, the principle that underlies the second law was discovered by the French physicist Sadi Carnot in the course of his work on heat engines, and represented an unexpected theoretical limitation on the efficiency of such engines. If the law were not true, an unlimited source of mechanical energy would be at our disposal. Early physicists were disappointed to discover that this was not the case. It is a human impossibility that deprives us of something we would have liked to have. The law of gravity might have been formulated in terms of impossibility: it is impossible to devise an engine (ruling out balloons and other floating devices) that will go upwards unless it is provided with an external source of energy (which may be stored "inside" the engine as chemical energy for convenience in transportation). The law of gravity was not formulated in this way, however, because until recently nobody had much interest in going upwards.

Rudolf Julius Emmanuel Clausius (1822–1888) was a German physicist who developed the kinetic theory of gases.

Sadi Carnot (1796–1832), French physicist, member of a distinguished family, one of whom, Marie François Sadi Carnot, became president of the French Republic and was assassinated in 1887. The assassinated president, also known as Sadi Carnot, is not to be confused with the physicist, who enunciated the Second Law of Thermodynamics in *Reflections on the Motive Power of Fire* (1824).

The state of the world we want, then, represents order for us; the antecedent possibility of getting it by accident is negligibly small. Yet many of us do get it, or something close to it, and not only in the plain evolutionary sense that we are well adapted to our environment and enjoy the benefits of civilization, but much more specifically. We form the intention of changing the environment in a specific way, and we bring about such a change; we paint paintings, compose musical works, write books, play games, build and furnish houses, travel (that is, change the environment by bringing new parts of it into view), undertake commercial enterprises. Drawing the line between what culture owes to the impersonal processes of evolution and the personal processes of decision is not always easy, and a plausible argument could be made for regarding decision as an individual version of cultural evolution, or conversely, cultural evolution as a collective version of decision.

But each of us can recognize some orders, for example—like the daily, monthly, and yearly rhythms of terrestrial life—that we owe to nature, and others—like the functioning of machinery, the disposition of our private belongings, the arrangement of books on shelves—that we owe to our own efforts or the efforts of people like us. Which class properly includes large-scale human phenomena like cities and armies is a question for debate, but the lines of causal determination of all but the largest-scale forms of order in our environment pass through human individuals. Such individuals, therefore, constitute a locus for the reversal of the cosmic tendency towards disorder.

Human agents are sources of negative entropy. When all is said and done, that is what makes them free. Even under such local violations the second law of thermodynamics continues to assert itself, since our brains are provided at birth with a far greater degree of organization than we are ever likely to impose unaided on the world about us, the thermodynamic hostility of the environment being as inexorable and merciless as it is. We need only as much surplus organizing power as is required to fight more or less successfully, for 80 years or so, a battle against disorder that in the end we will inevitably lose.

All order matters. What we sometimes call the order of nature—the relative densities of different substances, the alternation of night and day, the balance of hormones—consists just in those arrangements that if changed would affect our interests most profoundly. When we encounter serious lapses in this order we call them disasters. Most aspects of natural order are such that we can do little about them except on a limited and local scale. Human order, on the other hand, is something we are continually in the process of creating. We need set no limit to the degree of human order that can be conceived.

But material resources are limited, and the freedom of the individual, although it is in principle unfettered within the limits of its material resources, is in practice preoccupied to a considerable extent with the maintenance of often idiosyncratic conditions for the possibility of any action at all. This helps to explain why so many people in such apparently privileged circumstances achieve so little of lasting value. Maintaining the conditions for action—keeping ourselves continually poised to achieve value, even if we never actually achieve it—is the next best thing to acting, and even better than acting unwisely. It embodies in itself a kind of value. To use our earlier terminology, a state of the world so arranged that from it we could move, in the most economical way possible, to *any* desired state of the world, is itself a desirable state. Think of the child's wish: "I wish that whatever I wish would come true!" The value attaching to such a state is of the kind that has traditionally been called a *means* or *instrumental value*, as distinguished from the *end value* of the state of the world that is the ultimate objective.

The practical problems of the theory of value, moral, political, and aesthetic, lie in deciding which states of the world have end values attached to them, which states instrumental values, and how the limited resources of human agents can best be deployed to bring these states about. To put it differently, the fundamental problem is to find out what matters to the agent, how it can be reconciled with other things that matter to him or her (or other agents), and how the fact of its mattering can be accommodated in action.

48. The Capacity for Order an Unconditional Value

If we had an independent criterion for order, and if every order embodied a value—if order mattered only positively—we would have an easy solution to the problems of the theory of value. The overriding moral principle would be "Seek to achieve order," and the theory of value would become a branch of thermodynamics. Such a view has been advocated by the American physicist R. B. Lindsay, who introduced the idea of a "thermodynamic imperative."[3]

The difficulty with this idea is that while every value can be represented as an order, every order cannot be represented as a value. According to the definition given above, maximally ordered systems represent extremes of value along some dimension or other. But that might be just making the best of a bad job, and the desired state of the world might lie along some other dimension altogether. Any change in the actual situation would be a change for the worse, but we still might want to exchange that situation for a totally different one. In such a case we would have to retreat to a point at which the shift into another dimension of value could be accomplished, a strategy that is familiar from the cliché about things getting worse before they get better.

The idea of an imperative inspired by a thermodynamic argument need not be abandoned, however, just because what thermodynamics recognizes as order is not necessarily what we value. The surplus energy of the environment is bound to show up as order, and for us the significant thing is that we are able to have a part in determining to some extent what the nature of that order shall be. If the source of this personally determined order is our freedom as agents to manipulate the world, to which we have access through our bodies, then a genuine moral principle (or at least a general principle of value) emerges: that this freedom, and the bodies that exercise it, should be safeguarded.

The state of the world in which freedom and bodily efficiency are optimized must have an imperative attached to it if any subsequent state of the world is to be available as a value. In other words, failure to value freedom is incompatible with the realization of any other value. The question at issue here is not whether one agent's freedom is better than another's, but whether freedom in the most general sense—the ability not necessarily to suspend the causal order but to halt or reverse temporarily and locally the universal trend toward disorder—is to be regarded as an unconditional imperative for any conscious production of value. This chapter has been devoted to showing that this is an inevitable conclusion.

Human consciousness is not the only source of local negative entropy. The other sources, however, have either disappeared or settled down into an ecologically stable relationship. Human beings are the only animals engaged in the systematic and continuous production of new order. At the same time the largest fund of conscious awareness, at least in the world known to us, appears to be vested in human beings. Consciousness itself, Schrödinger thought, may simply be a concomitant of the emergence of novelty.[4] When children are learning to ride bicycles, they are conscious of the adjustments in position that are necessary to prevent them from falling off; once they have learned to ride, these adjustments become habitual and they no longer enter conscious awareness. The implications of this view are far-reaching. It suggests a critical difference between free action and other forms of adaptive behavior.

> *Erwin Schrödinger* (1887–1961), Austrian physicist. He formulated the basic equations of wave mechanics, but also wrote a series of philosophical essays, including *Nature and the Greeks* and *What is Life?* He won the Nobel Prize in 1933.

If the order sought is a standard one, for a species or for an individual, then its achievement can be programmed. Like all adaptive processes, the process will involve feedback, but the nature of the feedback will determine the nature of the adaptive response, which can therefore be automatic or habitual. If, on the other hand, the order sought is not a function of the present state of affairs but is open—if it is not yet required in Köhler's sense[5]—then the achievement of a good outcome is best served by a conscious entertainment of alternatives. From an evolutionary point of view, this will be more efficient than the incorporation of a random factor into the program, which would otherwise be necessary. If we have few alternatives and if there is not much to choose between them, then randomizing is an acceptable solution.

> *Wolfgang Köhler* (1887–1967), German-American psychologist, one of the founders of the Gestalt school of psychology. The notion of "requiredness" is his (on the whole very successful) answer to the problem of the relation of facts and values.[6]

A program can be written, for example, for playing chess that will take into account alternatives following upon alternatives to any desired degree of complexity, but it has to terminate in the definite acceptance or rejection of the strategy being tested. This requires a prior decision about the object of the game. In a way, reason is a completely general program for the resolution of choice, but it needs to be supplied with a conception of the order that is to result, and consciousness contributes this. The order chosen, if the choice is free and rational, will by definition embody a value. For the individual and, if Schrödinger's conjecture has any validity, for the species, the selection among values is progressive, and so is the development of habitual, as opposed to conscious, choice. Habitual choice will be adequate once a decision about the desired order has been made and the mechanism for arriving at it put into operation.

Notes

1. Quoted in Charles Coulton Gillispie, *The Edge of Objectivity: An Essay in the History of Scientific Ideas* (Princeton, N.J.: Princeton University Press, 1960), p. 399.
2. "Thermodynamics," *Van Nostrand's Scientific Encyclopedia*, 3rd ed. (Princeton, N.J.: Van Nostrand, 1958).
3. R. B. Lindsay, "Entropy Consumption and Values in Physical Science," *American Scientist* 47 (September 1959), pp. 376–85.
4. Erwin Schrödinger, *Mind and Matter* (Cambridge: Cambridge University Press, 1959), pp. 4–5.
5. Wolfgang Köhler, *The Place of Value in a World of Facts* (New York: Meridian Books, 1959 [Liveright, 1938]), Chapter 3.
6. Ibid., pp. 72ff., 336ff., and passim.

X

Action and Responsibility

49. The Complexity of Free Action

Every manifestation of order that goes beyond the merely physical or biological can be traced back to an *agent,* an individual who is a locus of freedom. The agent's exercise of this freedom, either alone or in cooperation with others, modifies the subsequent state of the world—often predictably, but sometimes in a manner that is unpredictable on the basis of the most complete knowledge of its previous state. Freedom as understood here manifests itself only in agents, and for our purposes we need consider human agency, and therefore human action, only—even though nonhuman agents, if there are any, might take advantage of looseness in the causal structure of the physical world elsewhere than in the human brain.

If free action is to result in a change in the order of the world, it must have access to the world. This is effected by means of bodies. Bodies store and dispose of energy, enough by itself to produce minor changes but capable of amplification—by cooperation with others, or by means of more or less complex tools and machines—in order to produce major changes. Freedom to produce change (in other words, to realize value) depends on the availability of the requisite energy, disposed in a suitable way. This means that the agents must enjoy a material advantage over the world they seek to modify. The change brought about by the expenditure of this energy is a movement of the world from one state to another that is presumably preferable. For agents to control the situation it is therefore not enough for them to command the material resources. They must also have access to detailed information about the initial state, and they must know accurately how states of the world respond to given expenditures of energy. They must know how things stand and what scientific laws govern the case. The formulation of the laws need not be technically sophisticated. Consider the case of Phoebe: she knows that pottery is fragile, she has the energy of the gravitational field at her disposal, and she knows that objects released from

128

rest fall. She meets the conditions of free action: if she has a vase in her hand, she is free to drop it, and it will break.

You may think this a strange example; it suggests that two other conditions for free action must be added to complete the specification. First, Phoebe must want to break the vase. If she dropped it by accident, we would not say she had performed an action at all. Second, nobody must prevent her from carrying out her intention. When embodied in action, the idea of freedom turns out to be much more complex than it is in its abstract form. We cannot claim that an action is free unless the agent:

1. intends to achieve a given end by it,
2. is not restrained or constrained by another agent,
3. has suitable resources of energy and material at his or her disposal,
4. has sufficient information about the state of the world at the time of the action, and
5. knows enough of the laws governing the behavior of that world to be able to foresee the likely consequences of the action.

This is a specification of what I call *complex freedom*. Taken by themselves, most of the conditions in the list are unproblematic; the force of complex freedom lies in their conjunction. The traditional notion of freedom was restricted to condition 2. Restraint means that someone is preventing you from doing something you want to do. Constraint means that someone is making you do something you do not want to do. But this is a thoroughly inadequate notion. If any one of the conditions on the above list is not met in connection with some action or set of actions, then the concept of freedom in that connection is empty.

Slaves are not free; most people agree about that. What is not always so clear is that the poor are not free either, and even the rich and powerful are not free if they are ignorant. Ignorant persons are free in one significant respect: they are free to investigate their circumstances in order to remove their ignorance. This is the situation of the scientist. To insist that the laws an experiment was designed to establish should be known in advance as a condition for the freedom of the experimentation would be absurd. But this does not invalidate condition 5, since the successful achievement of the scientific end does depend on a knowledge of the very ignorance it is meant to remedy, and of the regularities of the physical world against which those of the experiment are to be measured.

50. Morality as Interpersonal

Nothing has so far been said about morality. Before that subject could be approached it was necessary to establish, for the purposes of argument, that free actions are possible. Not all free actions are morally significant, but all morally significant actions must be free. A morally significant action is one for which the agent can reasonably be praised or blamed, rewarded or punished. The definition works best with praise and blame, since reward and punishment can be understood in purely behavioristic terms as stimulating or inhibiting future actions of the same kind. Praise and blame can be viewed in the behavioristic way too, if they are communicated to the agent, but they are regarded here as objective judgments. From my point of view as a subject it seems unfair to be blamed for something I could not help, for an action I was not free to avoid, and I am content for the time being to leave the matter on that level.

I restrict the adjective "moral" to actions affecting the freedom of other agents. This restriction needs defense on two grounds: its emphasis (1) on freedom, and (2) on others.

(1) Surely there must be other ways, you may say, in which my actions may offend morally: if they affect people's happiness or welfare, if they cause harm or pain. I agree that such actions are morally offensive, but why are they morally offensive? My project is to find a sturdy theoretical ground on which to base morality. If all the actions we intuitively recognize as immoral prove to have an element in common, and if that element alone also makes an action immoral, then instead of listing all the varieties of immoral action we can tie their immorality to that feature. This strategy is familiar in the sciences, where finding a formula that will generate a class of cases is recognized as more efficient than citing the cases one by one.

My claim is that the offense against freedom is the common element in immoral actions. Diminishing a person's freedom is immoral in itself, and other immoral actions have as a consequence some diminution of freedom. The cases just cited, of adversely affecting happiness or welfare, or causing pain or harm, all qualify as diminishing freedom if we augment the definition of freedom in the way I suggested in the account of complex freedom in section 49.

(2) Restricting moral consideration to action affecting others amounts to a rejection of the concept of a "desert-island" morality, but it still reflects accurately the ordinary meanings of morality that do not depend on transcendent presuppositions. The principal difficulty is with actions traditionally called *prudential*, such as giving up smoking because it is dangerous to health. In this analysis, some of these fall outside the moral realm altogether. Prudential considerations anticipate future possibilities as they may affect the agent, or his or her family or community, but they do not concern themselves with the impact of the agent's actions on others, except in the sense that these actions may provoke defensive or retaliatory reactions.

Prudential: "Prudence" is a contraction of "providence," from Latin *pro-,* "before," and *video,* "to see": seeing ahead, or foresight. It is thus the consequentialist virtue par excellence, since the basic demand of consequentialism is that we should look to the foreseeable consequences of our actions. Being prud*ent* is not the same as being prud*ish*—there is no etymological connection between the terms. "Prudish" comes from the same root as "proud." It was originally applied to women who had an exaggerated sense of propriety and correctness in social situations: deontologists one and all.

No action that is wholly reflexive, even if it enhances or impairs the freedom of the agent, is to be judged in moral terms. We might suppose that no such action is possible, except perhaps on the desert island itself. But on reflection many private actions come to mind whose probable consequences reach no further than the agent. Might we argue that someone who committed suicide, or became an incurable alcoholic, would commit a moral offense against a potential future self whose freedom was affected by those actions, even if they had no social effects (which is admittedly unlikely in such cases)? But becoming morally indignant with myself on account of actions affecting nobody but myself has some artificiality about it. Jekyll loathed Hyde, but that was because Hyde had murdered an innocent man. If an action of mine affects my future freedom—and many actions do—I may call myself stupid or clever, but I shall not, unless I have an exalted idea of my importance, consider myself to have done anything moral or immoral, or worthy of praise or blame.

Jekyll and Hyde: Names for the supposed good and evil sides of human nature, from *The Strange Case of Dr. Jekyll and Mr. Hyde* by the Scottish writer Robert Louis Stevenson (1850–1894).

I can blame myself for a genuinely immoral action, such as failure to help someone who is drowning. In this case I identify myself with, and take the part of, the other members of a society to which we both belong. But I cannot take their part against myself when no other person is involved, for according to this analysis they themselves ought to admit that my reflexive action carries no moral weight. Can I take my own part against myself, if for example I keep letting myself down, not keeping resolutions I have made, being self-indulgent in some way that causes me shame and remorse, failing to meet obligations to my well-being?

As in the case of the future self, this strikes me as not a moral issue. We may think of it in moral terms, as St. Paul does when he exclaims, "The good that I would I do not: but the evil which I would not, that I do . . . O wretched man that I am!,"[1] but only if we have set for ourselves (or had set for us) a prior and possibly arbitrary standard of behavior of which we fall short. In St. Paul's case what we have come short of is "the glory of God,"[2] which sets a high standard indeed; everything else is "sin," though in the passage quoted "the evil which I would not" suggests something more specific. Setting high standards for yourself is not a bad idea, and the feeling of having let yourself down may be a stimulus to greater effort. But this method of self-improvement should be used with care. Reinforced with disapproval, of familial or cultural or religious origin, self-reproach can be merciless and destructive.

Sin: Hamartia, the Greek word for "sin" in the New Testament, means "falling short of the target." Christian doctrine maintains that human beings are in a *state* of sin, from which they cannot escape without redemption. This may work against efforts at self-improvement or mutual help at the level of more local fallings-short, such as people's obligations to one another, because they seem minor in comparison.

The fact that many people have believed that reflexive actions can be moral or immoral, so that persons committing them have felt commended or blamed by society, is just another example of the overloading of the concept of morality. What has sometimes been in the back of their minds is that no action can be wholly reflexive, in the sense that its consequences affect no one but the agent, since God sees and judges all. But this does not follow. For unless God's freedom were impaired by witnessing the action—which, given the usual attributes of God, would be self-contradictory—the action would, if wholly reflexive, be amoral by this criterion even if God were looking. If morality is to be defined in terms of arbitrary standards laid down by God, the popular belief may be correct, but in this case "moral" ceases to have any useful meaning.

51. Moral Responsibility and Causal Responsibility

To help in setting the boundaries within which moral considerations properly apply, let us attempt a rudimentary classification of voluntary actions. Such actions, those performed by a free agent for a deliberate end, fall into four clearly distinguishable classes. These are not exhaustive, although they account for most cases, and they overlap, since actions are rarely simple.

(1) On the lowest level are what I call *sustaining* actions: actions that do not set out to increase or decrease the amount of order in the rest of the world but that concern the maintenance of the individual human organism, such as getting up in the morning, eating, taking exercise, working for a living. These actions would not take place unless they were voluntarily performed, but in themselves they serve no value beyond survival at an accustomed level of comfort. Working for a living, if the work is of the right kind, can be rewarding; the test of whether this work involves value above the sustaining level would be if the agent continued to do it even if he or she no longer had to do so for a living.

(2) Continuous with this class are *conventional* or *ritual* actions like putting on a tie, shaking hands, or applauding a performance.

(3) Third come distinctly *moral* (or immoral) actions, freely undertaken because of their effect on the freedom of others, such as giving to charity or shooting enemies. A notable subclass of moral actions are *enabling* actions, which are, in effect, sustaining actions done on behalf of another person. These may be immoral if what they enable the other person to do is something destructive of self or others. The action I enable, if its consequences do not reach beyond the agent who performs it, will not count as immoral by the rule of the preceding section, but the action I take to enable it may count as immoral, especially in cases where the agent I enable is weak-willed.

(4) Lastly, some actions are done for the sake of a quality in their results that changes the order of the world, without affecting the freedom of others, so that the world comes closer to the agent's conception of what it ought to be. To this class belong all actions done deliberately or casually for private satisfaction, from taking a snack or a vacation to playing chess or writing a novel. I call them *aesthetic* actions. This involves a considerable departure from the usual meaning of "aesthetic," though it encompasses that meaning. Actions in this class will be judged by the agent in terms of how his or her world looks or feels or tastes or sounds as a result, even if the rest of us are not inclined to call the result beautiful.

Aesthetic: Greek *aisthesis* means "perception"; the discipline of aesthetics (which is a relative newcomer to philosophy under

> that name) has traditionally had to do with the judgment of the perceptual qualities of works of art.

Few actions that are not simple fall neatly into any one of these classes. For example, going on a vacation for health or writing a novel for money would also count as sustaining actions. The point of the classification is to identify roughly the major reasons for acting at all. Sustaining actions preserve the status quo on the individual level. They affect freedom, but only reflexively and thus by this account amorally. Ritual actions preserve the status quo on a conventional social level. They do not increase or decrease anyone's freedom, though the refusal to perform them might do this. Specifically moral actions may preserve the status quo for other people (actions performed by an individual on behalf of the community are automatically moral, unless they are performed only for pay), but they may also change it. The majority of morally interesting actions are those that introduce changes into other people's lives. Finally, purely aesthetic actions will change the status quo for the agent, in ways pleasing to him or her, and perhaps also to other people, though in the pure case not in such a way as to affect their future freedom of action.

Sustaining, conventional, or aesthetic actions may become moral or immoral because they have an effect on the freedom of others, even though this was not intended. But the line must be carefully drawn here, because to hold an agent morally responsible for an improbable and wholly unforeseen consequence of an innocent act would be absurd. Moralists have always been fond of edifying stories about missing nails and lost battles, great oaks and little acorns. These have a legitimate point, but we cannot spend all our time in conjecture about the possible outcomes of minor actions. We ought to be aware of any likely outcome, and behave accordingly. In estimating what counts as likely, we should err on the side of caution and restraint rather than on the side of confidence and daring where the freedom of others is concerned. In the case of consequences affecting only the agent, as we have seen, moral considerations do not apply. But somebody may well be the causal agent of an event without being its moral agent, even though the event is one that, if brought about deliberately, would lead us to condemn the agent as immoral.

Consider the following cases. In the first, a reader of this book notices that a pattern of white spaces between the words (you can see such patterns if you half-close your eyes) resembles the profile of the uncle who abused her as a child. This provokes a psychotic episode during which she shoots her roommate. In the second, I heave an old television set I want to get rid of out of my apartment window; it crushes a passerby. In the first case I am a contributory causal agent of the death of the roommate, because if I hadn't written the book just as I did she would still be alive, but by no stretch of the imagination could anyone maintain that I was in any way the moral agent of her death. In the second case everyone would agree that I am the moral agent of the death of the passerby, even if I did not know anyone was there, even if the street was generally deserted at that time of night. I would be considered morally irresponsible even if nobody was hurt.

Moral responsibility is thus a special case of causal responsibility. The term "responsible," by itself, is ambiguous, and one of the tasks of ethics is to decide at what point the moral meaning becomes operative. Morally sensitive people will be concerned about the possible consequences of their actions, but to what lengths should such sensitivity go? At one end of the scale, someone who removed a sign saying "danger" at the edge of a cliff because it obstructed the view would rightly be thought to have done something immoral. At the other end of the scale, someone of no public importance who refused a drink at a crowded bar because doing otherwise might corrupt the young would not be thought to have done anything particularly moral.

Responsible: "Answerable" or "liable to be called to account." A person who is responsible generally acts in a considered way and is willing to give an account of his or her actions. A general failure in these respects counts as irresponsible. But we may also ask who is responsible for committing or failing to commit some specific act, in order to allocate praise or blame. The person who is responsible in this sense may well turn out to be irresponsible in the previous sense.

But consider the case of Albert Szent-Gyorgyi, the Hungarian-American biochemist who, when awarded the Nobel Prize, insisted on investing the money in "shares which had to go down in the case of war,"[3] because of his belief that war was wrong. Was that a quixotic gesture to be dismissed, or a moral example to be followed? The question can be taken in two ways. The first has to do with the consistency of the action with the belief, the second with the validity of the belief itself. Here our concern is with the first. The question is not only what are the probable consequences of my action, but also how much do I know (or want to know) of its probable consequences. Investing in stocks is not generally considered a particularly moral or immoral activity. Investment may be prudential (and to a degree moral also) with respect to the future security of the investor's family, but most of us do not pay too much attention to the remoter consequences of our involvement with the economy. Yet that involvement is voluntary, and if it leads, even indirectly, to a restriction on other people's freedom, to their exploitation or even death, the responsibility is partly ours.

52. Responsibilities and Rights

The doctrine that we bear partial responsibility for even such remote consequences of our actions may seem harsh, and to put fetters on our freedom rather than enhancing it. But if I wish to be morally reasonable I must surely ask not only whether I can perform such-and-such an action with moral impunity, but whether the manifest wrongs suffered by so many people in the world are in any way the consequences of my actions. Although every moral action is performed by a single agent, its consequences are not necessarily restricted to a particular person, and the actions that affect such a person may have been performed by many agents. Morality is a collective as well as an individual matter. If once again we reject the transcendent and supernatural, we are left with the fact that somebody, or some group of persons, is responsible for the present state of the world.

Leaving out of account uncontrollable events like earthquakes and storms, human beings are evidently in charge of their environment. They take pride in this. We are told that natural resources are still adequate, though only just and, if numbers continue to rise, not for long, to feed the present population of the earth. Whose fault is it, then, that poverty and deprivation, even starvation, are so pervasive? Someone may say that such conditions are nobody's fault, since nobody's actions brought them about. But somebody's action *conjointly with the actions of many other people* did bring them about, and somebody's inaction *conjointly with the inaction of many other people* failed to prevent them. If agents cannot be free unless they have energy and material at their disposal, if some agents lack these things, and if I have surplus energy and material that I refuse to make available to them, knowing as I do that they need them and that I have no use for them, am I not morally implicated in their plight?

But the argument here is getting ahead of itself. The view that those actions and only those that affect the freedom of others are to be called moral or immoral needs defense, and the crucial question of why anyone ought to act morally at all has yet to be approached. My purpose in this chapter has been to draw attention to the complementarity of the notions of action and responsibility. If agents are free in the full sense, then they are responsible for everything that follows from their actions, but they are morally responsible only for those consequences that are foreseeable and that affect the freedom of others.

If a consequence is foreseeable, then the agent has already staked his or her responsibility in performing the action even if that consequence does not in fact ensue. For this reason no separate discussion of intention is given here. If we assume that an agent's intention in performing an action is to achieve its probable consequences as he or she understands them, we have an adequate basis for moral judgment, which cannot be evaded by the excuse that what was really intended was not the probable consequence at all but some improbable consequence. If agents take risks, and gamble successfully for a lesser probability of benefit to themselves against a greater probability of harm to others, we say simply that they were lucky, not that they acted morally. And if they miscalculate the probability of the consequences, either wilfully or in ignorance, we say they are culpable if better information was in fact available to them.

I do not deny that practically we are justified in treating those who only intend to commit crimes more leniently than those who really commit them, but that is a jurisprudential difference and not a moral difference. Jurisprudence is the foresight of the law, whose resources might be wasted in pursuing merely possible offenders. But it would overload those resources beyond measure if we all waited for the law to catch us out in immoral actions. Those who do immoral acts because they can get away with them legally offend doubly, in the acts themselves and in the likelihood that their attitude, if general, would strain the legal system.

Before closing this discussion let me refer once again to another concept that is sometimes set over against the concept of responsibility: the concept of rights. The concept of a natural right, a right enjoyed by everyone simply by virtue of being a human being, and regardless of the dispositions of other human beings, is in my view empty. A belief in natural rights is possible only in a context of strong transcendent principles, having to do with the divine governance of the world, perhaps, or with the uniqueness and primacy of human existence. We have only to think of people in danger of being swept away by floods or eaten by wild beasts, far from any possibility of human help, to see the futility of asserting their unconditional rights to life, liberty, and the pursuit of happiness. Rights come into being in a social setting, and, as has often been pointed out, they have their own correlatives in the form of duties or obligations.

Responsibility has a double meaning: my responsibility to do my duty is different from my responsibility for having done whatever I happen to have done, whether duty or not. The individual recognition of moral responsibilities imposes moral duty, and the collective acknowledgment of duties guarantees rights. A declaration of human rights signifies the acceptance of participation in a human community, the members of which are prepared to assume responsibility for their actions as they affect others. If morality were a legal concept, this would be enough for ethics, but from the philosophical point of view we need to follow the analysis to a more fundamental level.

Community, society: Latin *communis* means "shared or common"; it is connected to *moenia,* "city walls," and to *munus,* "an official duty or function" or "a gift," from which we get "municipal" and also indirectly "remuneration" (office-holding has been associated with the giving of gifts for a long time). So a community originally had a common location and a common administration. "Society" is from *socius,* "acting together," hence a fellow in an enterprise. The difference between these concepts was developed into a theory by the German sociologist Ferdinand Tönnies (1855–1936); *Gemeinschaft* (community) for him was affective, natural, and organic, *Gesellschaft* (society) was contractual, artificial, and mechanical. To a rough approximation we might say that moral relations will dominate in a community, legal ones in a society.

Notes

1. St. Paul, *Epistle to the Romans* 7:19, 24.
2. Romans 3:23.
3. Albert Szent-Gyorgyi, "The Brain, Morals, and Politics," *Bulletin of the Atomic Scientists* 20 (May 1964), p. 2.

XI

The Idea of a Universal Ethics

53. The Development of Obligation

Why should we accept moral responsibility at all? We do attach imperatives to particular future states of the world; in the process these become values for us, so that (from our point of view) they ought to be the case. But can we affirm the existence of future states of the world to which we ought to attach imperatives? The formulation of that imperative would read: "It ought to be the case (that I think, or that everyone thinks) that it ought to be the case that x." This reiterated "ought" is not yet provided for. The weakness of many contemporary ethical theories is that their analyses are restricted to the second "ought." They tell us what we mean when we say "x ought to be the case," or "x is good," or "x is right," but they do not tell us whether that is what we ought to mean, whether we should attach an imperative to a state of the world in which such things are desirable or good or right.

In ordinary language the term "ought" is much too strong to be used for the objects of our private desires. I may want something very badly without being inclined to say that I ought to have it. But this is a difference of tone and emphasis. Wanting something to be the case and thinking that it ought to be so lie on the same continuum, and not so far from one another at that. In most cases wanting is immediate and spontaneous, while the conviction expressed by "ought" is arrived at only after deliberation. Yet we can easily think of instances contrary to these generalizations, such as obligations whose force is almost instinctive, and desires that become explicit only after reflection.

Ought, obligation: "Own" and "owe" and "ought" come from an Indo-Germanic root meaning "to possess," so "ought" originally had to do with giving people what was rightly theirs.

"Obligation" is from Latin *ligo,* "to bind," *ob-* meaning "over against," so that what I am bound to do is manifest or obvious ("obvious" being itself from *ob-* and *via,* "a way," something that is "in the way," that you can't miss). Although there is no direct etymological link between the terms, the conceptual connection is of long standing in ordinary usage: "*A* ought to do *x*" is equivalent to "*A* is under an obligation to do *x*." This works well as long as *x* is something in or for which *A* has a clear interest or responsibility. But in the impersonal "it ought to be the case that *x*," the corresponding obligation is not so clear, nor is it clear who incurs it.

The difficulty with separating the concepts of wanting and obligation too radically is that wanting (willing, desiring) is the phenomenological basis for value, to which all moral principles must be referred for their validation. To seek some other ground for obligation, such as reason, justice, or social conscience, leaves open the possibility of flat rejection. If people do not want justice, if justice simply does not matter to them, no appeal to it will be convincing. Conversely, those who are convinced by such an appeal are those to whom justice already matters and who attach value to states of the world in which justice is realized.

But someone to whom justice does not matter at first may be brought to see that it really does matter. The theory of value rectifies the experience of desire, just as scientific theory rectifies the experience of perception. And just as the trained scientist perceives the world differently from the way in which an uninformed person perceives it, so the moral agent trained in the theory of value wants a different world from the world the unreflective person wants. In one sense, and a very fundamental one, they all see the same thing (patches of light and shade, shapes, colors) and want the same thing (satisfaction or freedom from pain). The difference is that, in the case of the person trained in science or values, the unanalyzed perception and the unanalyzed desire, which are complex, have yielded to rational analysis. They have been shown to be explicable in terms of universal principles that, when apprehended, are seen to embody more fundamental but equally compelling truths about the way the world is and ought to be.

In the light of the theory I do not say that the object of my private desire ought to be the case; I make the object of my private desire what rational considerations tell me ought to be the case whether I want it in the direct sense or not. At the same time I do not have to deny my primitive conations, I have only to reorganize them in a larger context. The situation is like that of the observer who sees that a stick partially in water looks bent: I need not deny that the stick looks bent, but I place this untrained perception in the context of my knowledge of refraction.

The principle in the light of which my desires have to be modified, if my behavior is to be moral in the sense of this book, is the equivalence of human freedoms. If I want to do anything at all, I must want to be free to do it; I must attach an imperative to the state of the world in which that freedom is assured. I need not have a separate and conscious desire for this state in the abstract. Wanting it is implicit in wanting anything at all. On reflection this may be made explicit, but the original wanting takes no account of abstractions. If I only ever wanted one thing, all that would be implicit would be a desire for the conditions necessary for obtaining that thing, so that the argument for freedom in general would not hold. A necessary assumption, then, is that I want a variety of things, some of them as yet unspecified. In that case, whatever my goal may be, the proposition that I ought to be free becomes a truth for me.

What we now need is some way of showing that other people ought to be free, and of making this proposition also a truth *for me*. If this can be done, then I shall have a rational basis for moral action, a ground for attaching an imperative to the values of justice and equality.

To many people the proposition that everyone ought to be free is at least as self-evident as the proposition that they themselves are free, and they may become impatient with argument. Their intuition is sound, but their impatience may betray an unacknowledged awareness of the difficulties involved in any justification. In this case, as in the case of individual freedom, the best strategy is a shift in the burden of proof. Most moral problems arise because people choose to overlook the consequences of their actions as they affect the freedom of others, or because, while taking account of the adverse consequences, they nevertheless assert the right to impose these consequences on others. This generalization has to be understood in a sufficiently complex sense if it is to be adequate. The agent may be a group or even a class of persons, the action may be a failure to act, and the consequences may affect any of the five conditions of freedom listed in the previous chapter: intention, absence of constraint or restraint, availability of material resources, information, and knowledge.

We might then try out the following preliminary form of the required principle: *nobody has a right to disregard the freedom of others*. The burden of proof on people who wish to deny this is to show how they arrived at the position of privilege in the moral community that entitles them to do so. Only within such a community can the term "right" have any meaning. If under attack the attempt is made to shift the burden of proof back again, by demanding evidence for the denial of the right to disregard the freedom of others, we may answer that however the moral community is constituted (as distinct from the social or legal communities), it cannot be part of its constitution that any individual should have rights that other individuals do not have. The alternative universal proposition ("everybody has a right to disregard the freedom of others") would not qualify as a principle of community at all, let alone of moral community. To the further objection that the agents in question do not care about the moral community, we can reply that they are in that community whether they like it or not. To claim exclusion from the moral community is equivalent to claiming privilege within it.

Privilege: Latin *privilegio* meant "a law for one person, a private law," from *lex*, "law" and *privus*, "single or special," connected with *privo*, "to deprive." The association of privacy and privilege with deprivation is one that should be taken seriously. If a place or possession is private to me, then someone else is deprived of it; this is fine on a personal level if the "deprived" person has access to places and things just as good as mine, but it becomes morally questionable if social arrangements systematically exclude and deprive whole classes of people for the benefit of a privileged class. We tend to call such excluded people "under-privileged," as if what society needed were more privilege, when actually it needs less. Marx's polemic against private property rested on the deprivation that ensues when land and the means of production are held privately.

The force of the principle is thus equally well expressed if we say instead: in the moral community we admit no privilege, nor do we admit arguments intended to establish privilege. This is of an exemplary simplicity, but in ethics, if we remember the conditions for a generally applicable theory, that is a virtue. The principle has something in common with the Golden Rule and the categorical imperative, and this is not surprising. But the Golden Rule is inadequate, since it makes everything depend on the preference of the individual agent (which is all right for art but not for morality), and the categorical imperative is much too opaque to be practically applicable. "Act only according to that maxim by which you can at the same time will that it should become a universal law."[1] The difficulties attendant upon the concept of universal law and the conditions of its application would be enough to reduce the agent to impotence if this were all the guidance available. What prevents impotence from being the natural condition of moral agents is that they have conative impulses. These impulses do not drive people toward metaphysics; they drive them toward concrete states of the world that are seen as values.

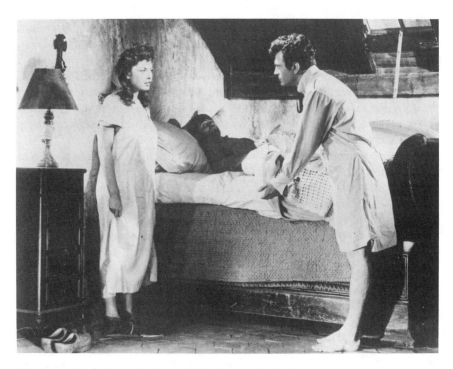

The Seven Deadly Sins: Gluttony (1953; director Carlo Rim)
An unexpected overnight guest (Henri Vidal) discusses sleeping arrangements with the wife of the house (Claudine Dupuis); her husband (Jean Richard) is already in bed. In spite of the flirtation between the wife and the guest, the latter's true interest is in a large cheese he has glimpsed at dinner. The consequence is that the husband is cheated—but not in the way the audience expects.

54. The Principle of Indifference

This is of greater importance than it may appear at first. Except in special cases, ethics cannot tell people what to do, if telling somebody what to do is a way of initiating action. People who are at a loss for anything to do do not need moral instruction; they need love or vitamins or psychoanalysis. Most people want to do many things, some of which may have direct or indirect effects on other people. Moral rules are mainly useful in restraining them from doing those things that adversely affect the freedom of others.

That is why most moral rules have traditionally been expressed as prohibitions: thou shalt not kill, thou shalt not commit adultery, and so on. The world is crowded, and the problem for each agent is to pursue his or her ends without thwarting other people in the pursuit of theirs. Sometimes that cannot be helped. If only one of something is available and if I and another person both want it, one of us must be disappointed. Let us assume that neither of us has any antecedent title to the thing in question. Should I step back and let the other person have it? This might be a gallant act, or even a morally worthy one, but moral considerations would not require it. Moral considerations would come into play only if I deceived my competitor into thinking that the object in question was not what it seemed, or hampered access to it in a way that caused harm, or by some other means subverted the opportunity for fair competition.

Such direct incompatibility of ends is not the most frequent source of moral difficulty, although because many interpersonal problems, especially sexual ones, take this form, it is more dramatic and more easily recognizable than most cases of conflict. The deprivation of freedom generally takes place in more subtle ways. When it comes to impairing people's freedom, it may be more effective to make them depressed and unhappy than to restrain them physically. This is not so much because unhappiness is painful as because it may destroy motivation and thus inhibit action. To say that inflicting pain is wrong misses the point, as all hedonistic theories of ethics do. Pain is only a symptom. Its evolutionary function is presumably to prevent wounded animals from running about and doing themselves further damage, and to induce them to stay still and make recovery possible. Pain following injury inhibits action in order to protect the potentiality for action. Physical or psychological pain inflicted without consent on one person by another merely inhibits action without protecting anything. This is what makes the action morally wrong, not the pain simply.

Hedonism: Greek *hedomai* was "to enjoy oneself, take one's pleasure." Hedonism is the view that pleasure is the highest good. Two main versions of hedonism are found among the Greeks. According to the Cyrenaics (Aristippus, about 435–356 B.C.E.), we should aim for intense pleasures of the moment, and according to the Epicureans (Epicurus, 341–270 B.C.E.), we should aim for calm enjoyment and freedom from pain.

Similarly, lying, fraud, and stealing are not wrong because we so describe them; they are made so by their probable effect on the freedom of others. Nothing is morally wrong in the enunciation of an untrue proposition, considered simply as such, even if it is done with the intent to deceive. Similarly, nothing is wrong in the removal from one place to another of a physical object, considered simply as such, even if it does not belong to the person who moves it. Under some circumstances these actions may become morally wrong—indeed they are almost certain to, since misinformation and the loss of property tend to affect the conditions of other agents' freedom of action. But their being wrong is not because they are the kind of action they are. We cannot condemn whole classes of actions with no consideration of circumstances. Moral offenses are committed one at a time. The intentions and probable consequences that constitute a moral offense are not essential characteristics of the actions to which they are attached; they are determined by the conditions in each case.

The principle of the equivalence of freedoms on which the foregoing analyses rest may be expressed as a principle of indifference between any pair of freedoms taken at random. *No argument is capable of showing that one person's freedom ought to be exercised at the expense of another's.* This new formulation is probably preferable to those given earlier in the chapter, since it reduces the complex case of the maximization of freedom in general to a collection of pairwise cases of the reconciliation of individual freedoms. In this form, which stresses the symmetry of any situation in which one human being's freedom confronts another's, the principle is anticipated in a well-known passage from Hobbes: "when all is reckoned together," he says, "the difference between man, and man, is not so considerable, as that one man can thereupon claim to himselfe any benefit, to which another may not pretend, as well as he."[2]

The central point is in the expression "can thereupon claim," which puts the burden of proof in the right place and preserves the status of the principle as a testable hypothesis. It also reminds us that if we insist on finite and hypothetical principles, limiting cases may arise to which they do not apply. Many people have tried to circumvent the restriction on possible arguments for unequal freedom expressed in the principle of indifference. But the history of tyranny and its overthrow provides evidence that, to make only the most modest demands on it, leaves the principle unfalsified. If some being were capable of coercing others absolutely, he or she would be an Absolute Tyrant who could simply ignore the principle and claim title to anything and everything. But such a being would be outside the moral domain. His or her behavior would be amoral rather than immoral. This distinction is already used in the case of persons who flaunt the various conventional moralities.

The only possible candidate for the title of Absolute Tyrant in human affairs is God, and this conclusion is fully compatible with traditional theology. These considerations apply to only one among the conditions for free action, namely, the absence of restraint or constraint. Parallel arguments could be constructed for the availability of information, material resources, motivation, and so forth, leading to an Absolute Deceiver and other analogous beings, each of whom would turn out to embody a possible aspect of God. God is commonly assumed to be an Absolute Benefactor also, which prevents the misuse of these powers. On a human level altruism, sympathy, compassion, and the like can frequently be counted on to temper any inclination to extreme ruthlessness or brutality. They cannot, however, always be counted on, and this makes them unsuitable as a basis for morality. Someone might be absolutely selfish or absolutely merciless; fortunately, no finite being can be absolutely powerful.

55. The Moral Community

This analysis is relevant to the vexed question of what moral relation people have, if any, to other animals. If human beings are free, some animals are no doubt also free, albeit to a lesser degree because their range of possible achievement is severely restricted in comparison with that of human beings. But if this is true, ought not the principle of indifference to apply to them too? In this case the answer is not quite as simple as in the case of God, but animals may be considered to bear to us a relation analogous to the relation we are presumed to bear to God. We can, practically speaking, afford to ignore their freedom and claim any benefits we like with respect to them. In so doing, we put ourselves outside *their* moral domain, or deny them any rights in ours, which amounts to the same thing, .

This is not a generous attitude to take, although most of us who are not Buddhists or vegetarians do in practice take it. The moral community within which the principle of indifference operates was established by an appeal to the symmetry of human freedoms taken in pairs; the symmetry breaks down when God's freedom is paired against a human being's, or a human being's freedom against an animal's. The Buddhist preaches abstention from doing injury to all living things because of a belief that life itself is a principle of community. But those who do not share this belief cannot be rebuked by an appeal to symmetry, although a human being who wished to exclude another human being from the moral community could be so rebuked. At the borders of that community it may be necessary to exclude or include by a decision rather than by a rational analysis, as is vividly shown in Vercors's novel *Les animaux dénaturés*, in which an anthropologist is brought to trial for the murder of a child he has had by a member of a tribe of humanoid apes. A conviction would confer human status on the tribe and heroic status on the anthropologist, who has arranged the whole episode with this in mind. On the other hand, an acquittal would mean that he would escape justice, but lose his case. At the trial the central issue is the definition of the human; no agreed-upon definition is forthcoming, and the judge concludes that being admitted to the human community is more like joining a club than passing a test. He declares the tribe human—but, since the declaration was not yet in force at the time of the murder, the anthropologist is acquitted after all.

Vercors: Pen name of the French novelist Jean Bruller (1902–). His *The Silence of the Sea* is a classic novel of the French resistance in World War II.

The term "community" can be interpreted in a stronger or a weaker sense. In the stronger sense the members of the community are mutually responsible, actually or potentially, while in the weaker sense some members may take up a responsibility for others that is not reciprocated. I say "potentially" to allow children, who are not yet responsible, to be members of the community in the stronger sense. In the weaker sense of the term, human beings and some animals may be considered to belong to the same community. Animals take no responsibility for the welfare of human beings, except in special cases (faithful dogs and horses), but many people voluntarily assume responsibility for the welfare of animals. The point about community may be accentuated by the observation that kindness to animals makes sense while kindness to plants would not ordinarily be thought rational except on the far-out fringe. But the consideration of intermediate cases—for example, kindness to insects or to fish—suggests that kindness to animals may be more sentimental than rational in the minds of most people.

Most people have a vague empathy for the larger, warmer, and furrier kinds of animal, similar to (and sometimes stronger than) the empathy they feel for other human beings. This seems morally compelling to people for whom moral compulsion is primarily an emotional matter. The intellect may reinforce the emotions by an appeal to the values inherent in all nature, or something of that sort, but unless we are, like the Buddhists, prepared to take that seriously and extend our altruism to rats and cockroaches, such arguments have a hollow ring.

The theory advocated here denies that any values are inherent in nature; they are all brought into being by conscious subjectivity. This does not mean that human values are the only values. Animals no doubt have their own values, and so do God and the Martians, if they exist. The trouble is that we are trying to devise a practical morality, and we have our hands more than full with human affairs. The consequence of restricting our consideration of values to human ones is that God, the Martians, and the animals are out of the moral sphere altogether.

Considerations of symmetry and consistency would therefore require people who eat meat or use insecticides to accept the justice of the situation if a powerful extraterrestrial being of advanced evolutionary status decided to make a meal of them, or exterminate their families because little human beings crawling about the newly acquired colony of earth filled the more squeamish members of the superior species with irrational panic. At the same time, being a vegetarian or a Buddhist would probably not cut much ice with the extraterrestrials; it would at most warrant a short-lived indignation unavailable to the rest of us.

The argument that we do not need to exploit animals for food or for research, and that seeking alternatives would be more humane, does have serious weight, but I do not think it is moral weight. To countenance suffering wilfully inflicted, outside the moral community, is a defect of character but not a moral offense. This is a sensitive issue. I think it likely that there is a psychological link between character and morality, in two senses. (1) Those who are indifferent to suffering in the vicinity of the moral community (that is, in animals sufficiently like us, for example, those having central nervous systems) will probably be deficient in their moral concerns within the community. (2) Similarly, people who are scrupulous within the moral community are likely to be moved by the plight of animals who are mistreated and in pain, and to wish to avoid involvements with institutions (food processing, cosmetics research) that sanction the infliction of such pain.

The case for the enlargement of the moral community to include animals has not, I believe, been made. If this makes morality sound callous, remember that one task of this book is to lighten the burden of moral argument—which is at present saddled with responsibility not only for morals but for taste, good breeding, and kindness to animals—so that it can more effectively perform its fundamental task of preserving human freedom. Morality can only be weakened if its indignation is constantly brought to bear on small children, butchers, and experimental psychologists.

Surely, you may say, all suffering unnecessarily inflicted is wrong? I agree: "wrong," as you remember, means "twisted" (it is related to "wring"), just as "right" means "straight," and it would be a twisted mind that enjoyed or even condoned avoidable suffering. How are we to construe "avoidable" here? How much of the unimaginable suffering animals must undergo in nature could be averted, with all the resources in the world? What about human suffering, close at hand in abusive families, or far off in countries ravaged by war and famine? All our resources of feeling and of moral action would be quickly exhausted if the object of morality were taken to be the avoidance of suffering. That is why I say that morality is not about suffering, it is about freedom. Our moral resources can, if focused, make a difference to the freedom of some agents. The community of those agents must be limited if these resources are not to be dissipated beyond recovery.

The limits set to the moral universe by God on the one hand and by animals on the other hand do not define it precisely enough. For various practical purposes criminals, the mentally ill, and the senile must also be excluded. Such exclusions must be handled carefully, and not made into excuses for oppression. The difference between us and them must be considerable enough to make the asymmetry indubitable. If there is any doubt, they must be given the benefit of it. The respect in which we treat them differently will amount to no more than this: that we shall not feel obliged to lend them active help in getting what they appear to want, whereas we might for others. But when all these special cases have been taken account of, the resulting community of human beings is one in which the principle of indifference can form the basis for a genuinely universal ethics.

Such an ethics addresses itself not to all, but to each. It calls upon us to recognize that if we are to act rationally we must desire the freedom of others as much as our own. If we choose not to act rationally, we read ourselves out of the human community, thereby depriving ourselves of the rights to which membership in that community entitles us. Rationality requires that we be able to give reasons for our actions. The principle of indifference says that we cannot give valid reasons for any action that requires assigning our freedom a more privileged status than the freedom of others. The universality of the system rests on the fact that everyone holds his or her freedom as a value—an instrumental one to be sure, but nonetheless a value. The applicability of the system to particular cases rests on the fact that freedom is defined in a suitably complex way.

56. Three Moral Rules

As a guide to action, ethics is principally negative, in that it prohibits interference with the freedom of others. But in some cases interference itself can be negative—if, for example, my failure to come to someone's aid when I am able to do so results in a diminution of that person's freedom in relation to that of others. This is obvious if the person in question is drowning, less obvious if he or she is just poor. In such cases the prohibition becomes a requirement by double negation.

We can distinguish three kinds of situation in which universal moral principles may be invoked, and three kinds of answer that may be given to an appeal for guidance in action.

(1) If I find, within reach of my causal influence, people whose freedom is restricted in some way (not counting the exceptions enumerated above), if I have at my disposal the resources necessary to remove that restriction, and if I can do so without bringing about a more serious restriction on the

freedom of *other* people, then I ought to do so. Agents must weigh carefully the nature of the deprivations they set out to correct, and the likely side effects of their actions, for which they may have to assume moral responsibility. For example, if in order to secure a special form of economic freedom for a privileged minority in an underdeveloped country, it became necessary to ravage the whole country and kill many innocent people, the agents of this liberation would be considered to have acted immorally, no matter how praiseworthy their intentions in the absence of the side effects.

(2) If no overriding imperatives of the kind referred to above intrude—if, that is to say, I have done what I can for the freedom of others—then moral principles have a merely negative force. If my action has any effect on others, that effect ought not to reduce their freedom. I will not find it easy to decide when (if ever) I have done what I can for the freedom of others. Here, as in the case of moral and causal responsibility, the argument needs to be supplemented with a pragmatic cutoff beyond which a disregard of other people's instrumental values for the sake of my end values is justified.

Pragmatic: From Greek *pragmata,* "affairs" or "business," often in the sense of "a bad business"; it is derived from *prasso,* "to achieve, to do" (originally "to pass through"), and connected to *praxis,* "doing" (see pp. 53–54). It thus has the connotations of hard-headed, efficacious, practical.

In this and in the previous case, the situation of the others in question must be factored into my moral deliberation. An important set of qualifications has to do with the voluntary or involuntary status of the agents whose freedom I am considering. For example, if some scheme of agreed-upon compensation is in place, so that people who lack freedom in some respect obvious to me are having it made up to them in ways I don't know about, then my concern about their freedom, and my efforts to optimize it, may turn out to be merely officious.

(3) If I meet the conditions set out in (2) but my action does not affect other people, or affects them, within reasonable limits of probability, neutrally or positively, then I can do what I like. Moral principles give me no guidance. In this situation, the theory of value is forced to take up entirely different considerations, the discussion of which I defer until the next chapter. As to affecting others positively, we should remember Russell's remark about the Golden Rule and not assume too readily that our benefactions will be welcome to the recipients. In the moral world do-gooders may be as big a nuisance as evildoers.

The assertion that there are circumstances in which I can do what I like may be a hard saying in a society of Puritan origins. The third rule really means what it says: if morality is a wholly interpersonal concept, then *if* the conditions are met, a private individual can do anything whatsoever, and so can groups of consenting individuals who all want the same thing. Two caveats must be noted. (1) Making sure the conditions are met is harder than we might think. (2) That an action is not immoral does not necessarily make it admirable or prudent.

By "groups of consenting individuals" I do not only mean those who do in private what traditional moralists would have condemned. The group can be large; it can include classes of people related to one another in contractual ways. (1) Though it may affect everyone's freedom, a collective decision to limit or ration goods need not be immoral if everyone has had a voice in it. (2) Suppose that an individual or group *A* wants to do something that is ruled out because of its probable consequences for the freedom of another individual or group *B*. *A* may be able to go ahead with the desired action if *B* voluntarily accepts compensation for this loss of freedom. This will normally involve an increase in *B*'s freedom in some other respect. The trading of freedoms in this way may become quite complicated, but this need not spoil the simplicity of the rules.

Note here that in spite of the reference to groups the rules still apply in the first instance to individuals. If I join in a group action I do so as an individual and am morally responsible as such. I do not take up in this book the question of the morality of state action, though I follow Aristotle in thinking that ethics and politics lie on the same continuum. Let me mention just one way in which state action is often held to be immoral, for example by persons of libertarian inclinations: by imposing taxes the state automatically reduces the freedom of individuals, money being in our society the resource of choice in assessing complex freedom. In so doing, however, the state need not violate the principle of indifference. If individuals are more and less free, and if the state does something redistributive, which limits *A*'s greater freedom for the sake of *B*'s lesser freedom, that is only relatively exercising *B*'s freedom at the expense of *A*'s, if the prior situation it means to correct was one in which *A*'s freedom was systematically exercised at the expense of *B*'s. Needless to say, not all projects for redistribution meet this condition; all I mean to show is that a redistributive project need not be incompatible with the principle of indifference.

If we take the rules seriously, severally and in their joint implications, it follows, for example, that a personally corrupt individual who was genuinely solicitous for the welfare of others would be morally preferable to a personally upright individual who was indifferent to the welfare of others. The point of this example is not to defend corruption, but to put the moral emphasis where it belongs, so that the upright but selfish person cannot use rectitude as an excuse for avoiding moral exertion of other kinds. It is just one example among many in which the consistent application of the rules produces a result different from what might be expected on a traditional view.

57. The Pragmatic Cutoff

More needs to be said about the "pragmatic cutoff": am I ever justified in relaxing my vigilance about the possible remote consequences of my action? or am I ever entitled to ignore another person's instrumental plight in order to get on with the pursuit of my end values? Imagine a great artist completing a great work, say Michelangelo and the ceiling of the Sistine Chapel. Imagine for the sake of argument that nobody else is about and that he hears a child crying in distress. Children are special cases of the potentiality whose fulfillment requires freedom in my complex sense. Michelangelo gets down, attends to the child, frees it from the dangerous entanglement that was about to suffocate it, and climbs back to where he was working. Now imagine, again for the sake of argument, an infinite supply of such children in distress, one after another. No sooner has Michelangelo put brush to palette than another cry imposes a fresh moral obligation, and this continues day and night. When, if ever, is he entitled to say, "Enough of that! I have to finish my painting," and leave the next and all subsequent children to their fate?

The function of such implausible examples is to push the conceptual issue under discussion to its limits. Can we expect to find a rule that will cover the case? I do not think we can. That is why I have called the cutoff pragmatic. "Pragmatic" means practically workable, as opposed to what may prove to be the unrealistic expectations of pure theory. We might agree that Michelangelo would be wrong to ignore the first cry for help, but think it reasonable (abandoning the artificial conditions of the example) for him to expect that after a few times someone else will come along to relieve him of his unwelcome responsibility. He might interrupt his work long enough to help set up a child rescue service. One function of collective arrangements is to take up the moral slack when obligations become too onerous for individuals. But the initiative for such arrangements has to come from individuals. It is often prompted by just such personal challenges.

The effect of leaving the cutoff pragmatic is a challenge in itself. I cannot hide behind a rule. If I decide to set the cutoff fairly high, so that manifest discomfort on the part of some others lies below the chosen threshold of my moral responsibility, I have to live with the knowledge that this is so. Many people succeed in doing this with respect to the homeless, the unemployed, the victims of war and disaster in other countries. The rest of us really have no ground on which to judge them morally inadequate, provided they have confronted the situation and decided what demands it makes on them and what strategy they mean to follow to meet those demands. We are in no position to condemn them even if we happen ourselves to be more sensitive and more active in doing good. That in turn is a claim we should make humbly if at all. (You are invited to examine your own behavior in these and similar respects.)

Nobody can be expected to carry the whole burden of the ills that beset others, nor even to take cognizance of them all. We would be overwhelmed and paralyzed if we knew of all the suffering that is endured locally, let alone far away. At the same time nobody has an excuse for complete indifference or inactivity. I shall never have done enough, but doing something is better than doing nothing. Where I come to rest between these extremes will be a function of my awareness and my sensitivity. Reading moral theory, if I let myself be challenged by it and do not take it as an academic exercise, should have the effect of making it harder to satisfy myself on this point.

Notes

1. Immanuel Kant, *Foundations of the Metaphysics of Morals*, trans. L. W. Beck (Indianapolis, Ind.: Library of Liberal Arts, 1950), p. 105.
2. Thomas Hobbes, *Leviathan,* ed. Richard Tuck (Cambridge: Cambridge University Press, 1991), p. 87.

XII

The Impossibility of a
Universal Aesthetics

58. Candidates for the Status of Universal Value

Freedom, as we have seen, is a universal instrumental value; end values are to be sought in the objects and states of affairs in whose pursuit freedom is exercised. Freedom stands for possibility, but this possibility is a possibility of future actualities. The distinction between instrumental and end values leads to a separation of moral questions, those having to do with freedom, from aesthetic questions in the broad sense, those having to do with the ultimate ends served by freedom. In an imperfect world freedom itself may seem a sufficient end, and for an agent to consecrate his or her freedom to the task of securing freedom for others has always seemed an honorable and meaningful course of action. But a life spent in such a task would be a purely moral life, not an aesthetic one, and sooner or later somebody must use freedom for an end beyond itself if so much devotion is to be justified.

A case could be made for the view that possibility itself is the free agent's most precious possession, better than any actuality that might emerge from it: to travel hopefully is better than to arrive. The traveler, however, is hoping for something, even if it is only an ideal and unattainable destination. As long as it remains future, a future actuality is still a possibility. The aesthetic goal may never be reached, but once conceived it is a particular possibility and no longer possibility in general. As a matter of fact, actualities—works of art, for instance—do emerge, so that this argument is academic. The discipline of aesthetics deals with such actualities and the principles according to which they are and ought to be selected for realization, or the attempt at realization. Most of what falls under our extended concept of the aesthetic will properly be beneath the notice of the discipline, though no sharp boundary will separate it from what does attract such notice.

A universal ethics is possible, since we recognize a universal instrumental value, namely freedom. But a universal aesthetics is not possible. It would require a universal end value, and no evidence shows us that such a value exists, nor do we have any plausible reason for supposing that it ever could. The conditions of aspiration toward *some* end are laid down. They form the basis for the argument about freedom. But the nature of the end is freely posited by the creative imagination, and although investigation into the scope of the imagination might place limits on the range of conceivable ends, we have no reason to suppose that, within that range, we would all have to alight at the same point.

Some biological and even intellectual ends, common to human beings with inherited constitutions and drives, can be posited without having to resort to the creative imagination. A descriptive study of values actually expressed might lead to the formulation of a universal goal: the state of the world an ideally rational agent would prefer if confronted with the set of all possible alternatives, the state whose realization, therefore, would be the object of the exercise of freedom. But this does not take us as far as aesthetics; indeed, it hardly takes us further than we have already come. For quite apart from the difficulty of formulating the alternatives (being sure we had them all), we would still be able to ask, supposing that such an ideally preferable state of the world had been achieved, what we would want then. One of the characteristics of the ideally desirable state would surely have to be the freedom to seek yet further ends, and this would restore the division between instruments and ends.

A strong tradition in the history of philosophy, to which Plato, Aristotle, Spinoza, and Whitehead belong, argues that we can point to an end toward which human aspiration moves universally, and identifies this end with God. This is a powerful idea, though the variation among conceptions of God argues against the thesis of universality. A God who exists is already actual, and nothing actual can be an end value in our sense, that is, one whose realization as actual involves movement toward the future. Conversely, a God who embodied the universal end value in this sense could not yet exist.

Alfred North Whitehead (1861–1947), English philosopher and mathematician. He collaborated with Russell (see p. 30) on the foundations of logic (*Principia Mathematica*). His later work, much of it written in America, developed a philosophy of process, solving the problem of the relation of matter to thought by attributing elementary thought-like properties to material entities.

An existing state can embody a value when agents aspire to preserve it, possess it, or in some other way change their relationship to it, but in this case the preservation or possession really forms the end value. So coming into the presence of, or achieving union with, God might function as an end value for those who are theologically inclined. In Whitehead's view, God is "the lure of feeling." This is a variant on a familiar idea in the history of thought, according to which the aspiration toward God serves as the motive power of the universe, the Unmoved Mover, the "one far-off divine event to which the whole creation moves," as Alfred Lord Tennyson put it in *In Memoriam*.

The idea of God has been used to justify some of the noblest (as well as some of the basest) of human actions, and has thus served in many cases as an end value, but nothing in the situation warrants a distinction between this value and others as religious rather than aesthetic. If the idea of God has arisen as a consequence of human striving towards the highest ideals, God might properly be regarded as a work of art. Voltaire said, "If God did not exist, it would be necessary to invent him." Without intending a mere parody on this remark (but keeping Voltaire's gendering of God for purposes of symmetry), we might say that if God existed he would be our greatest invention. On the other hand, if God already exists he presumably has his own values, among which might be union with his creatures, as theirs might be union with him. But to the extent that this union is conceived as atemporal, it means the end of value as we know it and is properly held at a decent eschatological distance.

Eschatology: The study of the last things, or the end of the world, from Greek *eskhatos,* "uttermost."

I do not intend to deny either the practical distinction between religion and art or the historical importance of religion to art. Just as the factual content of religious doctrine embodied early discoveries about the physical world, while its prescriptive content embodied early moral rules, so its ceremonial and liturgical content embodied an early concern for beauty. But the history of art is bound up with religion in a much more intimate way than the history of science or of morals, because the factual and prescriptive aspects of religion tend to be closed, and the received truth and the received law to change slowly, while the aesthetic aspect of religion is more friendly to experimentation. Art, accordingly, flourished under the protection of religion. Artistic innovation, having no cognitive content and thus posing no threat, could be dedicated to the glory of God, while innovation in theology or in morals would almost certainly be considered heretical.

And art served religion, by satisfying the aesthetic appetites of the people within the institutional framework of the church. The connection between order and value continues to hold here. Not only were the moral precepts of the church a reflection of the social order and a guarantee of its stability, but the example set by the church—especially in the lives of the saints, whose importance may have been far greater in aesthetic matters than in moral ones—offered to plain men and women a conception of the possibilities for order in their own lives. Imitation of the saints and devotion to them in their chapels and festivals offered opportunities for the practice of art, as opposed to its passive enjoyment. The decline of religion has had far more serious consequences for art, in the generalized sense understood in this book, than for morals. In its more formal aspects, religion is a civilizing influence, and mass culture, largely freed from this influence, has relapsed rapidly into barbarism.

59. The Nature of Art and Its Relation to Morality

We would nevertheless be mistaken if we argued, from these considerations, that religion is necessary to art, any more than it is necessary for science and morals. We can easily understand why so much great art has been religious. We may not so readily see that the art dignified the religion, and not the other way round, especially since artists have often insisted on giving God credit for their achievements. This tendency to underrate human creativity and to assume that, if something noble or beautiful emerges from the average squalor of the human condition, it must be explained by reference to transcendent principles, is unfortunate and can be harmful. Potentially creative people may become discouraged if they think they have to meet special conditions of inspiration. Plain men and women can and do create order without help from above. The practice of art is the creation of order in its most characteristically human form, an affirmation of freedom and a denial of any dependence.

Art always leads to novelty. This novelty cannot be total; creators and authors do not begin from nothing. A new order is only a reordering of material that was in the world all along, and the nature of the artist's material as well as the need to be understood prevents anything like a complete reordering. But an artwork can never be a mere reproduction or duplication of a previously existing order.

Creator, author: Latin *creo*, "to make", is connected to *cresco*, "to grow"; the root gives us not only "create" but also "increase" and "crescent." "Author" is from a Latin root meaning "to augment" (see p. 58). These origins are significant, reflecting as they do the idea that artists and writers work in the context of already existing works: imitating, borrowing, distorting—and eventually producing (if the new work is successful) something greater or better.

Art is the aspect of human activity that most characteristically looks to the future, and to a future that is not like the past. Art that does not do this betrays the function of art. In this lies one of the principal differences between art and science: a condition of the success of science is that the future should be exactly like the past. But the work of art need not—although it often does—serve anything beyond itself, or more accurately anything beyond the immediate satisfaction of the artist or spectator. To the extent that artists have didactic as well as aesthetic intentions, they create something that, while it is no less a work of art, is also something more. Art may have moral implications, but that is not part of its definition as art.

As far as that goes, nothing external distinguishes one manifestation of novelty from any other if neither serves an end beyond itself. Both are directed inward; neither by definition refers outside to any objective standard. But ordinary usage would not say that every creation of order for its own sake is art. Accordingly, in order to separate true art from play or aimless doodling as well as from the purely decorative aspects of crafts such as cooking and millinery, aesthetic theory appeals to such concepts as emotional expression and symbolic representation. But the decorative impulse, like the impulse to play, belongs to the same category as the impulse to create what are ordinarily called works of art, and the products of those impulses have their place along with artworks in the domain of end values.

That art is usually embodied in works—objects or events occupying space and time—has provided a convenient distinction between it and a good deal of merely aimless activity. Every object and every action is an event occupying space and time, but a work or a performance has traditionally been regarded as a special object or event. Some developments in modern and postmodern art have broken down this distinction by showing that nothing is sacred about the form that aesthetic activity must take. This is especially true of limiting cases like pop art, "happenings," and aleatory music, that is, music whose performance incorporates random elements. The institutional theory of art, according to which art is defined as what circulates in the art world, stands the traditional view on its head. The end values embodied in artworks are not sought because of their aesthetic character; instead, their aesthetic character derives from their having being chosen by members of a given community—say, New Yorkers—as end values.

The debate will continue as to what constitutes good art and what bad. Making the criteria for good art stringent and exclusive is surely desirable. However, the subject of our inquiry is not art as such but a value theory in which it is contrasted with morality, and the question for the theory is this: what actions are to be judged according to aesthetic criteria? The answer must be all genuine actions (that is, excluding reflex reactions) that are neither wholly sustaining actions nor judged according to moral criteria. In other words, all free actions whatever that are not necessary for survival and do not affect, more or less directly, the freedom of others fall into the extended category of the aesthetic.

Some of these actions can be lumped together as ritual or conventional, and in these cases the aesthetic judgment will stand for or against a culture rather than an individual. Such judgments are made less readily now than was once the case, doctrines of cultural relativism having undermined our confidence in our own conventional behavior as a touchstone of value. But if we are to have any aesthetics at all, we may just as well have an aesthetics of culture as one of individual action: the problems they pose are essentially the same. As far as the individual is concerned, conventional actions may be taken as culturally determined, and the problem of aesthetic life thus simplified.

If freedom serves any end beyond itself, this analysis shows that that end must be sought in the realm of the aesthetic. The reason why freedom ultimately matters is because it frees us to seek such an end. Since the argument for morality is that it preserves freedom, the relation between the moral and the aesthetic may be summed up in the following aphorism: *the function of morality is to preserve the possibility of art*. Free agents need not create works of art (in the broad sense intended here), but their ability to do so is the badge of their freedom. This idea is so fundamental that the exercise of this ability may be taken as the badge of their humanity itself.

The trouble with all this is that it lends support to an aestheticism that says, "I have tried to make my life a work of art," and indulges in gestures and vanity. When I reduce the sphere of the moral to its essentials and at the same time enlarge the sphere of the aesthetic, I simply mean that in a materially privileged society—one in which people have leisure to pursue activities not strictly necessary for survival—aesthetic criteria have to be invoked for the purpose of judging most of what most people do most of the time. Such criteria are relative to class, economic standing, education, and other factors. Strictly applied, the criteria may show that even more of modern life is ugly than already appears on its surface. But the ugliness with which we have unwittingly surrounded ourselves is not necessarily redeemed by a conscious attempt at the aesthetic life. Fatally bad art can easily be produced by aesthetic concentration, just as surprisingly good art is sometimes produced in the process of doing something entirely different.

Another way of saying all this is that the end beyond freedom, which freedom serves, is not art. Art sometimes emerges in the serving of such an end, and works of art are the enduring record of its having been served. The nature of the work often changes as it progresses, but the artist has a compulsion to continue until it is finished or until interest in that way of achieving the aesthetic end evaporates.

60. The Nonspecificity of End Values

What the end itself ought to be is not a matter of dispute, since no grounds for the unconditional settlement of such a dispute are available. What it has been in various cases we can learn from the testimony of articulate men and women in all ages. But already this way of talking is leading us imperceptibly toward the transcendent, by suggesting that in addition to particular ends, identifiable states of the world that are constituted as values, we might discover a supreme end or an ultimate value that would give a single order and direction to the life of the individual.

This would no doubt be gratifying if it were the case, and a good many people have been fortunate enough to find something functionally equivalent to such an end, such as the Holy Grail or the philosophers' stone. If they had ever attained it, they would no doubt have been quickly disappointed, since the felicity that was to follow the successful consummation of the quest could not possibly, in these cases, have been as exciting as the quest itself. Some religious people have cleverly averted the possibility of such disappointments by putting off the state of felicity until after death. The conditions of this afterlife are not generally specified in detail, but it is agreed that, at least for the elect, they will be better than the miserable existence to which we have become accustomed on earth.

The prevalence of this idea provides a clue to the structure of end values. Values are future states of the world, but at first all we know about them may be that they are better than the present state of the world. Our rejection of the present state sets us off on an exploratory path, along which we are able to recognize states as better or worse than the initial one and to modify our actions accordingly. This search process is usually guided by some conception of the desired end, as was suggested at the conclusion of section 46; the point is that the conception may be much less specific than was implied there.

Blank canvases represent to artists inherently unsatisfactory states of the world. Anybody can change that situation, given a minimum of equipment, but the artist knows which changes are satisfactory and which are not. Chimpanzees can paint, some of them rather well, but they find it hard to stop painting. They always spoil their work, reducing it in the end to formless grey-brown, if a human agent is not present to snatch the canvas away at an appropriate moment. Even the artist may not always know in detail what order is being sought until it appears, and the same is often true for ordinary people in pursuit of their own aesthetic ends. Still we all recognize, with some assurance, states of the world that do embody values and that we therefore wish to preserve.

Some empirical generalizations about such states are possible, but only at the crudest level, since what is acceptable depends on idiosyncrasies of physiology, taste, education, and the like. An individual's values may change, generally in a stepwise fashion, on exposure to progressively different experiences, and in this way tastes may be cultivated and judgment refined. What makes such a change a change for the better is a matter for dispute. The criteria that separate what is conventionally called "art" from all the other activities appropriately judged by aesthetic canons are complex. But we can safely leave them aside. As far as the conventional meaning of the term goes, this book is not about aesthetics at all.

61. An Apparent Case of Retrospective Evaluation

The existence of works of art as valued objects does pose a difficulty for the theory. Art criticism seems to be a pure case of retrospective evaluation, since the work is finished and cannot be tampered with. This appears to contradict the view that value is always future-referential. Here the question really is, not what should be brought into being, but what should be preserved, what should be exhibited, what large sums should be paid for, what should be reproduced in texts, or studied by art students, and into the presence of what works should people take the trouble to bring themselves. Museums dispose works of art in such a way that the value that consists in my having them temporarily incorporated into my world may be realized at will. All these considerations involve future states, as the theory requires.

In this light the work of art, regarded simply as a physical object, is not a carrier but a generator of value. In the absence of appropriate conditions, the work cannot be said to have any value at all. Chief among these conditions will be the presence of human beings able to recognize and seek the values that are generated, which often involve special knowledge and long experience. The converse of this proposition, which has been recognized and exploited by artists like Marcel Duchamp and Andy Warhol, who made artworks from ready-made or commonplace articles like urinals and

Campbell's soup cans, is that virtually valueless physical objects may acquire high value if people can be induced to regard them as works of art.

Marcel Duchamp (1887–1968), French painter. He was influential in Cubism, and in the nihilistic and absurdist Dada movement.

Andy Warhol (1929–1987), American painter and filmmaker. He was a leading figure in pop art, and is remembered for having said that everyone will be famous for 15 minutes.

Induced, not obliged: nothing can compel a given individual to attend to any particular art form, let alone agree with someone else's estimate of the value of a work in that form. That is the force of the title of this chapter. It denies the possibility of a universally normative aesthetics, that is, of a universally valid set of prescriptions about ends to be sought by free action, including the quintessentially free actions of the artist. Meta-aesthetics, the analysis of discourse about art, is untouched by this claim; it stands as good a chance of establishing itself as any metaphilosophical enterprise.

XIII

A General Theory of Value

62. Egocentricity and Temporality

The preceding chapters have served three purposes. They have dealt with several philosophical problems that must be taken into account in the construction of an efficacious theory of value, including the nature of value as distinct from fact and the freedom of the agent. They have indicated an essential division of values into instrumental and end values, and on the basis of this distinction they have limited the possibility of a universal theory to the instrumental (that is, the moral) side. And they have introduced in an unsystematic way the elements of a possible theoretical model for moral value. The structure of this model must now be made explicit.

First, let me make one or two general remarks about the main features of the theory and recapitulate some of the ways in which it is to be distinguished from scientific theory. Its two chief characteristics are (1) that it contains an essential ingredient of temporality, and (2) that it is egocentric. The theory's being egocentric does not make it *humanistic*; it does not say that humans are the necessary center of the universe, but that each human being is the contingent center of his or her own universe. And the theory does not say that human beings embody the highest value, but that each man or woman must decide for himself or herself what is the highest value.

To claim that each individual is the judge of value is only to recognize that, if other people or other beings make judgments of value and act on them, the acceptance or rejection of those acts and judgments is still the individual responsibility of each person who comes to know them. The individual cannot act on them and expect others—for example, those who formulated the judgments or set the example for the action—to take responsibility for the consequences of that action. To claim that each person embodies a value is often confounded with the claim that each person is the judge of value, but it is a quite separate movement of thought, which each person is free to make and which can be argued for on the basis of the theory, although it is not essential to the theory.

What distinguishes the theory of value from scientific theory is the element of temporality, for egocentricity is common to both. The scientific observer is as isolated in his or her observations as the moral agent is in his or her actions. Observation and action both take place in a complex human setting. The scientist depends on instruments and on a descriptive language that has been refined by centuries of development; the moral agent similarly makes use of machines and sources of energy, and of a language of request and command, which are shared with the rest of society. But the making of observations and the initiation of action are individual matters, even when the final outcome can only be achieved collectively. I choose to associate myself with a collective enterprise, and I have responsibility for my part in it. Perhaps I decide that I do not like the enterprise, and go through with it only because of the consequences of not doing so. Still, my honoring the commitment, even if it seems forced by the fact that the consequences of withdrawal would be worse than the consequences of continuing, is in the end my free individual choice.

This talk of consequences is a reflection of the temporality of value, every voluntary action being taken for the sake of and judged in the light of its probable consequences. While science throws light on the determination of events, the theory of value throws light on the consequences of action. The sequence may be the same, an action A causing an event E, but the value analysis precedes A, whereas the scientific analysis follows E. If similar cases have been observed in the past, then the scientist can predict that E will be a probable consequence of A. Unless such a prediction is possible, the agent will not know whether E is a probable consequence of A, and will not be able to assess responsibility for A as causing it. Ignorance of causal relations, however, is no excuse: if in doubt, the agent should conduct his or her own inquiry.

No separation of the range of activity of science and value is therefore possible. The distinction between them nevertheless remains: they deal with the same world, but from different temporal perspectives. To put it in another way, its location and date do not enter into a scientific observation essentially; the observation relates in the same manner to other observations of the same kind whenever and wherever it is made. The location of an observation of value is similarly irrelevant, but its date is integral to it and determines the possibility of its being effectively related to other observations.

Mattering is the phenomenological clue to value. The behavior of the verb "to matter" is the clue to it in ordinary language. "It doesn't matter" dismisses what is referred to from further consideration, as merely factual, or it expresses indifference between alternative states of the world. Extreme situations in which we come near to loss or disaster "show us what really matters." Heidegger makes "care" (*Sorge*) the characteristic mark of human "being-in-the-world," something we cannot humanly exist without.[1] We do not choose *that* things will matter, any more than we choose to exist; they simply do matter. Under some circumstances, we may choose *which* things will matter. We may also come to see that some things matter to which we were formerly indifferent, and that some things we passionately cared for do not matter much after all. But these realizations reflect changes in our situation, rather than properties of things about which we were at first mistaken and then enlightened.

> *Mattering:* Latin *materia* is cognate with *mater*, "mother." *Materia* is building material, mainly wood (the island of *Madeira* was so called because it had fine trees for shipbuilding), but also the substance out of which human beings are made. According to the Aristotelian theory of matter and form, the form of the child is imposed by the father on matter provided by the mother. The "matter at hand" thus came to mean the substance of argument or dispute. What is not material to the case is dismissed, does not matter. The idea is clear: what matters is what is important to us, what we care about.

63. Situations and Termini

The notion of situation is crucial. In earlier chapters the contrast between science and the theory of value was expressed principally in terms of "states of the world," in order to stress the temporal asymmetry involved. Because value enters only from an individual perspective, this was sometimes modified to "states of *my* world." But this formulation still preserves a separation between the subject and the world that, while necessary for analytic purposes, misrepresents the phenomenological situation. "Situation" consists of the individual *in* his or her world, the world encompassing the individual. When we say, in a discussion of questions of value, that the world is or ought to be thus-and-so, we really refer to the situation of some person or persons. Specifying a situation involves description, but of a more complex kind than that required to specify a state of the world, so that, for example, a change in situation might come about without overt change in the state of the physical world. The transition from x to y in the expression

$$x + iy$$

introduced in section 30 may express a change in the state of the subject instead of or in addition to a change in the state of the world. As far as that goes, the situation of an individual can never reflect adequately the state of the world, since that would require complete knowledge. The individual's situation may fail to reflect the state of the world in major respects (for example, someone who has cancer but does not know it) or may not reflect it at all (for example, a patient with catatonic schizophrenia).

The theory of value concerns itself with changes in situation, and hence only with such changes in the state of the physical world as these may entail. The change goes from x to y; it begins because x is different from y and ends when they have been brought into coincidence. The empirical foundations of the theory must therefore be in episodes that have their points of departure in something that "is the matter," as Dewey puts it,[2] and their terminus in some resolution of the initial dissonance.

The differences between Dewey's theory and mine deserve comment.

(1) For Dewey, something's "being the matter" means a *problem*. "Desires do not arise," he adds, "when things are going completely smoothly." For me mattering can and does occur in situations having no problematic aspects. Otherwise, value would be a function of the imperfection of the world. We might ask, suppose nothing were wrong? Suppose all agents had freedom both positively and negatively, so that nothing stood between them and the object of their desires? If value ceased to be operative under these circumstances, we would presumably all commit suicide or else be intolerably bored. Instead, we would invent new values, new ways of changing some aspect of the world; we would resort to art in its pure form.

(2) Dewey rejects the instrumental value–end value distinction on the grounds that instrumentalities become values in themselves, and that the claim to be pursuing end values may be used as an excuse for oppression, since I may consider my end values more important than someone else's instrumental values. The theory I present here would not allow that to happen, since the principle of indifference makes me attach to the freedom of any other agent importance equal to my own, and my own freedom is no less a value than any end I can achieve by exercising it. And although it may be that, in the struggle for freedom, freedom itself seems an end beyond which nothing matters, still when freedom has been won the question remains of what is to be done with it. The claim that freedom never will be won does not terminate the argument. That might be contingently true (although I do not believe it is), but the question would still be legitimate,

Bedazzled (1967; director Stanley Donen)
Avarice—petty avarice to be sure: the Devil (Peter Cook), who has arranged a date between a short-order cook (Dudley Moore) and the object of his affections (Eleanor Bron), intrudes by trying to collect money for the National Society for the Promotion of Depraved Criminals.

and it could not be answered without reference to some end beyond the instrumentality.

The pragmatic account, then, is not entirely adequate. Nothing need be conventionally wrong in order to start a value-driven process of change, and it may end without anything having being put conventionally right. The goal may not remain constant throughout, but may adapt itself in the course of the action, so that a situation which begins unsatisfactorily as

$$x + iy$$

may end satisfactorily as

$$z + iz.$$

The form of this last expression may be taken as defining the concept of *satisfaction*. I am satisfied when no further change in the situation is called for, and only then: when what is the case and what ought to be the case, with respect to the matter in hand, are one and the same.

The phenomenological situation may also be described in terms of acceptance and rejection. These are not strictly equivalent to mattering positively and mattering negatively, since we may reject something good for something better, or accept something bad for the want of anything better. But acceptance and rejection provide the dynamics of choice and action. The rejection of a situation ordinarily manifests itself in a movement out of that situation into some other, while its acceptance means the avoidance of any such movement. The movement may or may not be brought about directly by action, since situations can be counted on to change, sooner or later, if left alone. One possibility for a person who rejects his or her situation is to *hope* that it will change into an acceptable one, although the more unusual course is to take action, that is, to *work*. If an acceptable situation does come about, we may say that the process has reached a *terminus of satisfaction*. If neither hoping nor working for an acceptable situation succeeds in producing one, the agent can still end the process, in one of two ways: (1) by ceasing to hope or work but continuing to reject the situation, which may be called a *terminus of despair*, or (2) by changing the criteria of satisfaction and accepting the situation that was formerly rejected, which may be called a *terminus of resignation*.

The function of the theory of value is to guide the agent toward termini of satisfaction. The test of the theory's adequacy lies in its success in doing so, or, if that fails, in its ability to explain what went wrong. But if the test is to be fair, the agent must have followed the theory, that is, must have taken its hypotheses seriously. The test of a scientific theory is its ability to make predictions. If one of the hypotheses of the theory is that energy is conserved, if the prediction is based on the assumption that the energy involved in the process in question remains constant, and if in spite of this fact the experimenter takes no pains to protect the experiment from extraneous energy, the prediction will probably fail. Similarly, if one of the hypotheses of the theory of value is that everyone is free, if the guidance offered by the theory requires the agent to take account of the effect of his or her actions on other people and of their likely response, and if in spite of this fact the agent proceeds as though other people did not exist, the outcome is unlikely to be satisfactory.

One reason why disagreements in ethics have remained unresolved is that few ethical theories have been thoroughly worked out, and still fewer have been put into consistent practice by many people over any length of time. Some sets of rules deriving their authority from transcendent principles have had a measure of success, but even there the number of people following the rules faithfully has been small (they have generally been called saints), and the rules have gone by the board when different transcendent principles have come into conflict with one another.

64. A Schema for the Theory of Value

Table 13.1 assembles in one place the elements that have been introduced separately in the foregoing pages and shows the interconnections between them. It presents more clearly than is possible in a discursive account the moral theory toward which the argument of this book has been directed, but some things about it require clarification.

(1) The four levels differ somewhat from the four levels of Table 13-1. The distinction made there between the phenomenological and the descriptive is not necessary here, so they are merged into one, called the *experiential*. The theoretical level remains unchanged— that is, the propositions found in it are hypotheses. But the nomological level has been divided into two in the schema. The reason for this is that in moral inquiry we encounter two kinds of rule. *Ad hoc* rules, here called "inductive strategies," are generalized from the experience of attempts to satisfy desires. Moral rules properly so called are derived from moral principles. The reconciliation of these two kinds of rule is one of the major tasks of ethics.

(2) Although the hypothetical principles are given explicitly, the rules and other elements are indicated but not given in detail. The function of the schema is to show the structure of ethics, not to present a finished system.

(3) The factual elements of the individual experience of nature (which enter into complex descriptions but not into rules) do not appear in the schema. Learning to cope with them falls under the heading of prudence, not under the heading of morality. A factual element is present in the form of the desires of other people—also, by hypothesis, free agents—which constitute part of the setting for moral action.

(4) The schema is said to be simply for the theory of value, although it has to do only with moral value. This reflects the conviction that only moral values yield to this kind of analysis, aesthetic values (that is, in the language of this book, all end values) being incapable of generalization for everyone.

The impossibility of a universal aesthetics is embodied in one of the principles of the theory. Remember that a principle is just a hypothesis that is accepted as true. In addition to the metaphysical hypothesis of freedom, two explicitly normative hypotheses are required. The first is the hypothesis of the equivalence of freedoms, which we accepted as the principle of indifference, discussed in section 52. This principle forbids one person to override another's freedom for selfish ends. The other is the hypothesis, introduced in section 56, that no universal end value exists. If accepted as a principle, this would forbid the overriding of any person's freedom for transcendent ends.

We might call this new principle the *principle of immanence*. Transcendent ends that have been used in the past as excuses for the suppression of individual freedoms are by no means limited to religious ones; restraints

Table 13-1 General Schema for the Theory of Value

Levels	Descriptive Elements	Prescriptive Elements
Theoretical	Human beings are free, i.e., their actions can affect the course of events.	Nobody's freedom ought to be preferred to anyone else's. There is no end value such that all people should devote their freedom to achieving it.

Nomological (deductive)	Definition of free action as
	1. intended
	2. unconstrained
	3. materially equipped
	4. informed
	  a. as to the state of the world, and
	  b. as to the laws governing it
	
	Laws of psychology and the social sciences, etc.
		Rules for the preservation and equitable distribution of individual freedoms.
		1. requirement of self-knowledge
		2. injunction against murder and other, less obvious forms of interference
		3. requirement of sharing with respect to natural resources
		4a. injunctions against lying and other, less obvious forms of deception
		4b. requirement of universal education and access to results of research

Nomological (inductive)	Other people's strategies → Modified strategies (some ruled out as immoral or impractical)	Inductive strategies for the achievement of end values
Experiential	Other people's desires Satisfactions (acceptable termini, modified desires, etc.)	Original desires (raw conations)

have been imposed in the name of history, of the nation-state, of the family, of class or race solidarity. The principle of immanence insists that the individual agent's values can be found only within his or her experience and feeling. Value may never be imposed from without.

Immanent: From Latin *maneo,"* to remain," the prefix *in-* (*im-* when followed by "m") having the same sense in Latin as in English. "Immanent" is an antonym of "transcendent"; it means "remaining within" as opposed to "climbing beyond."

Both principles, of indifference and of immanence, are formulated negatively, which is in keeping with the role of morality as preserving the possibility of free action, and not in any way dictating the nature of that action. The search for positive moral principles, in the sense of directives toward a highest moral good for everyone, is vain. What could possibly be the object of such a search? The highest moral good for me is a situation in which I hinder none of my fellow human beings from the pursuit of their highest aesthetic goods, in which indeed I help them to the best of my power. It cannot include the pursuit of my aesthetic goods. But my unhindered or assisted pursuit of my highest aesthetic goods must by symmetry be part of their highest moral good. For anyone to share in detail the moral obligations of another hence becomes logically impossible. For everyone else has as moral a good the agent in question can have only as aesthetic, namely, the means to achieve his or her end values. Moral obligations are shared in principle, but the application of principle to individual cases does not lead to a particular good that will be the highest, morally, for all human agents. At best it leads to a formula that has as many instantiations as there are agents.

In conjunction with the definition of complex freedom in section 47, the deductive consequences of these principles are a series of rules governing the behavior of human beings toward one another. The only moral objectives one moral agent can entertain with respect to another are, first, to allow and, second, to assist the second agent to achieve his or her satisfactions in his or her way. In the table the rules are numbered to correspond with the elements of the definition of free action in the adjoining column.

The deductive movement from the principles through the rules meets an inductive movement from the agent's desires to a series of ad hoc strategies for satisfying them. This is where the rectification of desire that is the function of the theory takes place. If I have been convinced by the theory and have resolved to take it seriously, I will modify my strategies in the light of the restrictions the theory imposes on them; that is, I will consider whether the strategies are consistent with the rules, and if they are not I will discard them. This is the essence of moral behavior. The individual's responsibility is not primarily to follow the rules as positive injunctions. Two rules in the table that are positively formulated, (3) and (4b), require cooperative action, and their implications are mainly political. The function of the rules for the individual agent is to inhibit courses of action that are inconsistent with the principles.

The modified strategies (on which, as the table shows, the whole argument focuses) are the joint product of (1) the individual's strategies for the satisfaction of his or her own desires, (2) that individual's understanding of other people's probable strategies (from a knowledge of their patterns of behavior or from information about their desires), and (3) his or her consideration of the rules. We could modify strategies without considering the rules, taking account only of what other people are likely to do and taking advantage of their weaknesses. One function of the rules is to engender scruples about that kind of behavior. The unscrupulous person takes a moral risk in ignoring the rules. This is not yet necessarily immoral in fact, although it is likely to become so. But it may be judged immoral in principle, since a probable consequence of deliberately ignoring the rules is to become immoral in fact.

65. The Problem of Confirmation

This is a hypothetical model, subject to test. If we accept *these* hypotheses as true, and not some others, shall we get the world we want? But what world do we want? Ultimately each of us has to find his or her answer to that question. Other people cannot answer it for us any more than we can answer it for them. This being the case, we can choose any world we like. But other people will do so too, and we have therefore to come to a point of balance among these free choices. We have to respect the autonomy of other people's values and not attempt a Procrustean classification, even in terms of "happiness" or "goodness," which do not appear in the schema.

> *Procrustes:* A mythological figure, defeated by the hero Theseus. Procrustes had two beds, one short and one long; he would stretch short victims to fit the long bed and cut off the feet of tall victims to fit the short bed. "Procrustean" has therefore come to mean forcing something into a predetermined (or preconceived) pattern or category, rather than respecting differences.

What makes other people happy is none of my business, unless they invite me to consider it as such. My observance of moral rules clears the way for them to follow happiness if they want to, to the extent that this can be done without restricting the freedom of others to follow *their* own inclinations. But in one sense, according to the theory, I and all these others must want the same world. We must all want that world in which each of us has the best chance of getting the other things he or she wants. My empirically testable claim is that under the assumptions of this theory—namely, the principles that no justification can be provided for differential treatment of free agents and no transcendent objectives are to be imposed—the probability of the values involved is maximized. Another way of formulating it is to say that any systematic discrimination whatever, or any insistence on transcendent principles, will inevitably reduce the probability of the achievement of value for everyone. The verification of this claim is not easy—it would require a large-scale human experiment—but without waiting for that we are free to follow the strategy for scientific theory, and adhere to the principles until they are falsified by evidence. If enough of us did so, that would be the large-scale experiment. In this regard the theory advocated here has a considerable advantage over most of the available alternatives.

You may think that the concept of such a theory is utopian, that the situation is too complex, that the balancing of one freedom against another involves the comparison of incommensurables, and so on. The analysis needs to be supplemented on the practical level with a detailed consideration of cases, such as those provided at the end of this book. My main intention has been to clarify the rational foundations of morality, and to do this is in a way that encourages individuals to look to elementary moral principles for the guidance of their actions. If in every action individual citizens, individual legislators, and individual leaders were to keep in mind the principles of indifference and of immanence and apply them honestly for themselves, utopia would be upon us.

Notes

1. Martin Heidegger, *Being and Time,* trans. J. McQuarrie and E. S. Robinson (New York: Harper & Row, 1962), p. 274.
2. John Dewey, *Theory of Valuation* (Chicago: University of Chicago Press, 1939), p. 33.

XIV

Some Consequences of the Theory

66. Conventional Morality

Nothing prevents any individual from applying moral theory directly to his or her own circumstances. But the questions of detail raised by the attempt to do this may be too difficult for quiet resolution, or too complicated for a timely decision. In natural science we do not always have to go back to first principles, because we can (once we have grasped the structure of scientific theory) rely on other people's results without abandoning the ideal of understanding. Similarly in ethics we can follow rules formulated by others without abandoning the ideal of self-determination. The requirement here is that we should understand the principles from which the rules are derived and the conditions under which they are intended to apply. I take the working out of such rules to be the most pressing task of practical ethics. As things stand, too few of the rules people live by are warranted in terms of universally applicable principles.

In this penultimate chapter I wish to indicate briefly some of the more obvious practical implications of the theory of value sketched in the foregoing pages. The usual prohibitions of murder, lying, stealing, and so forth come out as expected, although not always for the usual reasons. Murder is the ultimate deprivation of freedom, and is therefore necessarily immoral. The problem of killing in self-defense is a symmetrical one in which the principle of indifference leaves the outcome open. I have no reason to give my freedom precedence over that of my attacker, but on the other hand I have no reason to give his or her freedom precedence either. Thus I cannot be condemned for taking my own part in the matter. My action is a reaction to restore what was formerly an equilibrium; the attacker who is killed in self-defense might be said to have committed suicide indirectly. Suicide is not immoral as such. If its consequences were limited to the agent who commits it, I could according to the theory have no morally grounded objection to it. But this is hardly ever the case. The suicide who leaves dependents traumatized or unprovided for, who paralyzes friends and family with grief, who places a burden on rescue services and emergency rooms, is immoral on many counts. People who are about to do away with themselves may not be interested in the morality of their action, but a lively sense of the consequences they will leave behind might have a deterrent effect.

Lying, however, is not necessarily immoral; it is so only to the extent that information required by some agent in deciding on a course of action is withheld or falsified. But how can the liar know, for any given lie, that this is not the case, since actions are undertaken in a total context any element of which may contribute to the agent's decision? For example, if I tell a lie that has no direct bearing on any act the person to whom I tell it is about to undertake, I may still be offending against his or her freedom in other ways: by removing myself as a trustworthy source of information in connection with future acts, and by undermining confidence in the truthfulness of others even though they are still trustworthy. So the prima facie injunction against lying stands. A parallel case could be made for promise-keeping.

Prima facie: Latin *facies* meant "shape, form, figure," hence "outward appearance," especially of the face (our word for which we obviously get from the same root). So "prima facie" means "on first appearance," "at first sight," in other words before contexts and conditions have been established, before reflective deliberation. Prima facie judgments are not to be confused with a priori ones! (See p. 32).

Similarly with stealing: to remove an object that contributes nothing to the antecedents of its owner's free action cannot be considered immoral, but to know that this is the case is virtually impossible. The concept of personal property reflects the fact that human beings have always created a material environment for themselves as a setting not only for free action but also for the sustaining actions that we have seen to be prerequisite to free action. Any wanton disturbance of that environment will have an indirect effect on freedom. The extension of the concept of property to a miserly accumulation of wealth is unjustified because it violates the rule of the equitable distribution of resources. But that is a rule whose enforcement requires collective action, so that individual enterprise in relieving the rich of their surplus possessions cannot be condoned.

Even in these examples, the theory introduces a complexity that simple general injunctions cannot adequately reflect. For the freedom of the agent is not determined solely by external considerations, and we may, as has already been implied, interfere with people's freedom of action just as effectively—and therefore just as immorally—by destroying their confidence in themselves or others, or causing them to be preoccupied with fears or regrets, or making them miserable, as by physical coercion or even murder. In view of the physical, psychological, social, and economic conditions that must be met and the inhibitions that must be avoided, any actual realization of individual freedom presents a whole series of opportunities for interference, of which only the most obvious are covered by conventional morality. We may interfere with the genuine exercise of freedom by encouraging an apparent exercise of it that is bound to fail, for example, by making people want what they cannot have. Freedom in action is always freedom to do a number of things, and is thus always relative to those possibilities. I may be free to do A or B if I choose A or B, but not to do C if I choose C. If I do not know this but someone else does, and that person now holds out to me the desirability of C, he or she acts immorally. Freedom can be diminished just as surely by an enlargement of desire as by a curtailment of opportunity. This is the inverse of the Stoic and Cartesian maxim that we should change our desires rather than the order of the world.

67. Cases Judged by Consequences

For the individual, then, the mark of moral responsibility is a sensitivity to the probable consequences of action as they affect the freedom of others. It is not an unthinking adherence to rules of conduct received from society. Mere conformity means that agents have learned nothing for themselves and have no reasons for behaving as they do, apart from the desire to avoid social embarrassment or other conditioned forms of distress such as shame or guilt. But people are always asking for such rules. Are promiscuous sexual relations wrong? Is doing drugs wrong? Is divorce wrong when there are small children? If such actions lead to physiological or psychological consequences that impair the freedom of some agent, the answer is yes, but a blanket condemnation is not possible in advance.

A likely consequence of unprotected sex with a partner about whose medical history you have any doubt is infection with a communicable disease like AIDS. If you contract the disease, no moral consequence immediately follows: you did it to yourself. But if you infect someone else, or die, moral consequences are all but inevitable (compare with the case of suicide, above). Another possible consequence of unprotected sex is the creation of a new agent; if the conditions of that agent's freedom cannot be adequately guaranteed, then again a moral offense has been committed. John Stuart Mill put the point forcefully: "to bring a child into existence," he wrote in *On Liberty*, "without a fair prospect of being able, not only to provide food for its body, but instruction and training for its mind, is a moral crime, both against the unfortunate offspring and against society."[1]

Drugs, and divorce involving children, almost invariably lead to the likely impairment of somebody's freedom. I need not make the case; you can do so yourself. But we cannot say that they always do. In all these cases, as in the case of lying, the prima facie injunction against the action, which is the rule received from society, need not be discarded, but the agent has to be on guard lest obedience to the rule should prove more immoral than breaking it. We can say that rules of practice always have exceptions, although a general moral rule such as the rule against interference with an agent's freedom has none.

I am aware that this insistence on consequences, the testing of the application of rules of practice (in the light of general rules) for every case, produces acute discomfort in many people. This is sometimes due to timidity about assuming the responsibility for moral decisions (as distinct from moral actions); this is modest and unobjectionable, although it is no excuse for shirking the responsibility. But such uneasiness sometimes reflects a conviction that no moral life—and perhaps no meaningful one— is possible without guarantees from a transcendent source, that the independent judgment of morality is beyond merely human competence, that the decline of belief in absolute standards is ominous and marks an age devoid of purpose and destiny.

This attitude is pernicious. Purpose and meaning and the destiny of human beings are where they have always been: in the human imagination. But the imagination of the holy men of old, the fathers of the country, and so on is no longer adequate to the situation, because the pace of change has accelerated to the point where every generation needs to redefine these concepts for itself, or come to the realization that they can safely be done without. Dogmatic and specific conclusions about purpose and destiny on a global scale are more dangerous than no conclusion at all. Each generation needs to assert this truth, if necessary against the crusading zeal of its elders.

68. Ideology and Political Morality

This brings me to political considerations. The theory is politically neutral, as it is ideologically neutral; it speaks of the freedom of human beings, not of blacks or whites, Christians or Muslims, Chinese or Americans, believers or atheists. And yet in the minds of most people the idea of freedom tends to be specialized as it applies to one of these groups or another, and the term has become a slogan, burdened with all the rhetorical and emotional tasks of propaganda. Not long ago—in the 1960s—America, the "land of the free," saw large segments of its population demonstrating for "Freedom, now!" At the same time America was fighting, in Vietnam, a war for freedom that deprived much of the Vietnamese population of its means of livelihood and caused the deaths of many innocent people. The concept of freedom is susceptible to radically different interpretations. But it is a complex concept, and these are simple interpretations and therefore partial ones.

Ideology: The term *idéologie* was coined by a group of French thinkers, the *idéologues*, whose principal member was Antoine Destutt de Tracy (1754–1836). Their aim was to develop a natural history and theory of ideas. But the term came to stand less for the study of ideas than for specific clusters of ideas, based on metaphysical claims and worked out in political practice. Because the ideas in question were often revolutionary, "ideology" acquired pejorative connotations.

The most striking recent illustration of conflict between partial interpretations is provided by the long-standing opposition between two great ideologies, which at the risk of serious oversimplification may be identified with socialism and capitalism. Even communism, although its state power in the old Soviet Union and Eastern Europe has collapsed, is not dead and survives intact in other places, such as China and Cuba. Two of the conditions of free action are the absence of restraint and the availability of material resources. Socialism emphasizes the equitable distribution of material resources, but at a price: that many individuals should be restrained. Capitalism emphasizes the freedom of enterprise, but also at a price: that many individuals should be deprived of material resources.

Socialism, capitalism, communism: These have become slogans rather than descriptive categories, though their origins are instructive. "Socialism" and "communism" derive obviously enough from society and community (see p. 138); although too much cannot be made of this contrast, we may note that socialism was meant to function politically within the system of state government, while communism envisaged the demise of the state, the "government of men" being replaced by the "administration of things." The root of "capitalism" is Latin *caput*, "head," which also gives "cattle" and "chattel"; wealth used to be counted in heads of cattle. (*Caput* also gives "chapter," so "chapter heading" is tautologous.) Capitalism assumes the accumulation of wealth and its multiplication by investment, but "state capitalism" and "welfare capitalism" are possible, so that capitalism need not always be unjust or exploitative.

The argument between these theories of social organization has usually proceeded in clichés, and it may be summed up in clichés. Socialism, says the capitalist, in its anxiety to liberate the working classes (who are often lazy and illiterate) places intolerable economic restrictions on the individual. A free enterprise economy is essential to the true prosperity of the working classes, who ought therefore to be content to leave things in the hands of their betters, and discouraged from collective action, if necessary by force. Capitalism, says the socialist, in its anxiety to keep the economy competitive (so as to satisfy the greed of the wealthy), allows an intolerable oppression of the working classes. The labor of the working classes is essential to the survival of the economy, which ought, therefore, to be considered to belong to them, and expropriated, if necessary by force. I make no apology for the extravagance of this language, which is a fairly accurate rendering of views still held by many people. The opposition extends to the level of definition: Roger Garaudy, a leading exponent of Marxism, once wrote: "For the bourgeoisie freedom is the maintenance of free enterprise, for the proletariat freedom is the destruction of this regime."[2]

Official representatives of both views have from time to time resorted to the manipulation of another condition for free action, namely, the availability of information. They have misrepresented the facts about the state of the world, about history, but above all about each other, as may be seen on a cursory inspection of what used to be taught about communism in American schools, and what used to be taught about capitalism in Russian schools. The result is that most of the common people of the world, both East and West, and in spite of the protestations of their leaders to the contrary, have been and largely remain in a state of effective bondage as far as their control over their eventual destiny is concerned. They have been and are in bondage to leaders no more intelligent and often less humane than themselves. This situation can be corrected only by the development of a morally responsible politics—which seems unlikely—or a politically sophisticated morality.

Bourgeoisie, proletariat: French *bourgeois* means "citizen," with connotations of property ownership, but its origins in the *bourg* or market village suggest small holdings. The *bourgeoisie* was not a land-owning class but gained power under capitalism by manufacturing and investment. Latin *proles* means "offspring" (compare English "prolific"); *proletarius*, in the classification of Roman citizens for taxation in time of war, meant a member of the lowest class, who had no money and could contribute only his children to the war effort.

Morality becomes political when its aims can be achieved only by the collective action of a whole society. I can abstain by myself from overt interference with the freedom of other people, but I cannot by myself provide more than a few other people with the material resources they require to achieve their private ends. If I find that I am overprivileged—for example, if I get much too rich—I can do something to put things right by philanthropy, as some of the great financiers of the Western world have done. But to correct the system in which some people get much too rich at the expense of other people requires collective action.

69. War and Revolution

It will not do to take such action precipitately, for example, by organizing a revolution. We should avoid violent adjustments that destroy more than they preserve. But unjust features of the system ought to be destroyed. Radical conservatism, the dialectical opposite of revolution, is equally unacceptable. Revolution coerces the freedom of moderates, conservatism suppresses it; in its radical form each therefore constitutes a morally objectionable basis for political organization.

The same argument applies to the waging of war. We cannot without oversimplifying say that war and revolution are always wrong. An intolerable situation might arise that could be corrected in no other way. But if it is wrong for one person to be the moral agent of the death of another, then the parties to a war should be sure that the benefits to be derived from it, judged according to the universal standard and not according to some local variant of it, are sufficiently great to expiate that wrong. This is difficult.

Many people think that the Second World War was, by this standard, a morally just war, mainly because of the atrocity of the Holocaust. But even if letting the Holocaust go unchecked would have been worse than fighting a war, reservations are plausible. Was war the only way to combat the Holocaust? Might more victims not have been saved in the absence of war, might the policy of extermination have been less hurried, might internal resistance to the regime have been strengthened? And if war was the best available strategy, even the morally best, did that make it a just war? Moral theories need to confront, though not many of them do, the possibility that in a given situation we can find no morally right thing to do, even though we must do something. If we choose the lesser of two evils, we must not forget that the lesser is still an evil.

Philosophers and statesmen have developed a body of doctrine about "just war," according to which wars are just if agreed conditions are satisfied in deciding to wage them (*jus ad bellum*), and agreed restraints are practiced in waging them (*jus in bello*). To satisfy the conditions of *jus ad bellum* a prospective combatant must have a just cause, act with right authority, and go to war with a right intention; the principle of proportionality must be honored (that is, the war must not do more harm than good); going to war must be a last resort, and the purpose of doing so must be to achieve peace. The main principles of *jus in bello* are discrimination (that is, targeting the enemy's soldiers, not civilians or other noncombatants) and proportionality again (but with a different meaning, in this case that the weapons used must be appropriate to the strategic and tactical circumstances).[3] But I think it unfortunate to speak of just wars at all. Even if we feel compelled to intervene on behalf of some innocent victims, we will certainly create others. Perhaps we should speak only of "justified war," in keeping with the principle suggested in the previous paragraph: one action may be better than another even though neither of them is good or right, and a course of action may be justified without being just.

Jus ad bellum, jus in bello: Latin *ius* (later *jus*) meant "right" or "law," and is the root of our "justice"; it also meant "broth or soup" (and is the root of our "juice")—probably an accident of linguistic development, though it is tempting to play with possible connections (the law smooths out injustices, renders the body politic homogeneous, etc.). *Ius* tends to refer to the idea of law or justice; particular laws fall under *lex*, "something written." (In the Bible, for example, "it is written" means that what follows is a commandment.) *Ad* means "toward" and *in* means "in," so *jus ad bellum* means in effect "justice on the way to war," and *jus in bello* means "justice while war is going on."

70. Knowledge and Power

The chief respects in which political action is necessary are, on the positive side, the equitable distribution of material resources and the provision of education, that is, teaching individuals how the world behaves and thus how to manipulate it successfully. Education, however, has a more complex function than at first appears. If people know what they want, education will teach them how to get it. But if they do not know what they want (and even sometimes if, for the moment, they do), education may make them aware of values they had not previously entertained, so that they come to want something, or something else. What education should studiously avoid is telling people what they ought to want. If it does this, it is not education at all but indoctrination. A good argument can be made for early indoctrination in a minimum of moral belief, but it is justified only if it is followed by education in critical methods of judging such belief, as soon as the child is old enough to understand them.

The temptation for those in power to assume that they know what is good for other people is almost overwhelming, but it is disastrous in a free society. The defense of indoctrination always rests in the end on the contention that people must have some set of values because they belong to a society or class: Americans cannot be true Americans if they are not instructed in the American way of life, workers cannot be true workers if the consciousness of the working class is not awakened in them, men and women cannot be true children of God if they are not taught the nature of sin and the necessity of grace. I do not deny that human groups—Americans, workers, children of God—may entertain genuinely collective values, but I do deny that, where the formation of an individual's values is concerned, apparent membership in a group can ever justify an a priori judgment about what those values should be.

Individuals must be allowed to create their values, and thus replenish the world's dwindling stock of them. Although they may seem to have the transcendent status that alone would warrant the subordination of the individual to them, the values represented by God, history, the nation-state, were simply human in the first place, conceptions entertained by men and women as to the possibilities of their future. We are rapidly using up our inherited futures; technology has in many cases left them far behind already. And we stand in need of new futures.

To be free involves a great responsibility. To repeat Sartre's formulation, "man being condemned to be free carries the weight of the whole world on his shoulders."[4] Human life is an awesome business, full of pitfalls. And it ends in death. But, as Spinoza remarks: "a free man thinks of nothing less than of death, and his wisdom is a meditation not upon death but upon life."[5] Within the confines of life we are free to seek our own conception of order, to change our world, inner or outer, so that it matches more closely our highest aspirations for it. Nothing could be less burdensome than that.

If this sounds like anarchy, remember that another collective institution, the law, stands ready to protect individuals from the excessive enthusiasm of their neighbors. Law is the fruit of political action on its negative side. The existence of the law modifies the agent's inductive strategies by introducing boundary conditions that impede the direct gratification of certain desires. The individual is not morally obliged to obey the law, as long as breaking it is not immoral in any of the direct senses discussed above. But the individual is morally obliged (as Socrates showed in the *Crito*) to abide by the verdict of the law, since to escape it would be to claim privilege, in violation of the principle of indifference.

The only justification for ignoring the verdict of the law would be evidence that the legal community was not coterminous with the moral community—evidence, in other words, that the law was giving systematic privilege to some segment of the community. All moral activity takes place in a community, and it is necessary to allocate, more or less equitably, the freedom left over when all the restraints imposed by the nature of the community itself have been taken account of. To put the matter in another way, as members of the community we collectively dispose of a limited causal space, and the task of the law is to equalize our rights to move about it. This observation may seem anticlimactic after the euphoria of the previous paragraph, which may itself have seemed cruel to those for whom freedom, in the full sense in which the word has been used in this book, is as yet an unrealized hope.

71. Science and the Augmentation of Freedom

Here enters the final contribution of science to values. Science and the technology that accompanies it manufactures freedom in the forms of expanded causal space. It does this in several ways: by prolonging life, by controlling population, by providing economical sources of energy, by devising new techniques of manufacture, by processing and preserving food, by moving things and people from place to place, by continually "doing more with less," to use a phrase of Buckminster Fuller's.[6] If its intellectual function is to help people understand the world, its social function is to help them control it. This is a familiar enough idea, but the question that it implicitly poses is not often enough asked: what is the point of controlling the world? Is it to give a few individuals a sense of power, or to make a few individuals rich?

Richard Buckminster Fuller (1895–1983) American engineer and architect. He devised the geodesic dome as the lightest and strongest structure to enclose a given space. A form of carbon, C^{60}, that occurs in spheres of the same configuration has been named buckminsterfullerene ("buckyballs"). Fuller had an original and trenchant philosophical streak that informed such works as *Critical Path*.

To this the reply must be: yes, those among other things. Nothing is wrong with the enjoyment of power or wealth, unless it comes at the expense of the enjoyment of other things by people to whom power and wealth do not matter. We must get this point in perspective. The old tags about power as corrupting and money as the root of all evil are too simple-minded. Evil and corruption come not from money and power in themselves, but from the dehumanization produced by the disregard for other individuals that so often accompanies the struggle for these things. This dehumanization can equally well occur in connection with the pursuit of other, apparently more innocent values, such as stamp collections and flower gardens, or in connection with the pursuit of what have come to be thought of as the highest values, such as holiness, or science itself, or even truth, if they serve as end values for individuals rather than as instrumental values for humankind.

The moral superiority of shared instrumentalities over private ends is my reiterated theme. The moral superiority of the shared instrumentalities is in no way incompatible with the aesthetic superiority of the private ends. But the theory of value is principally useful for the rectification of moral, rather than aesthetic, desires. Aesthetic virtues genuinely belong to the class of those that, in Aristotle's language, come about as the result of habit rather than as the result of teaching.[7] Aristotle's calling such virtues "moral" is one of the minor misfortunes of the history of ethics, since, as I have tried to show, moral conclusions can be drawn from the intellectual analysis of the situation of free individuals in a human community, which makes morality one of the intellectual virtues.

Given the priority of moral instrumentalities over aesthetic ends, the moral point of having scientific control over the world is to optimize the ability of *every* individual to reach his or her private ends—power for those who want power, wealth for those who want wealth, and privacy for those who want privacy, under the moral restrictions that the facts of competition and the probable consequences of particular actions impose. *And science can do this*. Except for a few scientists, it cannot provide a useful end in its own right; to suppose that science should be an end value for everyone is to fall into the fallacy of scientism. But as an instrumentality science might still be effective for the control of population and armaments, and for the provision of food and shelter for the entire human race. The means are at our disposal for the creation, if not of utopia, then at least of a world vastly more friendly than is now the case to the individual aspirations of human beings in all parts of it.

But this will never come about unless the appropriate values are invoked, and they never will be unless we come to a better agreement about the locus of value in the world and the basis for resolving disputes about it. The crisis described in Chapter III sprang from a failure of transcendent standards of value coupled with a rapid rise of science. The transcendent values human inquiry has encountered so far are not able to meet the challenge of science. I have attempted to provide a theory of value having a common root with science in the efforts of human beings to understand and control their environment. Such a theory can serve as a complement to science, by laying down the conditions for the moral coexistence of men and women in a world served by the achievements of science, so that they may freely pursue human ends of their choosing. The possible nature of those ends, and the possible satisfactions they can provide, are most adequately foreshadowed by the experience of art in its various forms. But even art cannot be allowed to place limitations upon them.

Notes

1. John Stuart Mill, *On Liberty* (Harmondsworth: Penguin Books, 1985), p. 176.
2. Roger Garaudy, *Karl Marx* (Paris: Editions Seghers, 1964), p. 149.
3. See James Turner Johnson, *Just War Tradition and the Restraint of War* (Princeton, N.J.: Princeton University Press, 1981), pp. xxii–xxiii and passim.
4. See note 1, Chapter III.
5. Benedict de Spinoza, *Ethics*, trans. J. Gutmann (New York: Hafner, 1949), p. 237. This is Part IV, Proposition LXVII.
6. See, for example, R. Buckminster Fuller, *Critical Path* (New York: St. Martin's Press, 1981), p. 133. The idea recurs frequently throughout Fuller's work.
7. Aristotle, *Nicomachean Ethics* 1103ᵃ14.

XV

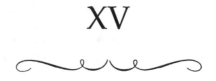

Conclusion: The Moral Life

72. Minimal Consequentialism

In Chapter I the moral theory to be worked out in this book was called "minimal consequentialism." In the body of the book this designation was for the most part quite forgotten, because the position was being developed in its own terms, as the plainly appropriate stance for an agent living in a world with other agents and needing along with them the conditions of free action in order to pursue his or her individual end values. The agent's experiences of wanting (Spinoza's *conatus*), and of acting and observing in the physical and social world, were appealed to as the empirical ground of the theory. The theory also built on the experiences of many generations of predecessors and contemporaries that come to us in the form of the sciences, natural and human.

Because of this preoccupation with the positive development, the argument did not, except incidentally, take polemical stances against other theories, deontological, virtue-based, and the like. The time has come to be more definite. Let me restate the central principles of minimal consequentialism so that its differences from these alternative views can be clearly seen.

As a kind of *consequentialism*, then, the position advocated here holds that the moral weight of an act attaches not to the kind of act it is or to the intentions of the agent but to the foreseeable consequences of the act, where "foreseeable" has the strongest possible force: if anybody could foresee an adverse consequence of my act, then I should foresee it or refrain from acting. Knowing the foreseeable consequences of my act will not by itself tell me whether it is wrong. But consequentialism holds that I have no way of telling this *unless* I know the foreseeable consequences; such knowledge is a necessary condition of moral action. Any ethical theory that claims to tell me the moral status of an act independently of its consequences is ill-conceived. There is to be no hiding behind rules or principles, no excuses on the grounds that the act was correct in itself, or done virtuously or with the best of intentions. The proposition that *considering the foreseeable conse-quences of an act is a necessary condition of its being a moral act* is the heart of the position. An act may be *immoral* without this; indeed, we could put the point more strongly and say that without this it *will* be an immoral act—an irresponsible act.

For an act that satisfies the necessary condition just stated it will be a sufficient condition for its being a moral act that it optimizes the instrumen-tal values of other agents causally affected by it. It will be morally neutral if it does not diminish any other agent's enjoyment of such values, morally negative if it does diminish and morally positive if it augments that enjoyment. However, positive action may be required even to maintain moral neutrality if inaction would contribute to the maintenance of some other agent in a condition of diminished enjoyment of instrumental value.

Necessary and sufficient conditions: If *A* always has to be true in order for *B* to be true (if *B* can never be true unless *A* is) then we say *A* is a *necessary* condition for *B*. If *A*'s being true is always enough to make *B* true (if nothing but the truth of *A* is ever needed in order for *B* to be true) then we say *A* is a *sufficient* condition for *B*.

Moral weight here is positively transitive, in that my acting in a way that enables another agent to act to diminish yet another agent's enjoyment of instrumental value implicates me. In deciding what to facilitate, I have to consider the consequences (as for any act): in particular what the agent I help is likely to do to others with that help, that he or she would not have been able to do without it. Part of the knowledge of the world required for free action involves knowledge of the characters and dispositions of other agents.

Transitive: Latin *transitio* means "a going across or passing over"; a transitive relation is one that carries over a series of terms. For example, if John is taller than Mary and Mary is taller than Bob, then John is taller than Bob—the relation "is taller than" is transitive. An intransitive relation does not carry over in this

> way: for example, if John likes Mary and Mary likes Bob it does not follow that John likes Bob—the relation "likes" is intransitive. In the moral case a transitive relation might work like this: if some bad outcome is the consequence of something you did, but your doing it was the consequence of something I did, then that outcome is among the consequences of what I did. Whether there are any such relations hinges on whether one person's act can ever be among the consequences of another person's act.

On the other hand, moral weight is not negatively transitive, if I may so put it. I need not yield to moral blackmail if another agent says, "Do as I say, or else I will commit such and such a terrible act." The difference is that in the positively transitive case I am treating the second agent as passive, assessing his or her probable action according to causal (or statistical) principles as if it were part of a natural course of events, whereas in the negatively transitive case the second agent is assuming an active position; I cannot be held to have caused an action undertaken freely by any agent other than myself. The exception to this is when the other agent acts under my orders, although in that case he or she might claim not to be acting freely, because my authority in a chain of command constitutes a form of constraint.

In keeping with its minimalist intentions, the position limits the application of moral judgment, in at least five ways. (1) It imposes no a priori conditions. No general end value or set of such values is posited that my acts are obliged to serve. (2) Its aim is less to achieve an ultimate good than to avert proximate evils and what might follow from them. (3) It declines to pronounce on any act until the consequences of the act reach beyond the agent's sphere, maintaining that *private satisfaction is untouched by moral theory until it has effects on nonconsenting others*. (4) These others, whose being affected positively or negatively brings my act into the sphere of the moral, must be *members of the moral community* and generally agreed to be so. (5) No universalizing claims are made as to the applicability of the theory elsewhere in time and space; its domain is the self-defined moral community as it has come into being historically.

A minimal approach suggests that limit cases—such as, for example, animals and first-trimester fetuses—leave the agent free to respect their freedom (to the extent that they can be said to have it) or not to respect it, until a consensus of those already belonging to the moral community is reached in favor of their admission to that community. An advocate of animal rights is free to work for change in the consensus, and can do so by setting a high example or by appealing to humanity or sympathy, but he or she cannot claim established moral status for animals, or hold those that who hunt or eat them are convicted of immorality, before that change has come about.

The main virtue of a minimal view of morality is that it is more likely than a more elaborate view to command agreement across a wide spectrum of beliefs and attitudes. The moral community's consensus about its boundaries changes slowly. In antiquity slaves and women were excluded, and in more recent times ethnic minorities, children, the mentally ill, and criminals have been excluded. Perhaps we will look back from some future time on the exclusion of animals as equally benighted. But to insist on the moral standing of the members of a disputed category before the consensus to include them is to misunderstand the purpose of moral argument, which is thwarted if it is cut off from its roots in the *mores* even though its eventual purpose may be to change them.

73. The Reach of Argument

I do not mean by this that moral issues are to be determined by majority vote; a valid argument is valid no matter how few of us have been convinced. But in moral theory, as distinct from scientific theory (remember the contrast between Bruno and Galileo in Chapter IV!), *the validity of arguments arises in part from conviction*, because the premises include imperatives that if not shared cannot be assumed as given. They cannot be reached by demonstration but have to be established by persuasion.

This view will naturally be contested by those who believe moral theory to be a matter of universal a priori truth. The trouble with a priori positions is that if they are in conflict no discursive means is available for resolving the conflict, which is therefore liable, in the end, to become violent. "Ethics from experience" means from experiences that anyone could have. The special forms of experience that constitute acculturation or indoctrination do not count, unless they are backed by the agent's observations that anyone could share, in which case they still do not count *as experience*, only as convenient ways of sharing the earlier experiences of others. And these must always be validated by the individual agent.

Surely, someone will say, first, it can't be right to leave morality in the hands of individuals! And second, what about the status of women and slaves back in antiquity, when the consensus about membership in the moral community hadn't yet included them—surely the inequalities in their status were already morally wrong, even then? To the first point I answer: who else is there? For better or worse, the fate of moral theory lies in the ability of individuals to convince one another by argument. The claim that some principles are valid prior to all argument is itself a claim that has to be argued. And to the second point I answer: on what grounds could the case against inequalities have been argued in antiquity? We can say now that such inequalities would be wrong now, and we might say now that they were wrong then, but that won't cut much ice if we couldn't have said then that they were wrong then. Well, we could have—if we'd had the arguments then that we have now. But an essential premise of the arguments we have now is some version of the indifference principle, and the indifference principle applies within the moral community. If we now say that the moral community even then ought to have included women and slaves, then the argument has come full circle.

Suppose, though, that at the time we are imagining there had been lone prophets—perhaps even some of the slaves or women themselves—who anticipated just the arguments we use today: would they have been right? Clearly we have to say yes, they would, and if only we had been there with them we would have joined in and tried to convince the others. As it was, perhaps, their voices were suppressed; perhaps they just died without convincing anyone. Something like this must have happened many times during the evolution of one moral truth or another. Historically, few such voices were recorded until recent centuries; human beings, even those who are oppressed, have often tended to assume that structures of oppression are natural and even right. (The point is illustrated starkly by the attitudes of many abused children and spouses toward their abusers.)

I cannot pursue here the psychological and political implications of victimhood, beyond remarking that these beliefs persist even today in many parts of the world, which might as well be in antiquity as far as the justice of their institutions is concerned. (We cannot distance ourselves quite so easily—the same may be true even quite close to home in the matter of economic justice.) We may hold that the moral community should include all human beings, but there are still plenty of human beings who remain to be convinced, and pinning that argument down seems for the moment more urgent than getting the animals and embryos in, worthy as this goal surely is for those whose convictions urge it upon them.

The point about moral values in past times may be made clearer by considering the corresponding case in science. If it is true to say now that matter is composed of elementary particles, and that hereditary properties are carried by genetic material in cell nuclei, we can argue that these statements must have been true even before arguments were available to establish them, because had they not been true we wouldn't be here now. Genetic theory, once confirmed, applies all the way back to the earliest organisms. This is because it is descriptive of a material world whose governing laws we have no reason to think have changed. Retrospective scientific judgments can therefore be justified. But value judgments, again, require an imperative component, and how are we to provide that retrospectively? Where shall we locate the imperative: then, or now? If now, we are in the futile situation of demanding that things should have been other than they were. But if then, whose imperative was it? Once our prophetic minority was out of the picture, the world would have had to wait once again for the emergence of the value in question.

My claim is that positions starting from any higher point than the minimal consequentialism that has been worked out in the foregoing pages will all be found to incorporate some element of the universalizing and the a priori, acquired by acculturation or indoctrination, passed down as tradition, promulgated as revolutionary doctrine, or in some other way superimposed on experience rather than derived from it, and hence not resting on experiences open to all. From such starting points argument about moral theory will eventually come down to a clash of views about human nature, virtue, divine law, social conduct, and the like. To the extent that means have been found to resolve such conflicts they have usually proved to incorporate minimal consequentialism: no deontologically correct act, no vaunted virtue, no received practice, can hold up argumentatively in the face of tragic or oppressive consequences. Argument can always be refused and oppressive practices enforced, but in this case the conflict is no longer on moral ground but some other, political, theological, or nationalistic.

Consequentialism has come under attack ever since it was first named by the English philosopher G. E. M. Anscombe in 1958, in an article dismissing it as shallow and corrupt.[1] Part of the case against it, especially in its utilitarian form (which is rejected here because other people's happiness is not my concern, although their freedom is), has always focused on its apparently formal and calculating aspect, as if it were lacking in some warmer humanity exemplified by more traditional and more pious views. A familiar personification of this lack is to be found in the figure of Mr. Gradgrind in Charles Dickens's *Hard Times*, who addresses the children in his school not by name but by number. I do not think minimal consequentialism can be accused of being heartless, but a general difficulty with theoretical approaches is that they are in danger of appearing lifeless. We have the structure of a moral life; what about its dynamics? This requires reflection of a different order.

74. Sentiment and Will

In discussing free action in Chapter X we implicitly assumed that the agent knows his or her own desires. The function of moral theory was said to be the rectification of desire. What I unreflectively want comes under the scrutiny of the theory, and I come to see that it differs from what is morally required. As a rational agent I then make the latter the object of my desire instead. But human beings are psychologically complicated, and knowing my desires has to go deeper than this. Why should I desire what is morally required? More simply, why should I be moral? Other questions quickly follow: why do I desire anything? why did I desire what I desired unreflectively in the first place?

In the history of moral philosophy more attention has been paid to questions of judgment than to questions of motivation to action, which tend to be relegated to psychology. But two important philosophical traditions throw light on the connection between judgment and desire. The first is the theory of the *moral sentiments*, to be found in David Hume and Adam Smith. The second is the theory of the *will*, to be found in Schopenhauer and Nietzsche.

Sentiment: Latin *sentio* is "to feel," so a sentiment is a feeling. Nothing would be lost by calling "moral sentiments" just "moral feelings"; something might be gained, since on the one hand "sentiment" has acquired the taint of sentimentality, which suggests false or exaggerated feelings, and on the other there has been a welcome movement in recent years to encourage people to acknowledge and respect their feelings.

Moral Sentiments

According to the theory of the moral sentiments, human beings have, among the passions to which they are naturally inclined to yield, innate feelings of sympathy for one another, which work (with the aid of reason) to counteract other passions such as cruelty and greed. The basis of morality, according to Hume, is a matter of feeling and not of knowing. We cannot, he thought, argue that anything *ought to be* the case on the basis of any number of propositions to the effect that something or other *is* the case. For him, argument is only a means to clarify imperatives already established by feeling. In his own words "reason is, and ought only to be, the slave of the passions."[2]

Passions: Latin *patior* meant "to suffer or undergo"; it gives us "passive" and "patient" and "passion." A *strict* opposition of these three to "active," "agent," and "action" is worth carrying through as far as it will go. An agent is one who acts, who does things; a patient is one who is acted upon, to whom things are done. "Being patient" in everyday language means letting things take their course, not intervening, letting the friend or the letter we're waiting for occupy the agent position. The exercise pays off in the case of "passion": it helps us to see that passionate behavior, which *seems* active, is really something that is happening to us, rather than something we are doing. In Spinoza's *Ethics* the chapter on the passions is entitled "Of Human Bondage," a title that was borrowed by the English novelist W. Somerset Maugham (1874–1965) for one of his best-known works.

We might agree that something other than knowledge is required in order to get the moral life under way without conceding that moral sentiments, indispensable as they no doubt are, have the last word. I can come to believe that some things ought to be the case without consulting my feelings; for example, I may be persuaded on purely intellectual grounds by the argument that everyone's freedom should be an imperative for me. Even the moral sentiments, although they account for characteristic judgments and attitudes, do not by themselves provide the dynamic component without which action will not begin. To get some insight into this we need to turn to the second of our two traditions.

Will

The philosophical treatment of the will in Schopenhauer and Nietzsche has its roots in Kant. As we saw earlier, Kant was impressed by two great basic features of the world, "the starry heavens above and the moral law within," which for him defined two autonomous domains, the realm of nature and the realm of freedom. In the realm of freedom the pure rational will sees what it must do according to the categorical imperative, and it comes to a conclusion like the principle of indifference: the second formulation of the imperative is "so act as to treat humanity, whether in your own person or in another, always as an end, and never as only a means." But Kant is a formalist, not an activist. If you must act, he suggests, do so in this way—but this gives no reason for acting in the first place. The realms of nature and freedom remain for him mutually external, linked only by the reflective subject whose judgment mediates the understanding of nature and the rational exercise of freedom.[3]

It remained for Schopenhauer, and then for Nietzsche, to recognize an overwhelmingly powerful force that drives agents to action, and to link it

The Seven Deadly Sins: Sloth (1953; director Jean Dréville)
Saint Peter (Noel Noel) comes to earth to see the effect of an experiment to counter the frenzy of modern life through laziness. The consequence of this general sloth is that everybody just stands around looking, and nothing is done at all.

with the domain of judgment in the person of the agent as the existential subject both of knowledge and of desire. I know the world as outer representation, said Schopenhauer, but I also know it, the same world, as inner will. In this character it carries me on—often, as we sometimes say, "against my better judgment"—and I cannot escape from it. Schopenhauer felt that this force of will was so powerful, so dark and sexual, that he was pessimistic about the possibility of its control by reason. Nietzsche thought it was powerful too, but welcomed this. For him the will carries us beyond good and evil, toward a higher form of being than the snivelling humanity that surrounds us.

Arthur Schopenhauer (1788–1860), German philosopher. He is remembered as a deeply pessimistic figure, who in a gesture of

> defiance scheduled his lectures at the same hour as Hegel's. Everyone went to Hegel's, but it is at least debatable that they would have been better off going to Schopenhauer's.

I visualize the contrast between these two thinkers in terms of an image from an amusement park: they are on a roller coaster, and as it comes to the top of each new loop Schopenhauer shrinks back into his seat, covering his eyes, and says, "Oh no! not again!," while Nietzsche stands up shouting and laughing, his hair flying, crying "Wheee!" The trouble is that neither of these attitudes is morally helpful. Schopenhauer avoids moral exertion because he thinks it hopeless, Nietzsche because he thinks it pointless. Nietzsche represents the will to power untouched by the moral sentiments. Unfortunately, too many innocent agents are likely to be trampled by the unrestrained exercise of such a will. To Nietzsche's credit he never actually did this; the whole thing gave him headaches and he eventually went mad, though this should not be blamed on his ideas.

No doubt we are thrust forward by time, by events, by desire, perhaps not as melodramatically as Schopenhauer and Nietzsche thought, but just as inescapably. A more recent version of the same idea is to be found in the Freudian concept of the drive, which complements the structure sketched in section 23; it is a constant ineluctable nonspecific force toward the satisfaction of desire, and is one of the aspects of reality, albeit an inner reality, with which the ego has to deal. We might reasonably conclude that the dynamic of the moral life does not need to be invented or explained because it is just given. Or, on reflection, we might say instead that the dynamic of *life* is given—that is its character as life—but that turning it to moral account is a challenge that has to be confronted.

Freudian drive: German *Trieb*, "driving force, motive power," was rendered as "instinct" (which is one of its meanings) by Freud's English translators, but this, with its associations to insects and birds, does not capture the dynamic energy of Freud's concept. The drive complements id, ego, and superego in what came to be called the "structure-drive" theory; it is like a power source that is turned on before birth and can never be turned off until death, with whose insistent and turbulent potentialities we have to deal at every moment of our lives, for good or ill—both of which it accounts for.

75. Self-knowledge

Among the conditions for free action under the hypothesis of complex freedom were included knowledge of the state of the world and of its likely behavior. But I am in the world, and if I act in it I must count as a part of it, so *my* state and behavior cannot be left out of an account of *its* state and behavior. A crucial part of the required knowledge is therefore *self-knowledge*. I have to ask not only what conditions obtain around me, but what conditions obtain within me; not only what is likely to happen, but what I am likely to do, unless I take steps to prevent it.

When the concept of complex freedom was first introduced, I suggested that fewer agents than is generally thought are really free. Although many people are unrestrained and unconstrained, not so many have sufficient resources. Still fewer have adequate information and knowledge. But the numbers drop drastically again when we strengthen the last requirement to include self-knowledge. By this fuller criterion hardly anyone has been wholly free since the beginning of the world. Yet everyone could be. The work required to bring this about is now clear:

· persuading those who constrain and restrain others to stop;
· arriving at an adequate and equitable distribution of material resources;
· making full information about their circumstances available to agents and encouraging corresponding habits of awareness and prudence;
· teaching each new generation the accumulation of human knowledge about nature and society; and
· seeing to it that everyone comes to a knowledge of self, as a part of early training that is considered just as important educationally as learning the world.

A utopian recipe indeed, given that what is taught and practiced in most parts of the world, if not by the official establishment then by family, religion, and popular custom and opinion, involves the exploitation of others, including family members and members of subordinated genders, classes, and races, hostility to outsiders, the settlement of disputes by violence, mindless consumption accompanied by a wildly inegalitarian distribution of resources, unreflective and often self-destructive habitual behavior, massive ignorance, and a general absence of self-critical understanding. Much of this is enshrined in cultures that we are called upon to respect because of their prevalence or antiquity. But no culture, not even yours or mine, deserves respect if it perpetuates or condones conditions like these, whose consequences for whole segments of the population mean an almost total lack of freedom to achieve even modest end values.

What can you as a morally concerned individual make of the immense discrepancy between the rationally preferable and the really prevalent? In the face of this apparently hopeless situation an old strategy is available that still works. It comes from Plato, who puts it into the mouth of Socrates in Book IX of the *Republic*. Glaucon, one of Socrates' interlocutors, has just had an insight about the ideal state Socrates has been constructing throughout the dialogue: "I think," he says, "that this State you have been describing never will come into being on the earth." "No," says Socrates, "but that does not matter: the form of it is laid up in heaven, and *anyone can become a citizen of it who likes, whether anyone else does so or not.*" The strategy then is this: I work out what would be the best way to behave for the good of all, and (to the extent that this is not suicidal) I proceed to behave in this way, regardless of the different forms of behavior of those around me. I thus constitute myself a member of an ideal moral community.

This principle has had an unfortunate history. It was appropriated by Christianity (like so many of Plato's insights) three or four hundred years after its formulation. The state of which anyone could become a citizen became the "kingdom not of this world" to which Jesus refers, and membership in it became conditional on extraneous beliefs about divinity, sin, redemption, and the like. When Plato said "laid up in heaven," he meant only that the form of the state was universal and belonged along with other Forms in the metaphysical domain he had invented to house them. The practice of Christianity shows that the strategy is psychologically possible. The unfortunate thing about the Christian version is not only that it infects a good Platonic principle with an alien religious tincture, but also that the community realized sometimes tends to be smug, and hostile to strangers who reject its message. Some Christians have risen above such pettiness and interpreted the idea of community with something like Plato's generosity, but they have been rare, and liable to conflicting impulses, since to relativize the principle to any set of doctrinal beliefs is to weaken its force.

If enough people resolved to behave consistently according to the minimal prescriptions offered in this book, to know themselves (and one another) as members of a worldwide moral community, such a community would come into being as a potent force for good. Something like it already exists among morally concerned people. I suggested earlier that to behave in such a way might sometimes be suicidal, and you may well become discouraged when people all about you are cheating on their income taxes or term papers or spouses, skimming from corporate or public funds, lying their way to private advantage, resorting to violence, or abusing themselves and others. But the private rewards of comporting yourself in such a way that if everybody did so the world would be a much better place are in fact real and substantial, and doing so, even in isolation, does make the world a marginally better place.

76. Morality in an Imperfect World

The world is still generally conceded to be in a mess. As I conclude this writing most of the old tensions are still in place, between Jews and Muslims and Christians, between Protestants and Catholics, between Hindus and Sikhs and again Muslims, between national and ethnic and regional groups, between rich and poor, North and South, left and right. Some of these tensions can be productive when those who experience them find a common basis for discursive argument; some have been destructive from the first and remain so.

What can moral theory have to say in such a world? The individual can live along with like-minded individuals in a better world, if only, given the realities of the external situation, a virtual one. He or she will offer an example to others, if they take any notice, which, given the complexity and variety of the contemporary scene, they are less and less likely to do unless the numbers of those offering the example become massive. But exemplary conduct apart, and we noted long ago that moralists cannot be counted on for this, what can be concluded or recommended? Sometimes, disappointingly little. No moral theory has an answer to every problem that presents a moral dimension, to every cruel dilemma that poses itself in an age of unrest and conflict. Moral philosophers have to admit that in many cases nothing we can do is right, and it may even be hard to discern the lesser of the two available evils.

The literature is full of cases of this sort: lifeboat cases in which one must be sacrificed to save the rest, hostage cases in which family members (or officials, or bystanders) are blackmailed into immoral acts to secure the victim's release, difficult-birth cases in which the mother's survival means losing the baby or vice versa. Such cases are typically used to challenge the moral theory a writer happens to be arguing against, by showing that it would lead to monstrous consequences. Many of them have been invented to refute consequentialism, especially in its utilitarian form. Can one of the alternatives in such a case still be "the right thing to do"? Often the monstrous consequences in such cases follow from the wickedness of the agents involved or the mercilessness of the natural forces in play. The best response to them may be not to contort our heads by inventing ever more fantastic elaborations of moral theory, but to work to educate future agents out of their wickedness or to protect human beings from future onslaughts of nature.

Still in every case, until the moral impasse is reached—and the force of the foregoing remarks is to insist that sometimes it cannot be avoided with the best theoretical will in the world—we can raise the questions: exactly what are the prevailing conditions? what will be the consequences of each possible course of action under the circumstances? whose freedom will be affected and in what ways? Moral theory will insist on no less. And just asking these questions seriously may clarify most situations. The first is the most often overlooked: when a moral problem is posed, we should always ask whether another way of looking at it would get us out of the impasse, whether framing and discussing the issue in a "different voice" (to use Carol Gilligan's phrase) would advance our understanding.

Independently of cases, contrived or otherwise, moral theory (as I have been propounding it) will raise with every agent two general questions:

1. How would you wish the world to be?
2. If it were that way, what would you do then?

A ready answer to the first but not to the second will indicate that the agent's action is driven by the imperfection of the world, that his or her end values are really instrumental values in disguise. It is the attitude of the dyed-in-the-wool reformer or evangelist, who would be at a loss if moral equilibrium were ever reached, who must always invent an *eskhaton*, an unreachable perfect future, to motivate action and give meaning to life. Such people tend to be dangerous. The trouble is that a genuine improvement in the state of affairs—for example, the collapse of communism—may appear to them as a disappointment, so that those who were energized by the form of imperfection embodied in communism now have to look for another cause, being unable to let go of the reformer's zeal and simply cultivate their gardens, as Voltaire's immortal advice would have them do.

Voltaire, pen-name of François Marie Arouet (1694–1778), French satirist and critic. His novel *Candide* mocked the politics and religion of his day; its last sentence was "Let us cultivate our gardens," that is, let us be tranquil and leave the world to go on its absurd way without us.

Moral theory would have each of us ask ourselves: Am I that kind of person? Or do I subscribe to any a priori view of the world, learned since childhood perhaps, relied on as a psychological crutch, that I have not submitted to critical scrutiny and challenge but under whose influence my actions might have an adverse effect on other agents, perhaps those of other races or beliefs or lifestyles? In thinking about morality we should have the wider context in mind, remembering that we are physical and social beings and that our acts have physical and psychological effects on others like (or even unlike) ourselves. My acts become truly moral only when I have taken all that into account. At the same time, as I insisted in Chapter II, the moral requirements imposed on agents must be relatively simple. What I call the "evangelist's rule" says that the wider the agreement desired, the simpler should be the formulation. For moral purposes, in the end, the aim must be for worldwide agreement. The three rules of section 54 are designed with this in mind.

If—and let us not consider it an a priori impossibility, wildly improbable as it must seem for the present—people did follow those minimal rules generally, if therefore a moral steady state were achieved, in which injustice and cruelty were at a minimum and the benign control of nature at a maximum, then agents would have to turn to the aesthetic dimensions of life, in the broad sense of the term, for guidance on most of their actions. The history of culture and civilization gives plenty of hints about what such a life might be like, although adopting it *as* one's life has heretofore only been possible at the price of ignoring the injustice and cruelty that obtain. Still the idea of the pragmatic cutoff suggests that we should keep the ideal alive, living with some of our energy as if the moral problems of the world were already resolved, on condition of spending some of the rest of it in continuing attempts to resolve them.

I have not paid much attention to the nature of injustice in this book, nor to the nature of justice, since on the one hand if the moral recommendations of minimal consequentialism were generally followed justice would be secure, while on the other hand as long as they are not generally followed justice needs to be secured by the law rather than by morality. The law operates essentially by rules that are a priori relative to the situation of the citizen. Ideally these should reflect the moral stance that the citizen would take on the basis of his or her experience and reflection, but under real social conditions as they are at present the law cannot trust the citizen to behave morally without encouragement or restraint, mainly the second.

An unfortunate consequence of an impersonal, rule-governed society is that laws—for example, the traffic laws governing green and red lights— are seen simply as commands ("you may proceed, you are forbidden to proceed") rather than as information ("it is safe to proceed, it is not safe"). The first view encourages the agent to think of the situation as involving only himself or herself and the law. The second, remembering that the morally relevant sense of safety is that of others, not one's own, requires that it be thought of in interpersonal terms. As Plato remarks, the numbers of lawyers and doctors in a city are inversely proportionate to its moral and physical health. A reasonable if apparently unrealistic ambition would be to make morality do more of the work of law, and law less of the work of morality, than is now the case. "Apparently unrealistic": this is no excuse for not trying. Adopting the minimal consequentialist position for ourselves would be a small first step in that direction; making it the basis of a pedagogy would be a considerably larger second step. We need not believe in the perfectibility of human beings or society in order to address their imperfections, even in a small way—and always starting with our own case.

77. Ethics in Theory and Practice: One Morality or Many?

Another familiar point not touched on in this book is that of professional ethics—medical ethics, business ethics, legislative ethics, and so on. It will be a fitting close to the argument to indicate why morality is one, not many, and why the agent is the same moral agent subject to the same imperatives whether he or she is acting in a private, public, or professional capacity.

I take my cue here again from Kant. I referred in section 20 to his late essay entitled "On the Common Saying: *'This May Be True in Theory, but It Does Not Apply in Practice,'*" where he holds firmly that "everything in morals which is true in theory must also be valid in practice." "We never grow out of the school of wisdom," he says, and we therefore cannot pretend that worldly experience in commerce or the professions gives us any better grasp than is available to the pure exponent of moral theory of "all that a man [or woman] is and all that can be required of him [or her]."[4] A commonly held view, especially in these multicultural times, is that we must allow for a pluralism of outlook in moral matters, as though the nature of obligation changed with changing languages or cultural practices or social roles. But Kant would maintain that as rational wills, free agents in the kingdom of ends, all human beings are equal and all are subject to the imperatives that reason imposes.

Disagreements about moral theory are obviously possible; as has been clear throughout, the position taken in this book is far from Kantian, Kant having been probably the strictest deontologist in the history of moral philosophy. The question here is not whether we agree with Kant's formulation of moral principles, but whether we accept the view that one set of moral principles operates in one set of circumstances and another in another. This is not the problem of "situation ethics," a polemical designation invented by (mainly Catholic) writers on ethics in an attempt to discredit sensitivity to outcomes in favor of a rigid adherence to rules. Moral action is always "in situation," as Sartre might say, and circumstances do alter cases. But do circumstances alter principles?

The burden of proof here is on those who might claim that they do: the corporate officer who agrees that depriving people of their livelihood, for example, would be wrong in general but does not hesitate in his or her corporate capacity to close a plant for the sake of the shareholders, or the public leader who would shrink from murder by his or her own hand but commits troops to armed action for merely political ends. To say that no plant should ever be closed, no war ever fought, would be too simplistic (though those would be good rules of thumb, suggesting that all other strategies should be exhausted first). It is instead to say that when these things are done *the same moral responsibility rests on their public or corporate agents as would rest on a private agent whose action had the same consequences.*

A recognition of something like this is embodied in what might be called the "Eichmann principle," after Adolf Eichmann, the Nazi official who implemented the "final solution" during World War II and whose excuse that he was acting under orders was disallowed when he was brought to trial. Responsibility begins with the immediate agent, the one who locks the workers out, or who turns on the gas in the death camp, but it goes all the way up the chain of command. If a consequence of my act contributes cumulatively with the consequences of others' acts to create a foreseeable effect on the freedom of others, I thereby become the agent of that effect. So that in cases like these the responsibility is not shared, if "shared" is understood to mean that the responsibility of each agent is lessened by the participation of the others. As Sartre points out, if I and 99 others commit some collective act, each of us acts with the strength of a hundred.[5] In a sense we are even *more* responsible—a thought that should give individuals pause before they throw in their lot with a corporation or a government or a branch of the armed services.

In a similar sense I am implicated in the practices of my culture. The suggestion that we live in a pluralist age, in which allowance must be made for historical differences—for example, in the treatment of women or children—must not be used as an excuse for turning a blind eye to oppression. If a cultural practice enslaves or maims or deprives one human agent who might otherwise be free, if it misleads one agent as to his or her situation or as to the state of the world, even if it does this in the name of the most venerable tradition, religious or otherwise, then it offends against moral principle.

Do we really after all have such a pluralism of values? If we set up a couple of contrasting lists:

kindness	cruelty
honesty	fraud
truth-telling	deception
fidelity	betrayal

will anyone be found to argue for the systematic superiority of the list on the right? And if we ask, why should we all prefer the virtues of the list on the left? the answer comes directly from consequentialist theory: because if everyone practiced those virtues, the world would be a much better world. And I repeat that even if you and I are the only ones to practice them, that will make a perceptible difference for the better.

In the end your moral world contains yourself as agent and everyone else as potentially affected by your acts. What others do to you, you must take as a given element of your situation, just as if it had come about naturally. Whenever you find yourself in a situation where action is called for, whether in a private, public, or corporate capacity, ask yourself at least the minimal consequentialist questions. The answers will not command or forbid you to act: the choice is still yours as a free agent. But they will tell you, if you have followed the argument of this book, what would and would not be a moral act. Knowing that is the capstone of your freedom. How you use it will have consequences for everyone.

Notes

1. G. E. M. Anscombe, "Modern Moral Philosophy," *Philosophy* 33 (124) (January 1958), pp. 1–19.
2. David Hume, *A Treatise of Human Nature* (Oxford: Clarendon Press, 1888), p. 415.
3. Immanuel Kant, *Critique of Judgment*, trans. J. H. Bernard, (New York: Hafner Press, 1951), p. 34.
4. Immanuel Kant, *Political Writings*, 2nd ed., trans. H. B. Nisbet, ed. Hans Reiss (Cambridge: Cambridge University Press, 1991), p. 72.
5. Jean-Paul Sartre, *Critique of Dialectical Reason*, Vol. I: *Theory of Practical Ensembles*, trans. Alan Sheridan-Smith (London: New Left Books, 1976), p. 393.

APPENDIX I

Popular Morality and the
Seven Deadly Sins

In Chapter XV I remarked that acculturation and indoctrination do not count as experience in the sense of my title, though if validated by individuals they count as a kind of sharing of the experiences of our predecessors. I meant by this that we have to experience desire and frustration firsthand (the *conatus* of Spinoza and the ways in which circumstances thwart it) in order to know what moral theory is talking about. If I am only conditioned to behave morally, either by punishment in childhood or later on by fear of punishment in this world or the next—if my acts are not the products of moral choices but of psychological and social pressures—then I am not a fully free moral agent. If I have thought the matter through, I may still be a prudential agent, and whether I have thought it through or not I still bear the moral responsibility for my acts. But fear of consequences for myself does not make me a consequentialist morally speaking; that takes assessment of foreseeable consequences in the light of an implicit or explicit theory of value.

At the same time, indoctrination (provided it is accompanied, or followed when the time is ripe, by an invitation to criticism) and acculturation (provided it builds on some firsthand experience) may be authentic routes to moral insight. If, as argued in Chapter I, reason operates mainly in the choice between alternatives offered to the agent from sources other than his or her own creative imagination, there can be no a priori limitation on the nature of those sources. Myths, parables, folktales, morality plays, literature, and more recently film and television provide examples, challenges, and even vicarious experiences that may contribute to the shaping of the agent's moral profile. Again, if this is a purely passive process—if someone simply takes the imprint of the surrounding culture—then the testing that is a part of the root meaning of "experience" will not have taken place. But if that person knows something of what it is to be moved by fear or pity, to use Aristotle's examples from the *Poetics*,[1] then these emotions may be experienced genuinely enough in the theater or at the movies, perhaps to a more intense degree than has been possible in everyday life. Aristotle thought such vicarious experiences "cathartic," that is, serving to purge or discharge pent-up emotions, but they can surely also be instructive, provoking serious reflection: What might I have done in similar circumstances? What might the effect of my action have been on others? How would I react if subjected to such emotional stresses in real life?

The trouble with vicarious moral experience is that it tends to be simplistic, to lack the complications and nuances, the immediacy of the problems and the force of the bodily sensations that accompany lived moral dilemmas. Still an extension of experience, even in simplified terms, is better than permanent confinement within the accidental limits of a narrow life, which would otherwise be the condition of most people throughout history. Folk wisdom, pageantry, ritual, and the arts have been of incalculable importance in enlarging the horizons of moral agents.

Such an enlargement of horizons can have morally undesirable effects if its emphasis is only on possibilities of gratification, without any counterweight in the form of the exploration of consequences and their implications for moral responsibility. How the media deal with questions of moral possibility and responsibility raises the question of their own moral role (and that of those who work in them). This is too weighty a topic for a mere appendix; it would require another book. But I take the opportunity offered by the illustrations that have been used in order to break the text in this book to touch on two aspects of popular morality and the media: the lore of the seven deadly sins and their cinematic representation. Readers will be readily able to think of other relevant examples of folk morality and of films on moral topics. Such cultural embodiments of ethical issues form an admirable basis for the discussion of problems in moral theory. Many films have implicit moral themes, though not too many have been made in which such themes are explicitly raised to the level of art; a striking recent exception is Krzysztof Kieslowski's ten-film sequence "The Decalogue."

The Ten Commandments, the Seven Deadly Sins: folk morality is patterned in traditional ways. In the New Testament the commandments are reduced to two:

> Thou shalt love the Lord thy God with all thy heart, and with all thy soul, and with all thy mind. This is the first and great commandment. And the second is like unto it, Thou shalt love thy neighbor as thyself. On these two commandments hang all the law and the prophets.[2]

"The second is like unto it" suggests that under its theological cover this passage expresses a single moral truth: that we should look outward from ourselves with intense concern toward others (or the Other). Doing so would, among other things, make consequentialists of us all; we could not fail to connect what we are and do with the totality of what there is on the one hand, and the fate of everyone on the other.

Such secular interpretations of sacred texts are an appropriate way of linking religious tradition with philosophical reflection. Religion is not necessary to morality, but that does not mean that all its pronouncements are morally useless. On the contrary, religious aspirations have frequently fueled moral reflection, out of just such a concern for the welfare of others, or for goodness or mercy more abstractly conceived. (They have also frequently fueled morally outrageous behavior, but that is another story.) If what defines the moral community is something like equal standing before God, that does not invalidate arguments about how members of the community should be treated.

The concept of sin has been intimately connected to religion; it has been seen as a falling-short with respect to God's will (see box on p. 132). Sin is the sort of thing that requires forgiveness, though it is said in the New Testament that one sin is unforgivable: blasphemy against the Holy Ghost.[3] The seven deadly sins are traditionally taken to be pride, anger, envy, lust, gluttony, avarice, and sloth. There are good consequentialist reasons for condemning these as immoral when they lead to action. Pride and envy can provoke the rejection of, or attacks on, the persons or reputations of others; anger and lust can lead to violence, in the latter case especially against women; gluttony and avarice can deprive others of needed resources; sloth can bring productive action to a halt.

But in these cases the sin is usually taken to lie in having the character or disposition in question rather than acting on it—a kind of deontology in advance. This attitude has been characteristic of the Christian West, following the doctrine of Jesus that "whoso looketh on a woman to lust after her hath committed adultery with her already in his heart."[4] Jimmy Carter, when he ran for president of the United States in 1976, caused some amusement when he admitted in an interview with *Playboy* magazine that he had sometimes done this. The amusement sprang from the contrast of this admission with Carter's rather pious image, but its roots no doubt went deeper. Do we really want to condemn ourselves to immorality because of private thoughts, unexpressed and not acted upon? Is not moral theory far more effective if restricted, as I have argued throughout this book, to the effect of acts on others?

There have been two notable cinematic treatments of the seven deadly sins, both multidirector films made in France, *The Seven Deadly Sins* (1953) and *The Seven Capital Sins* (1963). (The English film *Bedazzled* [1967] has some elements in common with these.) As might be expected, they treat the concept of sin lightly, but mainly with an eye to the consequences that follow from the acts these dispositions may lead to. Some twists that the directors give to their plots can be found in the captions to the illustrations in this book. The 1953 film adds an eighth sin. Its concluding segment, narrated, like the rest of the film, by Gérard Philippe, shows a cardinal of the church, along with an assortment of glamorous women and disreputable-looking men, entering what the viewer takes to be a brothel, with the scandalous imputation this implies. It turns out that he is going to have his portrait painted. The eighth sin is "thinking evil of others."

In conclusion I offer two observations. First, attitudes may dispose one to immoral action; thinking evil of others without justification certainly does, in the form of speaking evil (speech acts being full-fledged acts with consequences, as the work of J. L. Austin[5] and John Searle[6] has shown). Second, the attitudes and dispositions represented by the deadly sins may have unhappy consequences for the individual who has them; they are all capable of generating misery for the agent, who is consumed by envy, obsessed by avarice, made sick by gluttony, and so on.

The desire not to think potentially harmful thoughts and to avoid self-absorption and self-reproach is an admirable one, and I do not wish to suggest otherwise. To the extent that religion encourages in people a high view of what they might become (as opposed to encouraging a low view of what other people already are), its influence can be unreservedly welcomed, even if, as I myself hold, philosophy is capable of doing an even better job of this by itself. But I reiterate in closing that this is not properly speaking a moral concern. Morality is not always a matter of immediate gratification to the agent. The Socratic dictum that it is better to suffer evil than to commit it seems right, because when I do something that has an adverse but foreseeable and avoidable effect on someone else's freedom I commit a psychological offense against myself as well as a moral offense against the other. In the end, though, the reason for not doing it, in so far as this is moral, is to avoid the practical consequence for the freedom of the other. Avoiding the psychological consequence for myself makes my acting or refraining from acting morally no better or worse. And yet I am the better for it.

Notes

1. Aristotle, *Poetics* 1452^{b}32
2. Matthew 22:37–40.
3. Matthew 12:31–32.
4. Matthew 5:28.
5. J. L. Austin, *How to Do Things with Words* (Oxford: Oxford University Press, 1962).
6. John R. Searle, *Speech Acts: An Essay in the Philosophy of Language* (Cambridge: Cambridge University Press, 1969).

APPENDIX II

Case Vignettes

The following sketches are intended to serve as a basis for discussion. They are examples only; you could make up cases as good or better yourself, or extract them from the daily newspaper. I have limited myself to a presentation of the bare bones of the situation. Use each one as an imaginative starting point for further questioning and for working out the moral issues involved. Don't jump to conclusions! Here is one good way to proceed:

1. Go over the facts as presented and try to put yourself (or, even better, yourselves) imaginatively into the situation of the agent, asking what other information you might need about the circumstances in order for the action you decide on to qualify as free.
2. List without prejudice all the alternative possible actions you can envisage, even those that at the outset seem obviously immoral; and only then
3. Argue each possibility in terms of its feasibility, imaginability, and likely consequences. Whose freedom will be affected? What resources will be needed, of character or otherwise? Will any apparently negligible consequences add up, if everyone takes the proposed course of action, to some non-negligible effect down the road?

You need not come to a definite conclusion, individually or collectively, about these or any other cases—until you find yourself actively involved in one. That is when the habit of thinking that moral issues are important is likely to pay off.

Case #1: The Baby Test Case

You are a health professional on a hospital ethics committee. Babies born in your hospital are routinely tested for the human immunodeficiency virus (HIV). The question before the committee is whether mothers should be told when their babies' tests are positive. The hospital social workers argue that mothers whose babies are identified as HIV positive (who may not have known their own status) will avoid contact with the health care system and not bring the babies in for checkups, whereas they would bring them in if they were not so identified. The legal aides are concerned about the issue of forced testing. You feel that you have knowledge at your disposal that is important for someone's freedom, but whose? What do you recommend to the committee?

Case #2: The Pedro Case

You are an explorer in the Amazon jungle and come upon a clearing where bandits are gathered. Ten blindfolded prisoners are tied to trees and Pedro is aiming his rifle at the first. The bandit chief explains that they are all going to be shot. You protest. The bandit chief says he'll make a deal with you: Pedro will give you the rifle, and if you shoot one of the ten—take your pick!—he'll let the other nine go free. If you refuse, or miss, Pedro will shoot them all. What should you do?

A variant of the above: The bandit chief says that if you don't accept his deal Pedro will shoot the ten victims and then you and your party too. Does this change your decision? [Adapted from Bernard Williams.]

Case #3: The Case of the Scrupulous Lover

You are a college student and have had a few sexual encounters over the years. Now you have met the ideal partner and think you have a good chance of developing a mutual long-term commitment, possibly a permanent one. The relationship is not intimate but may soon become so. You have never to your knowledge been at risk for exposure to AIDS, but there are many things you don't know about your former partners and you have never been tested. Should you be tested now, before taking your new relationship any further?

Case #4: The Case of the Reformed Applicant

You are an applicant for a job that you need very badly, not only for your own sake but for that of your family. Years ago, in another state, you were either (1) hospitalized briefly for depression or (2) jailed briefly for possession of illegal drugs. Nothing like this ever happened again, and as far as you know no record of it has followed you to your present address. On the job application you are asked if you have a criminal record or a history of mental illness. You are pretty sure, given what you know of the company and the attitude of its personnel office, that if you tell the truth you won't get the job. Do you check "yes" or "no"?

Case #5: The Unexpected Paternity Case

You are a single man who recently had a brief affair with a single woman. The affair is now over and you have not seen the woman for several months. Through a mutual friend you learn that she is pregnant. You have good reason to believe that the child is yours. You also learn that the woman has decided either (1) to have an abortion or (2) to put the child up for adoption. She has no intention of coming after you for support. You find that this news arouses strong feelings on your part. Do you have any right to act on them?

Case #6: The Case of the Convenient Grandmother

You are a student whose family is modestly well off. Your parents can afford to send you to the local state university but not to the Ivy League school you have set your heart on. You are admitted to the Ivy League school, which offers you a financial aid package the size of which depends on family income. The figures show that you will not get enough to take the strain off the family budget. Your father has a great idea: his mother, your grandmother, who lives on a small pension, is willing to claim you as a dependent; you can use her address, and given her income level you will get full support. Do you accept this arrangement?

Case #7: The Under-the-Table Case

You are an academic, not terribly well paid but in a high enough tax bracket to make April 15 a painful day. You are invited to give a prestigious series of lectures to a business organization. You give the lectures, and the president of the organization presents you, in private, with a large honorarium check in a plain envelope. As he thanks you and passes over the envelope he winks at you. Nobody has asked for your social security number. The check is drawn on a general purpose account and on the stub it says "payment for goods delivered." Do you report this honorarium on your income tax return?

Case #8: The Case of Sibling Cooperation

You are soon to graduate but must finish the paper for one last course in your major. Your future may well ride on the grade you get in this course, but you find you have a real block and are beginning to feel anxious. You go home for the weekend for your mother's birthday. Somebody proposes a family outing to one of your mother's favorite places, but you say you really can't go, you have to stay home to work on the paper. Your mother is visibly disappointed. An older sibling, who went to college in a different part of the country but majored in the same subject, says, "Don't worry about it, here's a paper I wrote a couple of years ago that aced the course, all you have to change is a couple of references." Do you accept this friendly offer?

Case #9: The Whistleblower Case

You are a summer intern in a small firm. You become aware that a senior executive of the firm has been billing the government fraudulently, to such an extent that an audit would probably mean heavy penalties for the firm and criminal proceedings against the executive. Other people on the staff have noticed this but have done nothing about it and advise you not to either. Without the income from these billings the firm might well go under. What do you do with your knowledge?

Case #10: The Case of the Innocent Shoplifter

You have been shopping in a large department store. When you get home, you find in one of the bags a piece of jewelry that you looked at but decided not to buy. Evidently it must have fallen in without anybody noticing. You decide you rather like it after all. You are afraid that if you take it back this will be interpreted not as the correction of an innocent error but as remorse after a theft your conscience can't live with. What do you do? Does the value of the item make any difference? Suppose two cases: in one of them it is priced at $5, in the other at $500.

Case #11: The Purloined Drug Case

You are a worker whose income only just meets expenses when your spouse falls seriously ill. Prescriptions are not covered by your insurance and the only drug that will meet the case is far beyond your means. As luck would have it, a friend who works in the local drugstore leaves a set of keys at your house; they won't be missed for a while and it would be easy for you to make a surreptitious visit after hours. You know the layout and the pharmacology well enough to be sure you get the right stuff, quickly enough to run no risk of being caught. You have reason to think your spouse will die without the drug. What should you do? [Adapted from Carol Gilligan.]

Case #12: The Case of Telephonic Translocation

You have landed a part-time job as a telephone salesperson and have spent a couple of days learning the spiel and familiarizing yourself with the product and the sales operation. The last thing your instructor tells you is that you are supposed to begin each call by saying, "Hello, I'm calling from New York as part of a promotion by the X Corporation." The problem is that you're in Bridgeport, Connecticut. How do you handle this situation?

Index

[Note: Page numbers in square brackets refer to definitions or biographical sketches set off from the main text in boxes.]